AD(H)D and Schizophrenia

AD(H)D and Schizophrenia

Ursula Davatz

It did not come easily: Ursula Davatz has worked on schizophrenia and ADHD/ADD for more than three decades, chipping away at the diagnosis schizophrenia bit by bit like a sculptor, to uncover the process that confirmed her hypothesis drawn from over four decades of clinical observation and countless therapy cases; that ADHD and ADD are genetically inherited conditions which in a high number of cases lead to various mental health problems as a result of unfavorable interactions with their family and educational environment.

Content

Why You Should Read This Book 15
Luc Ciompi 15

Biography 24
Ursula Davatz 24
The potential of schizophrenia 26
Incompatible new territory? 28

Guiding Principals 32

SCHIZOPHRENIA 45

AD(H)D – Genetic Vulnerability 47
Introduction 47
Characteristics of children with ADHD and ADD 50
ADD 52
ADHD/ADD and education 52
Conflict behavior of adults with AD(H)D 56
Conflict resolution and debriefing of parents with AD(H)D 57
Typical labels attached to children with ADHD and ADD 59
Difficulties in learning rules 61
Cooperation instead of power struggles 62
Dealing with learning difficulties 65
Traumatic school experiences 67
Adolescence – endless quagmires 68
Conflict management in adolescence 69
AD(H)D and use of drugs 70
Cannabis – a risk factor for psychosis 71
Cannabis as a problem-solver 73

Guidelines for parents of adolescent cannabis users 76
Career choice – a decision-making process 77
ADHD and ADD – a genetic predisposition to mental illnesses 78
Gene-environment interaction as a determining factor 81

Family Environment as a Risk Factor 84
The "why" question 84
How do family systems function? 84

Family Constellations 87
Emotional focus 87
Sibling positions 87
The oldest child with structural responsibility 88
The middle child as an intermediary 89
The youngest child with emotional responsibility 90
The only child 92
Talent as a factor in emotional overfocus 94
Gender as a positive factor in emotional focusing 95
Gender as a negative factor in emotional focusing 97
The black sheep 98
The therapeutic child 100
The comforter child 102
The replacement child 103
The planned child 105
The disabled child 106
Early childhood disease as a factor in emotional focusing 107
Fatal adaptation 109
They cannot speak for themselves 110

Pathogenic Family Interaction Patterns 112
The triangle 112
Revolving-door conflict 113

| Content | 9 |

Split loyalty 115
Illness in the family's interest 117
Triangulation persists after divorce 119
Strategies for dealing with split loyalty 120

Stressful Communication Styles 123
High expressed emotions 124
Associative communication 125
Concealing communication 126
The double-bind 127
Avoidance of conflicts – negation of perception – family group protection 128

Parenting Styles 130
Four distinct educational styles 130
Conflicting parenting practices 133
Problem-solving strategies of parents 134
Paternal withdrawal – lack of structure 136
Matriarchal leadership style – patriarchal dysfunction 138
Overinvolved mothers – helpless fathers 139

Competition of Instincts 142
Protective instinct overrules autonomy instinct 142
Avoidance of conflict by fathers 144
Puppy license by authority figures 146
Malignant puberty 147
Outsourced detachment conflict 148
Suppressed temperament – emotional monster waves 149
Mania – a big bang moment in the pursuit of autonomy 151

Biographical Stress Factors 154
First love 154
Love delusion 156

Intergenerational sexual issues 157
Psychological problems – physical symptoms 159
Phantom pregnancy 160
Sex as a tool of power 161
Failed career choices 163
Parental ambitions as stress factors 166
Failed exams as a stress factor 168

Biographical Stress Factors for Women 169
Female postpartum psychosis 169
Excessive expectations set us up for disappointment 171
To bear a child without the father's consent 173
Mothers' separation anxiety 174
The child as a pawn between the generations 175
Hyper-aroused mothers 176
Danger of infanticide 177

Unresolved Partnership Conflict 179
Female self-realization 179
Divorce as an escape fantasy 182
Unresolved father-daughter attachments 184
Indulgent fathers 185
Abusive father-daughter relationships 186
Absent or neglectful fathers 189
Conflictual mother-daughter relations 192
Compromised female leadership 194
Losing hidden patronage 197

Biographical Stress Factors for Men 201
Men and psychosis 201
Male postpartum psychosis 203
Masculinity and job achievement 206

Suicide – the only way out 207
Dissatisfied mothers casting a shadow 210
Helpful interventions by employers 212
Employment despite schizophrenia 213

Stress Factors in Old Age 215
Unfulfilled expectations 215
Unrealized potential 215
Missed opportunities 217
Delusional sexuality 218
Sexual trauma projected onto the third generation 219

The Brain and Adaptation Strategies 223
MacLean's triune brain 224
The brain – the social organ 231
The brain – the most adaptive organ 232
Memory function 233
Schizophrenia – intellectual high-performance 235

Behavior Patterns in Schizophrenia 237
Flight reaction 237
Behavior avoidance 239
Freeze reaction 242
From flight to fight reaction 244
Courtesy distance 244
Better mad than bad 246

Delusions to Avoid Painful Reality 248
Delusions of reference 249
Delusions of grandeur 250
Paranoia 253
Male delusional jealousy 256

Delusions of love 259
Disguised sexual abuse 263
Somatic delusions 265
Replacing delusions with actions 267

TREATMENT 271

From Mistakes to Rules 273
Therapy as a learning process 273
Anxiety is not helpful 274
Symptom-hunting is futile 275
Relationship versus medical model 276
When ordinary logic fails 276
Abstain from activism 277
Potential for change lies with the family system 278
Validating hardship 279
Emotional turmoil 279
Effective therapeutic coaching 280
Don't cut the umbilical cord too soon 281
Criticism of therapy – vital feedback 282
Unfulfilled parental expectations 282

The Role of Systemic Therapy 284
How does systems therapy work? 284
Systems therapy – a resource-based method 285
Parents as a resource – not an obstacle 286
Loyalty conflict – fear of what? 288
"Yes, but…" – resistance 289
Blind obedience 291
Fake consent 293
Guided family groups 294
Therapy of marital conflict 295

Therapeutic Tasks for Parents 297
Pseudo-mutuality 297
Division of tasks between parents 298
Fathers' task 298
Mothers' task 299
Differentiation from the family of origin 300
The toxic triangle 301
Defocusing on illness 304
Ambivalence hinders detachment 305
Dealing with guilt feelings 307

Disentanglement of Family Issues 311
Unresolved family issues 312
Suffocated conflict creates monster waves 313
Paternal incompetence 315
From functional helplessness to competence 318
Marginalization of fathers 320
Tug-of-war in partnership 322
Fathers' impact on therapy 323
Divorce does not do away with split loyalty 326

The Deeper Function of Madness 328
The obsessed diplomat 328
Obsessed diplomat as guardian 329
Liberating the obsessed diplomat 330

Differentiation – Tool for Change 333
Differentiation from the family of origin 333
Differentiation from deceased parents 335
Therapy with the help of a lie 337

Psychotropic Medication 339
Medication as an agent of change 339
Covert drug administration – a no-go 341
Medication intake lies with the patient 342
Parents, stay out of it! 344

Vocational Rehabilitation 346
Rehabilitation programs are not sufficient 346
Standard procedures are not effective 346
Job coaching – the alternative approach 347
Parents as obstacles to job coaching 350
Successful cooperation with employers 351

Final Words to Parents 353
Learning from mistakes 353
Courage to accept imperfection 353
Ready for change 354
The best of all things possible 354

Glossary 357

Bibliography 365

Why You Should Read This Book

Luc Ciompi

For more than five decades, I have been working in search of a theoretical and practical concept to explain psychosis and schizophrenia and have conducted my own long-term studies of this disorder, developed the concept of affective logic, and have helped patients rehabilitate by establishing the therapeutic community of Soteria in Bern, Switzerland. I therefore read this book with a degree of curiosity and interest, but also a certain amount of skepticism, since it proposes yet another "completely new understanding" of this enigmatic illness.

I only mention this because there have been countless attempts at explaining psychosis over the decades that have disappeared without a trace. The first of these concepts was termed *premature dementia*, which Emil Kraepelin disentangled from the previous jumble of psychiatric disorders at the end of the nineteenth century by defining it as a mental illness that inevitably leads to *dementia*. Just a few years later in 1911, this concept was pushed aside and replaced by Eugen Bleuler's new, considerably more dynamic and more promising concept of the split in the individual's mental state, which he called *schizophrenia*. Bleuler, recognizing a certain *pathoplastic* influence of biographical traumas on the brain, assumed that there had to be a hidden meaning behind the apparently incomprehensible symptoms of delusion and hallucinations. He also did not rule out a certain potential for improvement and even a cure for this illness. However, after Bleuler, there followed decades of stagnation dominated by the belief in a genetic, endogenous disease arising for entirely unknown reasons "from within" a person and completely resistant to any external influence attempts.

It was not until after World War II that this rigid understanding of psychosis once again began to shift. First, psychoanalytical paradigms began appearing that attempted to explain schizophrenia psycho-dynamically and tried to treat it with modified analytical techniques. Psychotic symptoms were regarded as encoded messages with symbolic, dream-like meanings that were rooted in archaic fear of annihilation and existential anxiety. We must express our gratitude for this approach because it has given us insight into the so-called flattening of affect evidenced in chronic schizophrenia patients. It could be largely interpreted as a protective and defensive measure against overstimulation and mental overload while high levels of sensitivity and susceptibility continue to flourish beneath the surface. In a few individual cases, psychoanalysis produced some remarkable successes, but it proved to be so costly and time-consuming that therapists were able to treat only a few cases over their entire careers.

This problem led some pioneers in the 1960s and 1970s to begin looking into the family situation of their patients. Among other things, they observed destructive *relationship traps* or "emotionally distressing dilemmas", known as *double-binds*, which were deemed capable of disturbing sensitive individuals to the point of mental ill health. Family systems therapies, which also underlie this book, were developed on the basis of those insights. The key factor to this approach lies in its endeavor to take the patient's entire family and social system into account and include it in the treatment.

It was around the same time that the large-scale longitudinal studies of schizophrenia conducted by me and other researchers confirmed the key influence of environment on the course of the illness. Considerably better outcomes than had generally been assumed could be observed if favorable environmental conditions were created. Studies of hospitalization and institutionalization should be considered in the same context. They showed that permanent hospitalization of people with schizophrenia in prison-like institutional settings with low levels of stimulation, as was the standard practice at the time, led to almost identical symptoms of indifference, hopelessness, and affective flattening not only in people with chronic schizophrenia, but also in other patients with entirely different diagnoses. For decades, it had been assumed that this was specific to schizophrenia. Wide-ranging, transcultural comparative studies and those of twins and adopted children also documented both the pathogenic influence of genes and environmental factors. Considering this book's subject, studies of what are known as expressed emotions, to which I will return later, are of particular interest in this regard.

For the past two to three decades, such environment-related studies have been sidelined by advances in modern neurobiology. Imaging processes now allow researchers to look into a patient's brain and identify entire series of deviating neuronal or neurophysiological findings in schizophrenia patients. The frontal lobe and other structures that regulate emotions appear to be affected. There has even been occasional talk of a revival of Kraepelin's old hypothesis that schizophrenia is a disease of the brain. However, it has usually remained unclear whether the findings were the cause of the illness or a consequence of the drug treatment and long-term hospitalization in low-stimulation settings. It is also impossible to ignore the fact that modern neurobiological research has so far yielded very little of practical use for the treatment of psychosis; what it has yielded is out of proportion to the time and effort involved. That is probably why the focus has once again returned to predominantly milieu- and family-related approaches in addition to the current "biological wave". These approaches focus primarily on the chances of recovery or improvement in symptoms and are developing innovative methods focused on resilience and empowerment to reactivate long suppressed personal, family, and environmental resources.

It is against this backdrop that Ursula Davatz once again presents a modified version of her explanatory model for schizophrenia based on pathogenic family environments. Her explanation draws on the image of an *emotional monster wave* that builds up over the course of generations in certain families and eventually plays a key role in the outbreak of psychosis. How plausible is this understanding of psychosis, which is both very old and also very new?

All the different explanations of schizophrenia notwithstanding, there are a number of reasons why we should take note of, and give credence to, Ursula Davatz's provocative theses. First, it should be clearly stated that most of the aforementioned paradigms are not mutually exclusive. The majority of them can mainly be understood as complementary aspects of the same, complex illness. They arose from very specific perspectives and were then erroneously made into absolute truths. If Davatz's assumption is correct, and there is much to indicate that it is, then the central issue is no longer which of these approaches is the best or the only true one, but rather what common features they share and how their overlapping aspects could best be used for therapeutic purposes.

The phenomenon of highly tense emotional states in the environment and within the individual in advance of schizophrenic psychoses at the center of Ursula Davatz's hypothesis undoubtedly represents a common factor of considerable practical and theoretical interest. Not only is it not inconsistent with any of the previously mentioned paradigms, it also correlates with general clinical experience and is backed by numerous recent and older research findings. The latter include the aforementioned research into expressed emotions in more than 20 methodologically exceptional studies from various corners of the earth that have consistently shown that the emergence of psychotic symptoms correlates extremely closely with a critical increase in massive emotional tension in particularly sensitive individuals (Vaughn & Leff 1976, Kavanagh 1992). Equally significant is the fact that current neurobiological research is increasingly showing that emotions influence our thinking to a previously unimaginable extent (see, e.g., Panksepp 1991, LeDoux 1998, Damasio 2000, Ciompi and Panksepp 2005). Recent research on stress and trauma as well as studies on neuronal plasticity have also shown that environmental influences, in particular emotional trauma, can permanently alter the brain's microstructure and functioning. Epigenetic studies have further led to the conclusion that it is not genes alone that are responsible for the development of mental ill health, as previously assumed, but that they interact with certain environmental factors. Field studies conducted by Tienari et al. across Finland in the 1980s revealed that adopted children genetically susceptible to schizophrenia only developed schizophrenic psychoses if they grew up in a particularly tense family environment. In harmonious families, by contrast, the probability that the disorder would develop was no different than in the average population.

A further argument that speaks in favor of Ursula Davatz's hypotheses, and which, in my opinion, can certainly be placed alongside the research findings mentioned above, is her wide-ranging clinical experience and wealth of case studies. Her many decades of training and practice in the assessment and treatment of schizophrenia patients and their families have allowed her to develop a clinical eye for pathogenic family structures and the pathogenic effects of emotional tension, which less experienced therapists may fail to see, or which may appear to them as merely coincidental. The author is, first and foremost, not a theoretician, but a clinician and therapist with a wealth of intuition and empathy who, as her comprehensive inventory of family stress situations shows, is particularly adept at flexibly handling diverse types of disorders. Her fundamentally systemic approach to treating her patients by incorporating their entire social and family situation is not just a theory cut off from the real world. Quite the contrary, clinical observation is Davatz's most important tool. If this experienced therapist has, over the course of many years' work, reached the increasingly unambiguous conclusion that tsunami-like *emotional monster waves* play a role in psychotic episodes, then we need to take note of this observation. Incidentally, the manner in which she also incorporates the *turbo function* of the over-stimulated limbic system during psychotic episodes, as well as a number of congenital adaptation mechanisms such as the fight or flight reflex, into her hypothesis is one of the finest and most astute syntheses of current neurobiological and evolutionary psychosis research I have come across to date.

There is yet another obvious argument for taking Ursula Davatz's theses seriously: they correspond almost entirely with the basic assumptions underlying my concept of affective logic, which I proposed for the first time more than 30 years ago and have continued to develop ever since. Affective logic deals with the interactions between feeling and thinking. Emotions are regarded as biologically anchored energies, or, more precisely, evolutionarily anchored situation-dependent patterns for distributing energy that ultimately drive all of our social and interpersonal affairs. At the same time, they have complex triggers and filtering effects on our perception, attention, memory, and combinatory thinking. This energetic and dynamic understanding of emotions enables us to apply the central insights of systems theory to the dynamic processes of psychosocial systems and construct a theory of the *non-linear dynamics of complex systems* or *chaos complexity theory*, a shorter, though less precise term. The mental system, the familiar normal system of feeling, thinking and acting, can go through a sudden non-linear shift known as bifurcation as can happen with other complex systems. A new and totally altered functional pattern can be triggered when energetic tension reaches a critical threshold. In sensitive individuals with such predispositions, for example, an unstable love relationship can suddenly and without warning *flip over* into hatred when the pressure from rising emotional tension reaches a critical level. What had been a long-term peaceful coexistence can turn into all-out war, and normal everyday behavior (and this is the salient point) can turn into psychotically altered patterns of feeling, thinking and acting. Reducing the level of emotional tension in dealing with patients and their families can very obviously also reduce the psychotic *derangement*, as has been repeatedly confirmed for more than 30 years in the therapeutic community of Soteria in Bern, where the concept of affective logic is applied (see Ciompi et al. 2004). The approach of affective logic and the theory of a pathogenic role of *emotional monster waves* (developed separately) are thus mutually compatible and complementary.

One should further bear in mind that the influence of emotional factors on the dynamics of psychosis has in principle been known for a long time, although they were for decades eclipsed by the prejudice that schizophrenia was primarily a cognitive disease. However, upon closer inspection, Eugen Bleuler's famous "four A's" (affect, ambivalence, autism and association of thought), which he described as the key symptoms of schizophrenia, are all characterized by emotions. Bleuler repeatedly stressed the key role of affect in the development of all mental health disorders. Studies of brain waves conducted by Wielant Machleidt approximately 20 years ago consistently showed that extreme fear in the form of a latent (and generally complexly encoded) core feeling lies behind most psychotic disorders. Machleidt therefore assumed that schizophrenia is primarily an affective illness and published *Schizophrenia – An Affective Illness? – Fundamentals, Phenomenology, Psychodynamics and Therapy*. The book contains in-depth discussions by a number of authors (including myself) of the significance of emotion on schizophrenic psychosis. Ursula Davatz is therefore not alone in putting forward such concepts. In fact, they go back a very long way, though they have, for various reasons, been repeatedly obscured by other theories.

As is to be expected from such a prominent author as Ursula Davatz, this book naturally features both the strengths mentioned above and a few critical points. She sometimes makes statements that appear to run the risk of overgeneralization. One such example is the claim that parents systematically inhibit the desire for autonomy of their adolescent child with psychosis. Sometimes, one comes away with the impression that the author has succumbed to the temptation to see her theses as absolute. Some experts might also express more than disapproval in light of the author's postulate that the *long-sought genetically inherited vulnerability of schizophrenia* is the increasingly diagnosed *Attention Deficit and Hyperactivity Disorder (ADHD)*. Most ADHD specialists vehemently refute any close link whatsoever between schizophrenia and ADHD. However, as far as I am aware, there is a widespread lack of specifically empirical studies into this important question. Likewise, the broad overlap the author describes between ADHD and what used to be called early childhood psycho-organic syndrome (POS), which for decades was regarded a clear risk factor for schizophrenia, has so far not been subject to closer investigation.

Such concerns notwithstanding, I believe Ursula Davatz's book makes an important contribution to solving the age-old scientific conundrum of what exactly schizophrenic psychosis is and what the best treatment approach might be. Davatz's approach in no way represents, as a superficial observer might conclude, a nostalgic relic from family systems research of the 1970s and 1980s, even though it does take up certain key ideas from that period and explores them in greater depth. Rather, this book forms the basis of a concept that will last into the future, because it takes a great deal of what is currently happening in the vanguard of neurobiological research on emotions to create a working hypothesis that makes sense for clinical practice. In view of the impact of affective states on our thinking and behavior, which can now be investigated more precisely than ever before, a treatment approach based on the patient's emotional life appears increasingly promising. In addition, Davatz's model could become a fruitful starting point for further systemic research into psychosis, something we currently need more of.

For the aforementioned reasons, I hope this book will not only be read by professional psychotherapists, persons with schizophrenia and their relatives, but also by neurobiologists, those studying emotions, and sociologists. I also hope it receives the broad recognition it deserves from a wider audience interested in the riddle of schizophrenia.

References

Ciompi L.: Affektlogik. Über die Struktur der Psyche und ihre Entwicklung. Ein Beitrag zur Schizophrenie-forschung. Klett-Cotta, Stuttgart 1982.

Ciompi L., Hoffmann, H.: Soteria Berne. An innovative milieu therapeutic approach to acute schizophrenia based on the concept of affectlogic. World Psychiatry 3: 140–146, 2004.

Ciompi L., Panksepp J.: Energetic effects of emotions on cognitions – complementary psychobiological and psychosocial findings. In: Ellis R., Newton N. (eds), Consciousness and Emotion, John Benjamins Publishing Company, Amsterdam/Philadelphia, 23–55, 2005.

Damasio A. R.: A second chance for emotion. In: Lane R. D., Nadel L.: Cognitive neuroscience of emotion. Oxford University Press, Oxford 2000.

Kavanagh D. J.: Recent developments in expressed emotion and schizophrenia. British Journal of Psychiatry. 160: 601– 620, 1992.

LeDoux J.: Das Netz der Gefühle. Wie Emotionen entstehen. Hanser, München-Wien 1998 (The emotional brain. The mysterious underpinnings of emotional life.) Simon and Schuster, New York 1996.

Machleidt W., Haltenhof H., Garlipp P. (eds): Schizophrenie – eine affektive Erkrankung? Grundlagen, Phänomenologie, Psychodynamik und Therapie. Schattauer, Stuttgart/ 1999.

Panksepp J.: Affective neuroscience: A conceptual framework for the neurobiological study of emotions. In: Strongman K. T. (ed.): International review of studies on emotion, Vol. I. John Wiley & Sons, New Jersey, 59–99, 1991.

Tienari P., Sorri A., Lathi I., Naurala M., et al: Interaction of genetic and psychosocial factors in schizophrenia. Acta Psychiatrica Scandinavica. 71: 19–30, 1985.

Vaughn C., Leff J.: The influence of family and social factors on the course of psychiatric illness. A comparison of schizophrenic and depressed neurotic patients. British Journal of Psychiatry. 129: 125–137, 1976.

Biography

Ursula Davatz

In 1971, I began my training as a psychiatrist with Christian Müller in Lausanne, Switzerland. As a student of Eugen Bleuler, he was regarded as one of Switzerland's leading researchers in schizophrenia. In collaboration with Luc Ciompi, he was head of a research project on the long-term course of schizophrenia. Aldo Calanca, then senior physician, drew my attention towards social psychiatry and the environmental aspects of schizophrenia. In 1972, I took up a job in Maxwell Jones' therapeutic community at Dingleton Hospital in Melrose, Scotland. My next step was the 3,000-bed St. Elizabeth State Hospital in Pontiac, Michigan, USA. From 1975–77, I partook in a psychiatric residency training program at Michigan State University in East Lansing.

Fortunately, my supervisor Sham Hague granted my request to establish a multi-family therapy group with three families and their daughters who had been diagnosed with schizophrenia. After just two sessions, he allowed me to proceed on my own. In need of more experience and knowledge, I registered for a training program in family therapy run by the Ackerman Institute in Detroit, where I met Murray Bowen. His family systems theory immediately fascinated me, and I asked him for a job as a trainee. He mentioned the postgraduate fellowship program at Georgetown University in Washington, D.C., which, however, was restricted to US citizens, though he suggested I apply anyway. A few weeks later, I went for my interview and was accepted. After completing my training as an American psychiatrist at Michigan State and finishing my residency in Pontiac, we packed our VW camper and moved with our two children to Washington, D.C. Heavily pregnant with our third child, just one month to go till my due date, I started my new job as a fellow at the Georgetown Family Center. It was a groundbreaking moment in my career.

My own family system was undergoing significant changes at the time: I had started a new job, moved from Michigan to a new residence in Washington, D.C., and was expecting our third child. My pregnancy prompted Bowen to make the comment that pregnant women were unable think of anything else but their own belly, a comment which he – as a skilled therapist – presumably intended as a provocation. His remark did in fact fire my ambition, and I immediately started writing an article entitled "Fusion between Mother and Child". It later became the topic for my first book *Fusion and Differentiation*, about fusion behavior in animals and humans.

Murray Bowen, a creative mind in the field of schizophrenia and family systems research, had become famous for his research project at the National Institute of Mental Health (NIMH), where he had hospitalized parents together with their sons and daughters who had schizophrenia and monitored them over an extended period of time. These longitudinal observations then served as the basis for his family systems theory. Being able to watch him in family sessions was an incredibly valuable experience for me. He skillfully steered the therapeutic process in the sessions, which were broadcast to an audience in a large auditorium. At annual conferences with researchers from other fields such as biology, cancer research, primatology, cytology, etc., I had the opportunity to encounter these different disciplines and their use of systemic thinking.

At the Georgetown Family Center in Washington, D.C., Bowen assigned me all the families whose member(s) had been diagnosed with schizophrenia and who had been referred to him. Over a period of three years, I had the invaluable opportunity to work with these families under his competent supervision.

Time and again, Bowen instilled in me the notion of systemic thinking, and my training as a fellow in systemic therapy was the fundamental experience of my entire career as a physician and psychiatrist. Systemic thinking has given me innumerable valuable insights not only into mental illness, but also into somatic and psychosomatic disorders.

The potential of schizophrenia

From the very beginning of my professional career as a psychiatrist, I was especially drawn to the diagnosis of schizophrenia, which also became the origin of this book.

Schizophrenia has been the subject of a great deal of research, yet it is still not entirely understood. It occurs in all populations of all cultures around the world and affects about 1% of men and women. Both are equally affected, although men tend to be diagnosed earlier.

Schizophrenia, however, is a diagnosis that professionals are reluctant to make, and patients and their families often fiercely resist the finding because it stigmatizes not only the patient but also the family, and implies incurability.

Despite decades of research and treatment of this disorder, most professionals and almost all laypeople still assume that schizophrenia is incurable. This attitude is supported by the oft-quoted statistical outcome, the so-called prognostic rule of thumb that says that one-third of people with schizophrenia recover spontaneously; one-third stagnates with significant symptoms at a lower level of functioning; and one-third becomes severely impaired, has constant relapses and is therefore repeatedly hospitalized. Ten percent of the last group will even be permanently hospitalized. For two-thirds of patients, this statistical rule of thumb does not offer an optimistic perspective, a fact that patients and their families find extremely difficult to deal with.

The perception of schizophrenia as dangerous and life-threatening is also evident in the widespread popular belief that the treatment of the acute phase must always take place in an inpatient setting. However, patients consider in-patient treatment in a psychiatric hospital insulting and a violation of their human rights, and usually oppose this therapeutic measure vehemently. Hospitalization thus often occurs too late and can only be undertaken against the patients' will. Moreover, relatives often fear aggressive reactions from their affected family member and are scared that contact may break off for good if they forcibly commit them to a psychiatric hospital. They perceive compulsory admission not only as degrading to their family member, but also as a threat to the reputation of the family as a whole. For these reasons, the treatment of schizophrenia is often unnecessarily delayed, though deferred treatment and involuntary hospitalization often lead unnecessarily to chronification, the worst of all possible therapeutic outcomes.

Nowadays, most research on schizophrenia focuses exclusively on neurochemistry, neuropsychology and genetics. Over the past three decades, as Luc Ciompi mentioned in his foreword, there was little interest in the psychosocial aspect of this illness. Nearly all studies of schizophrenia and their family systems were published in the 1960s and 1970s, and hardly any research has explored the psychosocial aspect since. However, the family plays an extremely important role in the development of schizophrenia, a disorder that is a multifactorial, multistep process. As Thomas Beck said in 2012: "The reform of psychiatry got stuck halfway and medical diagnostic in psychiatry tends to alienate itself from any kind of biographic and relationship-oriented thinking whatsoever."

With this book, I am following a path that differs to the one taken by research and treatment practiced today. I include the entire family system over several generations and analyze its patterns of interaction. I also consider the patient's individual biography and the stress factors prior to the onset of the illness. Furthermore, I draw connections between genes and environment. I analyze the genetically transmitted vulnerability factor of AD(H)D in interaction with the psychosocial factor of the family system.

With this longitudinal history, the gradual build-up of the illness over three or more generations can be traced. The dysfunction of the projection process within the family system becomes apparent in one of its most vulnerable members. Moreover, the book should demonstrate my hypothesis that the genetic predisposition to AD(H)D, a disorder characterized by high levels of sensitivity and extraordinary susceptibility, results in affected individuals absorbing all the stress of the family system. The ultimate outcome is the development of schizophrenia in adolescence of the AD(H)D child.

This research approach, based on the family system and the personalized biographical history of the individual who suffers from schizophrenia, stands in explicit contrast to the customary statistical data collection which nowadays is standard practice in psychiatric research.

Schizophrenia and its outcome is thus greatly influenced by the biographies of the patient's parents. The extreme behavioral symptoms exhibited by persons affected by schizophrenia tend to bind the family together. On the other hand, the irregular behavior allows them to exert control over their ill family member to protect their standing with friends and the public at large. There are very few other diseases that legitimize and condone to the same extent the patronizing behavior towards affected individuals and the overstepping of personal boundaries on the part of the family system. This, in turn, gives rise to intense emotional escalations, thus further exacerbating the patient's illness.

In colloquial terms, behavior that deviates greatly from the norm is referred to as "schizophrenic" to keep social norms intact. Under such circumstances, "schizophrenic" is equal to "crazy" and is therefore used as an insult. Persons labelled as such are devalued and degraded. Moreover, they lose social legitimacy, and are at risk of being ostracized. For this reason, the naming of this disease, and the concomitant shaming in public, is feared by patients and their families.

Incompatible new territory?

When I mentioned my hypothesis regarding the origin of schizophrenia to my former supervisor Werner Saameli upon my return from America in 1980, he made the remark: "If you can prove this, you deserve to win the Nobel Prize." More than three decades later, a large-scale, cross-disorder study with over 60,000 patients conducted by the Psychiatric Genomics Consortium Cross-Disorder Group has in fact lent support to my hypothesis. This genomic cross-disorder cohort study has revealed the same genetic constellation – what I call risk factors – for five different serious mental diseases: schizophrenia, manic-depressive psychosis (or bipolar disorder), severe depression, and AD(H)D. The researchers were surprised, but I consider the implication obvious: AD(H)D with the highest genetic determination of 30% represents – to my mind – the inherited vulnerability of the other four mental disorders. I believe that specific interactions between the social environment and the AD(H)D genotype are determining factors for the development of the different mental illnesses. My hypothesis is therefore as follows:

AD(H)D represents the genetic factor that can lead to schizophrenia as a result of unfavorable interactions with the family environment.

One might call this an epigenetic process. Because of the effect of the social environment on certain genetically determined personality traits of children with AD(H)D, the pathogenic development of schizophrenia will be enhanced. However, there is no direct causal link between AD(H)D and schizophrenia. The fact that 80% of adults diagnosed with AD(H)D have different additional mental disorders also supports my hypothesis.

However, every AD(H)D expert and publisher I approached with my hypothesis rejected it. One publisher responded: "But there could, of course, be an entirely different explanation for it." Another publishing house wrote that it did not publish books by authors who thought they knew all the answers. When I offered my manuscript to Fritz Simon, a publisher, psychiatrist and systems therapist, he wrote: "Indeed, you are entering new territory that appears to be too foreign to be compatible with commonly accepted theories in today's psychiatry." His publishing house also rejected my book.

Nevertheless, I stand by my hypothesis: schizophrenia must be interpreted as a multistep, multifactorial-process disease in individuals with AD(H)D, interacting with their family context. Children with AD(H)D are highly sensitive to emotions within their family. They have strong impulsive reactions to parental distress. During the detachment phase of puberty under stressful conditions, they develop tsunami-like *monster waves* of emotions, exhausting their ability to adapt, and triggering schizophrenia instead.

As far-fetched as it might seem, schizophrenia patients feel obliged to help the system and usually try to help their parents to detach from their families of origin on a subconscious level. They are functionalized members of the family, so to speak. These entanglements can be traced back three or more generations.

Dysfunctional relationship patterns force the system to reduce the tensions within the family by projecting unresolvable problems onto one of their members, most often the child with AD(H)D. The highly sensitive and most susceptible member thus becomes the black sheep in the family. These children consequently assume a role their families impose on them, which becomes their sole purpose in life. The process of individuation and entry into adulthood is thereby hindered or altogether arrested. In the further course of the illness, the affected individual's life, cut off from the world outside, consists primarily of fulfilling their function on behalf of the family. Schizophrenia patients cannot ignore the cry for help, even if it is only implied. They are tempted to follow the siren call for affection of the neediest voices and take the role in the system as *obsessed diplomats*, a term which refers to their tendency towards mediation behavior within the dysfunctional family systems. Moreover, the family's preoccupation is mainly with their sick member.

The hidden mission of schizophrenia, which is to reveal the dysfunction of the family system as well as the impaired parental relationship, is closely examined in this book. Understanding schizophrenia from this broader, interrelated perspective means dealing with the disease in a way that no longer perceives it as a hopeless, incurable diagnosis, but rather as a manifestation of intergenerational entanglements encrypted in family systems. This unorthodox perception of the much-feared illness offers a better understanding within the family system and a new way of regarding those "crazy individuals". Using individual real-life clinical examples instead of analyzing statistically collected impersonal data with a theoretical search key – a method which neglects all biographical socio-interactive factors – it can be demonstrated how family systems research allows us to decode the development of this long-term illness and makes it easier to grasp its complexity. The frequent question as to whether schizophrenia is ever curable must be answered affirmatively; it is indeed curable if the persons concerned have trust in family systems therapy, and the parents are willing to learn.

As a psychiatrist with four decades of professional experience treating countless families with schizophrenia, conducting research, and exploring the mental development of this complex disease, I have come to believe that outpatient treatment with systems therapy can achieve amazing, almost miraculous results with little trauma at low cost.

Guiding Principals

1. AD(H)D – Genetic Vulnerability
   Children with AD(H)D are particularly sensitive to fear-inducing parenting and educational styles.

2. AD(H)D – Genetic Vulnerability
   Conflicts can never be resolved in the heat of a battle.

3. AD(H)D – Genetic Vulnerability
   Rituals and regular daily structures are particularly useful for learning rules and provide a sense of security in children with ADHD.

4. AD(H)D – Genetic Vulnerability
   For parents and educators, the number one rule is: get your own emotions under control before you deal with ADHD adolescents.

5. AD(H)D – Genetic Vulnerability
   Youngsters with ADHD and ADD are not only more susceptible to schizophrenia when they consume drugs, they also get more easily addicted than those without ADHD. They tend to use the drugs as self-medication and become hooked on them.

6. AD(H)D – Genetic Vulnerability
   Cannabis use in adolescence as a problem-solving strategy in a stressful family environment ultimately becomes a decisive risk factor for the development of psychosis.

7. AD(H)D – Genetic Vulnerability
   My hypothesis from decades of clinical observation and countless therapy cases: AD(H)D is a genetically inherited condition which – in

70% to 80% of cases – may lead to many different mental health problems in individuals as a result of unfavorable interactions with their environment – an epigenetic process.

8 Family Constellations
   Characteristics that distinguish a child from its siblings in a positive or negative way may lead to increased emotional focus on that child by the entire family system.

9 Family Constellations
   Gifted children attract parental expectations and emotional focusing.

10 Family Constellations
   Children who are born at a time of traumatic circumstances have the Herculean task of comforting the family system throughout their life; they become what we call comforter children.

11 Family Constellations
   Children who are subject to emotional focus remain stuck in their functional role in adolescence in order to compensate the disfunction of the family system, thus they cannot detach themselves to become independent adults.

12 Pathogenic Family Interaction Patterns
   Detachment conflicts, combined with incessant parental partnership rivalry, cause continuous emotional turmoil within the family system from which there is no escape for family members with schizophrenia.

13 Stressful Communication Styles
   Environmental factors are crucial for the development of schizophrenia, even more so than genetic factors, a significant epigenetic process, which should not be ignored.

14 Stressful Communication Styles
The adaptive benefit of staying loyal to the family and remaining under the protection of the family system, represents the evolutionary strategy of kin-selection.

15 Parenting Styles
Discrepancies between paternal and maternal parenting practices is significantly increased in families with schizophrenia.

16 Parenting Styles
Mothers' criticism of fathers' lack of involvement and fathers' sarcastic mocking of overinvolved mothers are usually a sign of unfulfilled expectations in both families of origin, and thus unresolved attachment problems.

17 Parenting Styles
Deeply ingrained patterns between anxious, overinvolved mothers and conflict-shy, passive fathers ensure the destructive cycles in family systems with schizophrenic offspring,

18 Competition of Instincts
Mothers as well as fathers should be pillars of strength for their teenagers, and not in quest of love and understanding for themselves.

19 Competition of Instincts
The problematic triangular relationship between father, mother and child inhibits youngsters in adolescence from finding their own identity.

20 Biographical Stress Factors
The first sexual relationship encounter represents a milestone for every human being, a chance as well as a risk factor at the same time.

21 Unresolved Partnership Conflict
The father-daughter relationship described above is reminiscent of a Trojan Horse: from the outside, the affectionate behavior on the part of the fathers appears to be an unselfish and truly benign act of care towards their daughters. Yet, it may also serve the purpose of hiding the fathers' emotional hardship, a shortage of love and affection during their own childhood. From this point of view, it constitutes a patronizing act of exercising power over their daughters, weakening their personal development to become autonomous adults and infringing on their growth potential.

22 Unresolved Partnership Conflict
An unmet need for affection in males during their childhood may undermine their daughters' female strength and autonomy.

23 Unresolved Partnership Conflict
Females whose personality reflects the emotional shortfalls of their own fathers' families most likely transfer their unresolved attachment problem with their father to their partners, and from there to the most sensitive child.

24 Unresolved Partnership Conflict
An indulgent father-daughter relationship tends to undermine female autonomy.

25 Unresolved Partnership Conflict
A good father-daughter relationship, though it might be an excellent starting point for a female's successful professional career, can later become a stumbling block when fathers keep their daughters in a position of dependency, thus undermining their autonomy.

26 Unresolved Partnership Conflict
Middle-aged women who develop psychosis generally suffer from an unmet need for affection and support, dating back to their family of origin. This may lead to deep-seated anger towards their partner for not receiving the expected support they feel entitled to request.

27 Brain and Adaptation Strategies
Hearing voices can be interpreted as an internal dialogue, originating from unresolved conflicts, intense anger, a bad conscience or fear of punishment for one's own aggression.

28 Brain and Adaptation Strategies
Learning is continuously optimizing cognitive and behavioral adaptation to an ever-changing environment.

29 Behavior Patterns in Schizophrenia
Brain activity in a heightened state of arousal is an attempt to search for quick-fix problem-solving strategies on a cognitive level.

30 Behavior Patterns in Schizophrenia
The habitual flight response of people with schizophrenia is most probably related to their genetically determined sensitivity resulting from their ADHD or ADD. However, it can also be related to a fear-inducing parenting style experienced during their upbringing, as well as to current stress factors in their environment, which leads to a system overload.

31 Behavior Patterns in Schizophrenia
Psychosis usually obscures parental conflict and prevents detachment issues of the adolescent from being brought forward and resolved, instead all negative emotions of the affected family member are inwardly concealed and conceptually projected outwards onto strangers in form of delusional ideas.

32   Behavior Patterns in Schizophrenia
Families of individuals with schizophrenia quite often mention, sometimes even with pride, that their child never went through puberty.

33   Delusions to Avoid Painful Reality
Delusions can be referred to as creative self-deceptions for the sake of achieving family cohesion. They are attempts on a mental level at fulfilling the unachievable mission as obsessed diplomats to conceal the family secrets and taboos.

34   Delusions to Avoid Painful Reality
The adaptive function of paranoia can be interpreted as an appeal to the altruistic instinct of potential helpers in the sufferer's social environment.

35   Delusions to Avoid Painful Reality
All delusions primarily originate from a chronic painful emotional state, which is not acknowledged by the environment and cannot be expressed by the affected person. The conflicted feelings are therefore essentially outsourced as delusional constructs and projected onto the surroundings in which the person lives. They have to be viewed as and dealt with as such.

36   Delusions to Avoid Painful Reality
Delusions have distinct mental functions and must be understood as a cognitive adaptive behavior.

37   Delusions to Avoid Painful Reality
Delusional ideas are systematic mental constructions within an inclusive logic. They only function within closed cognitive systems and do not process any stimuli coming from the real world other than including it

into the delusional system. Any kind of new psychosocial learning is thereby being obstructed.

38 From Mistakes to Rules
Every therapeutic mistake makes the system reveal itself a little bit more clearly.

39 From Mistakes to Rules
„You never get a second chance to make a first impression" is a rule when encountering people with schizophrenia.

40 From Mistakes to Rules
Looking beyond symptoms towards a systemic approach is a prerequisite for successful treatment of families with schizophrenia.

41 From Mistakes to Rules
At first, calming down the emotional state of the family rather than just correcting the family member's irrational behavior and paralogical thinking is paramount.

42 From Mistakes to Rules
Schizophrenia is a chronic disorder that keeps reinventing itself within a closed family system. There is no fast cure for it, nor is a quick approach effective when trying to cure this chronic disorder.

43 From Mistakes to Rules
The therapeutic role is one of a trusted coach: professionals act as change agents for the family system.

44 From Mistakes to Rules
The most significant therapeutic coaching in the treatment of schizophrenia is achieved through active cooperation with the parents. As a

natural outcome, the sick family member will be able to develop, thus becoming the embodiment of a successful therapy.

45 From Mistakes to Rules
Address the family system in its current situation, and not where you would like it to be, before making any intervention or suggestions for change.

46 From Mistakes to Rules
Keep an eye on emerging unrest within the family system and respond to any potential crisis promptly but calmly. This is very reassuring for the family.

47 From Mistakes to Rules
Family therapists have to adopt an attitude of multidirectional partiality, as Boszormenyi-Nagy calls it, which involves empathizing with each member, and acknowledging his or her viewpoint and position within the family conflict.

48 From Mistakes to Rules
Always gain the mother's consent before attempting a therapeutic change of the mother-child symbiosis.

49 From Mistakes to Rules
Professionals don't always know what is best. Listening carefully to the family system and cooperating with it is therefore helpful.

50 From Mistakes to Rules
Once parents become aware of their unfulfilled potential and own up to their hidden dreams, they accept therapeutic help more readily, and the family system can once again continue to make progress.

51 The Role of Systemic Therapy
From a systemic point of view, parental changes in behavior are far more effective and efficient than any therapeutic attempt at controlling the schizophrenic symptoms of the family member.

52 The Role of Systemic Therapy
The resistance to therapeutic interventions should always be regarded as an inherent right to self-defense.

53 The Role of Systemic Therapy
The therapeutic change process cannot start as long as the parents avoid dealing with their own feelings of guilt.

54 The Role of Systemic Therapy
Parents always have to be reminded that they have to take full responsibility for all suggested therapeutic steps. They should never accept any proposed therapeutic prescription for change if they cannot fully stand behind it.

55 The Role of Systemic Therapy
Pretended parental consent to a therapeutic step is ineffective at best and can be detrimental at worst.

56 The Role of Systemic Therapy
For successful systemic therapy with an individual who has schizophrenia, the parents must reflect on their partner relationship conflict.

57 Therapeutic Tasks for Parents
To practice controversial exchanges at eye level with their teenager without resorting to paternalism, without devaluing their adolescent in conflict, and without manipulative interference on the part of mothers, is the most important challenge for parents towards

Guiding Principals 41

58 Therapeutic Tasks for Parents
Mothers of schizophrenia patients are usually overanxious and therefore cling to their caring role far beyond their offspring's puberty.

59 Therapeutic Tasks for Parents
Pampering and caring behavior towards the child with schizophrenia is very difficult for mothers to desist from; it feels entirely wrong. Even if mothers believe they have understood the concept of detachment themselves from their maternal role and handing over responsibility to the young adult, it is extremely hard for them to put it into action and then stick with it.

60 Therapeutic Tasks for Parents
The maternal instinct is so central for most women that it overrules reason time and again, no matter how hard or carefully one works on this issue as a therapist.

61 Disentanglement of Family Issues
The unresolved detachment process on the part of mothers is perceived by susceptible teenagers, leading to prolonged puberty features in psychotic adolescents.

62 Disentanglement of Family Issues
Children with schizophrenia often function as a cover-up in a highly encrypted manner for unresolved partnership conflicts and hidden attachment problems in the family of origin.

63 Disentanglement of Family Issues
For fathers who want to participate effectively and productively in the therapeutic process, it is essential that they engage with the identified patient on equal terms while also reflecting on their own biography.

64 Disentanglement of Family Issues
My advice to fathers: work on your unresolved issues from your family of origin in order to acquire the competence you're currently lacking in dealing with your pubescent child with schizophrenia. Be less dependent on your wife's or partner's approval.

65 Disentanglement of Family Issues
The crucial question is: can mothers abandon their overprotective caring behavior and make space for the fatherly role?

66 Disentanglement of Family Issues
Strengthening the fathers in their role through systemic therapeutic coaching with a three-generation approach may have a healing effect on the schizophrenia patient by resetting the family system.

67 The Deeper Function of Madness
Schizophrenic family members serve as objects of projection in the family's deception maneuver. They ultimately become scapegoats for all dysfunctions within the system.

68 The Deeper Function of Madness
The function of madness is to bring to the surface the fact that the system is in urgent need of an update or change.

69 The Deeper Function of Madness
As obsessed diplomats, family members with schizophrenia remain involved with the chronic conflicts of their parents as well as the extended family network, not knowing that they embody the connecting element in the intricate family system.

70 Differentiation – Tool for Change
It is of great benefit to the maturation process of schizophrenia patients

when parents address conflicts in their families of origin, even if their parents have long since departed.

71 Differentiation – Tool for Change
Reconnecting with the family of origin may resolve certain entanglements and lead to a reset of the dammed-up emotional undercurrents in the family system.

72 Psychotropic Medication
All psychotropic medications change the affective condition and mental state of a person; they are meant to control emotions and behavior.

73 Psychotropic Medication
I always advise parents against covert medicine administration. As tempting and instantly effective this approach may seem, it encroaches on the patients' privacy and undermines the maturation process of their personality.

74 Psychotropic Medication
It is the patient's responsibility to prevent a relapse – not the parents'. Relapses are inevitable but will not impede learning.

75 Vocational Rehabilitation
First place, then train.

SCHIZOPHRENIA

AD(H)D – Genetic Vulnerability

Introduction

In 1973, I encountered the clinical picture of psycho-organic brain disorder in early childhood for the first time. At the time, this condition was referred to as minimal brain dysfunction, or MBD. With my experience of schizophrenia patients, which I had gained as psychiatric resident in Lausanne with Christian Müller in 1971 and in Scotland at Dingleton Hospital with Dan Jones in 1972, I noticed that the descriptions of MBD symptoms matched those of schizophrenia to an astonishingly high degree.

Seven years later, in the early 1980s, upon my return from the Georgetown Family Center in Washington, D.C. to Switzerland as a senior staff member, I noticed when I took care of many patients with schizophrenia and their families, that both – patients and their family members – exhibited MBD symptoms more frequently than other families. This observation gradually led me to the conclusion that this brain disorder, currently referred to as ADHD, might represent the long sought-after inherited genetic *vulnerability* factor, which plays an important role in the development of schizophrenia. Schizophrenia researcher Luc Ciompi also observed the astounding correlation between cognitive disorders of schizophrenia patients and those of children with MBD/ADHD and recorded this in his book *Affekt Logik* (affect-logic).

The condition of AD(H)D, which had long been controversial even among child psychiatrists, is nowadays generally recognized as a genetically inherited condition, a functional brain disorder that exists from birth.

For quite a while, it was assumed that children with AD(H)D would outgrow this diagnosis, so the symptoms would disappear in adulthood. Today, we know that many of the features persist, yet adults have mostly learned to manage their symptoms. Realizing this, psychiatry now also had to deal with the topic of AD(H)D in adulthood. On top of this, it had been discovered that adults with ADHD often have an additional diagnosis of mental health problems. According to statistical studies performed by P. Baud, up to 75% of individuals with AD(H)D receive an additional psychiatric diagnosis in adulthood, with some estimates even reaching 80%.

With new techniques, AD(H)D brain dysfunctions can be visualized today through diagnostic imaging such as functional magnetic resonance imaging (MRI) and positron emission tomography (PET). This visual evidence was not possible previously and is most probably the reason why the syndrome was so long disputed by many experts but is now commonly accepted. By measuring oxygen consumption, or consumption of radioactively labeled glucose, both overactive and underactive brain regions can be identified. The same diagnostic imaging that had been used to visualize AD(H)D has also been used on schizophrenia patients and their families. Test results have revealed malfunctioning in the forebrains of AD(H)D patients as well as schizophrenia patients and their relatives.

Let us return to the symptoms of AD(H)D and schizophrenia. The very same symptoms which can be found in AD(H)D – slight distractibility, lack of stimulus inhibition, system overflow as well as the visual inability to differentiate between foreground and background or between details, and more significant features, are also found in schizophrenia patients and their relatives. Even before the manifestation of acute illness, these symptoms could be identified in a thorough neuropsychological evaluation as subtle indicators of a genetic vulnerability in both patients and their relatives. These symptoms were referred to by Süllwold as a basic functional disorder of the brain in schizophrenia patients. Even though a connection to AD(H)D was not established, these organic vulnerability factors of the brain, or basic dysfunctions, almost exactly correspond with those of AD(H)D.

Even the scientific findings of Eugen Bleuler in 1911 suggested that schizophrenia patients are hyper perceptive and therefore less likely to be visually deceived than healthy people. This indicates that Bleuler had already observed symptoms in schizophrenia patients that could be related to AD(H)D, which confirms my hypothesis that AD(H)D must be the genetically inherited vulnerability of schizophrenia.

To test my hypothesis that AD(H)D is the genetically inherited organic brain vulnerability of schizophrenia, I conducted a retrospective survey of schizophrenia patients with respect to AD(H)D symptoms in childhood. Parents of children with schizophrenia did indeed report symptoms of AD(H)D significantly more often than parents of children in the control group. These findings suggested that a diagnosis of AD(H)D can be at least suspected in the case of schizophrenia retrospectively. Some of my subjects had indeed been diagnosed with AD(H)D in childhood. Through clinical observation, I found that siblings or other family members of schizophrenia patients were often diagnosed with AD(H)D.

In a long-term study by David Goldblatt, in which various psychological factors were measured in childhood, attention disorder – the typical main symptom of AD(H)D – was the only factor that significantly correlated with subsequent schizophrenic disorders, a finding, which also supports my hypothesis.

According to statistics, 5% to 10% of all children exhibit features of AD(H)D. However, only about 1% of the population suffers from schizophrenia. An individual with AD(H)D will therefore not necessarily develop a schizophrenic disorder. Regarding AD(H)D, additional factors are essential for the development of schizophrenia. Based on my experience, these additional factors consist of parenting style and interactions with the school environment. Environmental conditions, however, can be changed. Managing the environment of children with AD(H)D therefore plays an extremely important preventive role. Diagnosis and medical treatment with Ritalin are nowhere near sufficient to impede the development of a secondary disease such as schizophrenia. To prevent children with AD(H)D from developing a secondary mental illness, more experts with knowledge of how to deal with AD(H)D children would be required in the educational system.

Characteristics of children with ADHD and ADD

In order to become better acquainted with ADHD and ADD, the following offers a brief summary of some of the most frequent symptoms. It also aids our understanding of the difficulties involved in raising children who have the syndrome:

ADHD
Attention deficit:
- Short attention span and easy distractibility. Difficulty in focusing on a given task in case of low interest
- Hyperfocus on something of high interest

Impulsivity:
- Heightened emotional irritability
- Decreased impulse control
- Sensation-seeking and extreme exploratory behavior, leading to the transgression of official boundaries
- Disruptive social behavior and a lack of respect for social boundaries in a relationship context
- Aggressive outbursts with antisocial behavior if needs are denied or limits are set
- Aggressive defensive behavior in environments of intrusive educational disciplinary measures

Hypersensitivity:

- Pronounced sensitivity to noise, smell, taste and touch
- Emotional hypersensitivity and high reactivity
- Lacking an affective filtering of environmental stimuli
- High emotional intelligence and hyper-social behavior, or aggressive defense reaction

Motor symptoms:
- Hyperactivity, the symptom of a restless child
- Lacking fine motor skills, i.e. displays signs of clumsiness and poor dexterity
- Poor motor coordination of sequences, impaired hand-eye coordination, clumsiness in all ball games
- Outstanding motor skills and pronounced hand-eye coordination

Cognitive symptoms:
- Visual cognitive disorders, i.e. decreased spatial perception and its opposite: particularly good spatial perception
- Inability to distinguish between foreground and background
- Auditory processing disorder caused by insufficient ability to distinguish between sounds
- Decreased serial memory

Insufficient channeling ability:
- Lacking the ability to focus when presented with excessive stimuli
- Fast over-stimulation through intake of many simultaneous stimuli leading
- to "sensory overload", thus increased sensitivity to stress

Difficulties with automation:
- Problems with going on "autopilot" and thus difficulties in learning rules
- Difficulties in learning from own mistakes

Insufficient adaptability:
- Intense reactions to all types of unannounced and unexpected changes
- Fear of new and unfamiliar situations

Learning disabilities:
- Dyslexia, reading and spelling disability
- Dyscalculia, difficulty understanding number-related concepts (incl. calculations)
- Disorder of serial memory, difficulties in left/right orientation
- Poor perception of time
- Reduced capacity for abstract thinking

Creativity:
- People with ADHD are often highly creative
- It is easier for them to break rules and transcend boundaries

ADD

All symptoms listed for ADHD are also present in ADD except for the motor hyperactivity and the impulsivity in terms of aggression. In ADD children, all impulsivity is inwardly directed and manifests itself in ruminating thoughts.

ADHD/ADD and education

A most impressive document of the educational difficulties often experienced by children with AD(H)D is a description by Jean-Jacques Rousseau (1712–1778), who worked unsuccessfully as a tutor for Monsieur de Mably in 1740; the original document can be found in *Les Confessions*, which was first published after his death in Geneva, 1782.

"I had about as much knowledge as was necessary for a tutor and believed that I had a talent for this; but during the year I spent with the Mably family, it became clear that I wasn't able. The gentleness of my disposition would have enabled me to practice this profession had it not been for my stormy outbursts. As long as things went favorably, and my efforts (which I did not spare) were met with success, I was an angel; when things went wrong, I was a devil. When my pupils did not understand me, I was beside myself, and when they were mischievous, I could have killed them. However, this was no way to make them wise and well behaved. I had two under my care, and they had very different personalities. Sainte-Marie who was between eight and nine years old was well presented with an alert mind and was quite lively, boisterous, mischievous, and malicious but a cheerful malice. The younger one, named Condillac, who was between six and seven years old, seemed almost stupid and was absent-minded, stubborn as a mule, and could not grasp anything. One can image that between these two children, I had a difficult time. With patience and cold blood, I might have achieved success, but lacking both, I didn't achieve anything noteworthy, nothing worth mentioning, and my pupils failed miserably. I was not lacking in perseverance, but I did lack coolness and especially wisdom. I could only make use of three means, which are always futile and often disastrous with children. These are feeling, rational reflection, and anger. Sainte-Marie soon made me succumb and brought me to tears; I wanted him to succumb as if it was reasonable to suppose a child could be susceptible to such emotions. I soon exhausted myself trying to reason with him as though he could have understood me. Because he sometimes made very subtle objections, I took him seriously when he disagreed. The little Condillac embarrassed me even more: he neither understood nor answered, nor was he concerned with anything, and he had an unprecedented stubbornness; never was he more triumphant than when he made me angry because then he was the reasonable one, and I the child. I saw all my faults, studied the minds of my pupils, I comprehended them very well, and I believe that I was not once deceived by their cunning. But what was the use of seeing the evil without being able to apply a remedy? While I saw through everything, I prevented nothing. I succeeded in nothing. Everything that I did was exactly what I should not have done. I had as little success for myself as for my pupils."

In 1740, AD(H)D was not yet an issue, nor was it a diagnosis for children or adults. However, in 2013 we would probably associate Rousseau's impulsive behavior with ADHD. He describes himself as a teacher lacking in patience and the necessary cold blood. He describes the personality of his pupil Sainte-Marie as "alert, lively, boisterous, mischievous, and malicious" – a child with ADHD. Condillac, too, is termed "stupid, absent-minded, and stubborn" – a child with ADD.

Rousseau describes situations that I come across every day, nearly 300 years later. I hear the same complaints from many desperate parents and teachers of children with ADHD and ADD. However, many are not quite as self-critical as Rousseau was in his written records. Rousseau recognized his personal failure as a teacher. Today, many adults lack that critical distance and self-reflection, condemning the stubborn children and punishing their uncooperative behavior with bad grades and admonishment; they usually do not query how they might change their own behavior to meet the children's need, which would make their attempts at educating them more successful.

Rousseau writes: "When my pupils did not understand me, I was beside myself, and when they were mischievous, I could have killed them". Rousseau did not beat his two pupils – probably because he realized in time that the use of violence would not have changed Sainte-Marie and Condillac. In fact, extreme parental measures such as violence fail to help with managing children with AD(H)D and are rather more likely to cause increased stubbornness and oppositional reactions as well as psychiatric illness later on.

If we consider the behavior of children with AD(H)D in the context of Rousseau's text and the education of his two pupils, we would probably agree entirely with his words. Emotionally charged, irritable behavior and overzealous arguing do not only lead to little educational success but will negatively affect the development of these children in all age groups. If their parents also suffer from AD(H)D but have not reflected on it, they do not recognize the problems they are causing, nor do they accept them. If teachers lack the knowledge and therefore the competence to deal with these children, they can indeed seriously impair the children's development.

To shed light on this serious educational problem with AD(H)D children, I have analyzed different parenting styles in families with schizophrenia and correlated them with the occurrence of AD(H)D. In families with schizophrenia, this study has shown a highly significant correlation between symptoms of AD(H)D and emotionally negative, fear-inducing parenting styles as well as succumbing behavior in conflict situations. This damaging mixture of AD(H)D symptoms in children and fear-inducing parenting style, as well as the yielding and non-consistent parenting behavior in conflict situations, obviously represents a combination of risk factors that promote the development of schizophrenia.

> Children with AD(H)D are particularly sensitive to fear-inducing parenting and educational styles.

In a study by Gutzwiller et al. (2005) on parenting styles and parent-child relationships and their influence on children's health, it was found that the children of parents with a mature parenting style exhibit less health-damaging behavior, such as the use of tobacco and cannabis during adolescence, and generally feel better. The study confirmed the significant influence of parenting on children's health as adolescents. Conversely, parents and educators who subject children with AD(H)D to immature and impatient parenting styles damage the health of these children.

It can be assumed that an environment rife with problems such as insecure emotional attitudes in parenting matters, unacknowledged conflict within the partnership and additional hidden problems from the family of origin hinder the healthy development of sensitive children with AD(H)D during childhood, and especially in adolescence.

Conflict behavior of adults with AD(H)D

The two main characteristics of individuals with AD(H)D are high sensitivity and difficulties in controlling impulses. In 1740, Rousseau had described this in relation to his two pupils and himself. Both characteristics contribute to high reactivity. If parents of children with AD(H)D also have AD(H)D, which is often the case because AD(H)D is genetically inherited, it can rapidly lead to escalating conflict situations. This is also consistent with the findings of Cupa (1997), who observed in families with schizophrenia that fathers reported conflicts three times more often than fathers from the control group. This correlates with the findings that families with AD(H)D in general are reported to have more conflicts, more divorces and more job changes.

In a study of 500 adults with AD(H)D and a control group of equal size, with matching ages and gender, Faraone and Biederman (2004a) found a significantly higher divorce rate and more frequent job changes with different employment relationships in a period of ten years.

Families with AD(H)D have not only more conflict within their family systems but also within the wider community in general. Relationships of individuals with AD(H)D are characterized by a high tendency towards escalation in conflict situations. If an individual expresses an opinion about an issue, the person with AD(H)D often interrupts them before the sentence is even finished. If both have AD(H)D, they simultaneously interrupt each other. The conversation is thus like a game of ping-pong, quickening back and forth until the nerves of one of them are raw. Verbal confrontations between spouses – and between parents and children with AD(H)D – often follow this pattern.

The arguments are usually emotionally charged. Both sides try to persuade each other with emotional fervor and make their voices heard at the same time, but neither of them listens. The result is that both discussion partners feel misunderstood. Both withdraw, because they feel left out. The conflict remains unresolved, and the relationship remains unreconciled.

If the partners resume the discussion on the same topic later on, the struggle continues because both persist in clinging to their opinion. Each party sticks to their preconceived ideas, secretly hoping for more empathy from the other.

Because of their impulsive mindset, individuals with AD(H)D also tend to immediately assign meaning to a statement or a remark – long before they have listened to the entire sentence. They seem to be unable to let go of their preconceived ideas. Such interaction patterns are usually perceived as stubbornness. They often lead to misunderstandings and conflicts within and outside of the family.

In patriarchal family structures, conflicts between parties are usually prevented from escalating and are halted in an authoritarian manner. However, if this *patriarchal conflict resolution strategy* – which resorts to fear-inducing authority – ceases to be accepted by the family members, conflicts continue unhindered.

The following therefore provides a brief outline of a conflict management checklist for a more successful outcome for AD(H)D partners experiencing conflicts.

Conflict resolution and debriefing of parents with AD(H)D

The following tips may be helpful for developing a partnership conflict resolution strategy on equal terms between parents who are affected by AD(H)D:

| Conflicts can never be resolved in the heat of a battle.

- Both parties must calm down before they attempt to resolve a conflict.
- In a calm state, the different perspectives and viewpoints can be presented in turn and explained.
- The conflicting parties should always try to comprehend his counterpart's point of view.

The debriefing should proceed as follows:
- The person who wants to talk about the conflict should first describe the circumstances and the situation as impartially and objectively as possible.
- The individual leading the exchange should not immediately start the discussion with his own point of view.
- Once he has outlined his standpoint as clearly as possible, the conflict partner should be given ample scope and be asked about his motives, his reaction and behavior in that conflict situation.
- If the conflict partner does not understand the other's motives, he should avoid accusing him of false claims and untruths.
- Instead, he should rather continue to ask the conflict partner questions until he can comprehend his motivation and behavior as objectively as possible.
- If the questioning individual has understood the situation of his partner's and their behavior well enough, he should validate it with appreciation, for example: "I can understand your reaction".

Understanding the other's behavior, however, does not necessarily mean agreeing with it.

- After a short break, the person leading the conversation begins with a description of his own point of view, but without trying to convince or dominate the conflict partner with his own narrative.
- If the counterpart reacts with counter-arguments, he should not

AD(H)D – Genetic Vulnerability

defend his point of view with further explanations but rather offer his own position as clearly as possible.
- It is advantageous to stand firm and reflect one's own point of view without intending to persuade or fight the other.
- The desire to persuade the other is always an indication that one is not quite self-assured. Seeking the other's consent indicates a relationship of dependency. A position of unresolved dependency does not allow for constructive debate.
- After presenting his own perspective, the person who talks must ask whether the summary of his viewpoint is understandable. However, this does not mean that the conflict partner agrees.
- Sometimes, the conflict partner does not accept further questioning since he immediately feels under pressure to agree. The conflict thus begins anew.
- The person leading the discussion should therefore always be aware that confrontational issues sometimes simply should be left as they are.

> The debriefing is not a power struggle over who is right and who is wrong, but rather an exchange of different viewpoints between equals.

Typical labels attached to children with ADHD and ADD

Children with AD(H)D can easily assume certain roles through their innate personality traits not only in the family but also in the wider social environment, for example in day care, in school, and in the playground. Their behavior often provokes negative emotional attention on the part of their surroundings:

- **The troublemaker or scapegoat** is a common behavior pattern of children with AD(H)D. They are often difficult to deal with at school

,and they easily become the subject of negative focus. Teachers usually respond to the lack of impulse control and distractibility of these children with punishment and social exclusion. In the case of disruptive behavior during class, they are ejected from the class more frequently than other children, and they receive bad grades in social competence.

- **The class clown** is another typical role inhabited by children with AD(H)D. They make a virtue of necessity and use their otherness to entertain their classmates. However, their teachers are usually not amused and not on their side because they feel that pupils playing the fool undermine their authority. Yet, in this way, they try to escape their social isolation, often without success.
- **Slowness and dawdling** (which are due to high distractibility), compulsive self-controlling behavior to avoid mistakes, and lack of motivation through lack of interest have fewer social consequences but hinder the completion of homework and learning in general. Despite their intelligence, their performance is often well below their IQ-level. This triggers incomprehension and criticism in teachers and parents.
- **Over-adaptation of hypoactive**, shy children with ADD – in contrast to hyperactive children with ADHD – hypoactive children with ADD are a slightly different challenge for educators. These children are mostly dreamers and withdrawn, especially when they are protecting themselves against injury. They are easily overlooked in the classroom as well as on the playground. They also lose out in competitions in school. In conflict situations, they are unable to defend themselves because of their sensitivity and shyness. As outsiders, they are socially isolated and often become victims of bullying and mobbing.

For parents and educators, it is often difficult to understand why children with ADHD and ADD do not respond to conventional educational methods, even though they are successful with others. These children require individualized educational methods. Educators should minimize the risk of provoking or fostering a secondary mental illness in these children because they are unable to deal with their innate personality traits.

Difficulties in learning rules

In the family and in school, the educational task is primarily a socialization process. Children are to learn how to adapt to the social environment, and teenagers should gradually integrate into adult society. At a societal level, all social classes are subject to the generally accepted rules of conduct.

For individuals with ADHD, it is difficult to conform to those norms at school and later in professional life as adults. They always present a deviation from the norm and resist all normalization processes. This makes them a great challenge for their parents and educators. However, deviations from the norm which create disturbances in the routine of an established system should not be considered an illness per se. Unusual thinking and behavioral patterns of teenagers are nowadays too often considered psychiatric symptoms. In the firm belief that they are a sign of impending disease, when in fact they belong to the phase of being an adolescent, parents and medical professionals try to correct them with medication and behavioral therapy.

Children with ADHD generally have trouble learning rules; they are simply unable to follow them for the sake of obedience. Rules must therefore always be negotiated carefully with them, considering their temperament, and adapted to their nature in terms of what is and is not possible. Rules should be established in a consensual manner and formulated concisely. Too many rules overwhelm children with ADHD and stifle their creative personality; excessive instruction can also cause them to erupt and ignore or go against every attempt at guiding them.

Successful education of children with ADHD continually needs reinventing. The educational methods must be adapted to their personality and the level of their development. Yet ADHD children never represent nor fit the norm. In fact, they resist normalization processes constantly. The rules which educators or parents require the children to learn should therefore be limited to the essentials. Educating them with simple rules, and being consistent about them, provides structure and allows for a smooth daily routine.

Parents who overload the system with too many rules end up not being able to enforce them at all. Yet yielding and granting too many exceptions, children quickly learn to break the rules and take the lead as they please. However, this often triggers feelings of guilt in the children, and anger in the parents towards the child.

> Rituals and regular daily structures are particularly useful for learning rules and provide a sense of security in children with ADHD.

Cooperation instead of power struggles

Regardless of social class and educational ambition, disobedience in children with ADHD is an enormous challenge for the parents. When dealing with defiant children, parents usually repeat their commands countless times, not realizing that they no longer have – or have never had – their attention. They continue giving orders, yet always without success until they lose patience. As a next step, they raise their voice and threaten the child with punishment in an attempt to make them obey. Mothers often lapse into the suffering role. They present themselves as victims of their disobedient offspring and thus try to instill feelings of guilt to encourage their cooperation.

Dealing with disobedience in children with ADHD is a strikingly daring art that requires tremendous self-control on behalf of caretakers such as parents and educators. They often tend to punish the frequently aggressive outbursts with the attitude: "That will not do. I cannot tolerate this behavior, otherwise the child will believe that anything goes". Yet if parents and educators do not reflect on their own conduct and ask themselves what has elicited the outburst, they will fail to identify why children can't obey. Teachers often neither accept nor admit their helplessness, although they are overwhelmed by the situation. As a result of their own powerlessness, they project their despair as anger and label the child as "bad", which is merely an excuse for their educational failure.

Another option is the withdrawal to relieve themselves of responsibility, which elicits feelings of guilt in the youngsters. However, neither teachers nor parents are aware what damaging effect it has on the self-esteem of that child, and they thereby lay the foundation for mental disorder.

Power struggles by parents and teachers with these children are common. Children with ADHD are said to be headstrong. Parents as well as teachers are often insufficiently instructed and prepared for dealing with this stubbornness because they lack alternatives to their traditional educational methods.

There is often no easy way of trying to divert children with ADHD from their set intentions. If parents or teachers nevertheless attempt to do so, power struggles will inevitably arise. Yet, these children have remarkable stamina and are often more persistent than adults, who quickly reach their limit. Out of desperation, they often become contemptuous and condemn the child for being a disobedient and adversarial youngster.

Adults who yield for the sake of peace often get angry with themselves. Yet, by caving in too often, they turn their youngsters into little tyrants who are always winning but live in a perpetually angry atmosphere. A survey on this issue which I conducted has shown that parents of children with schizophrenia have yielded during conflict situations more often than parents in the control group. This is yet another indication that these schizophrenia patients – even if undiagnosed – were as children most likely children with ADHD. Their intentions can not be easily redirected, and their parents therefore often give in with their stubborn youngsters when conflicts arise.

In trying to control aggressive behavior in children, parents and educators display an openly belligerent attitude as well. The situation tends to escalate into a power struggle, once again creating a negative emotional climate, not at all conducive to the educational task with highly impulsive children with ADHD. Parents as well as teachers therefore often give up or resort to rigid authoritarian punishment, condemning the children wholesale and, if still not successful, hand them over to child psychiatry.

Rather than engaging in a power struggle, adults should ask themselves: "Why are they refusing to comply with rules or requests? What could be done differently"?

Was the child given enough time to complete the task? Were the instructions only given in passing? Or was the adolescent emotionally excited and therefore not receptive? Were the instructions too complicated? Did they contain too many messages at once? Or were the caretakers themselves not fully convinced of their educational aim?

Suggestions

If you have found out why your child is defiant, start again from scratch. This time try to encourage the child to cooperate. Take your time, be patient, and always adhere to the following rules:

- Wait until you and your child have calmed down.
- Then get his attention.
- Make sure that you formulate the instruction as a rule in the sense of "I would like you to put your shoes in the shoe cabinet when you come home. Otherwise, someone might trip over them". Avoid a command coupled with a threat, "Put your shoes away, or else somebody might break his leg!"
- Give the instruction in a calm but firm tone. "C'est le ton qui fait la

AD(H)D – Genetic Vulnerability

musique." It's the tone of your voice that makes the difference. The instruction should sound neither aggressive nor irritated.
- The instruction should never be paired with criticism. Describe how you want it to be done and not how you *don't* want it to be done!
- If possible, always give a single instruction or one rule at a time.
- Make sure that your order does not contain any "double message".
- Your instruction should always match your emotional communication.
- Don't be sarcastic.
- If there is a power struggle, you should first ask yourself: "Have I made too many demands?"
- If you think that your requirements were adequate, make sure that you yourself are convinced that you have requested the right thing. If so, you need to remobilize your mental strength. It's not about persuading the adolescent but rather asserting yourself.

Dealing with learning difficulties

Inconsistent intellectual performance often poses a big problem for ambitious parents who have planned an academic career for their offspring with ADHD. Actually, they may have outstanding talents in specific areas, but their performance may be below average in others. Some may perform well at school because of their quick mind. However, they often end up failing when a task calls for sustained attention and continuous learning over an extended period of time.

Learning disorders and fluctuations are easily noticed at school because teaching methods and teaching aids are designed for average students. Performance and behavior are graded based on the class average. Because children with ADHD are easily distracted, and their willingness to learn essentially depends on their emotional state, their commitment to performing can fluctuate from high performance to complete refusal.

Children with ADHD are placed at a disadvantage because their performance is compared and graded in line with the class average, while their special abilities are often not considered. Teachers and parents react to the volatile performance curve with statements such as, "You could if you only put your mind to it."

For teachers or parents who wish to organize learning therapies for their children, the following rule applies: A lasting good relationship with the child is more important than therapy. If children oppose therapy, it should not be forced upon them against their will. Learning disorders can be evaluated and treated by special therapists; however, teachers and parents may also be able to master proper methods of handling learning disorders with the help of appropriate expert advice.

- Children with ADHD should not be judged by their mistakes and weaknesses, but rather receive appreciation for their strengths.
- Support and appreciation strengthen their willingness to better their weaknesses such as learning difficulties they experience at school.
- In cases of stress and impatience on the part of parents or teachers, the ability to learn and reproduce what they have learned is greatly impaired in children with ADHD. A steady hand, however, promotes their educational development and their fun in learning.
- Special talents in sports, music or drawing should be encouraged as far as possible but should not be misused as a "motivational bait", according to the motto: "You may only play football again when you've got a better grade in math." The ban on something they like to do will not motivate children with ADHD to work more for the math class; on the contrary, any motivation may vanish completely under such circumstances.
- To deal with exam-induced angst, children with ADHD must be taught to arrive on time for the examination proceedings, so that they

can calm down, concentrate, and prepare themselves before the examination starts.

Traumatic school experiences

Despite their high and sometimes even above-average intelligence, children with ADHD often perform worse at school than their level of intelligence would indicate. As a result of their attention deficit, they have a learning disability, which educational experts often wrongly label as a lack of motivation. If their impulsive temperament causes additional behavioral problems, teachers usually give up and expel them from class. The chance of higher education for these children is thus significantly reduced.

Traumatic experiences at school also give rise to defensive behavior later in life. Even the smallest injustices, or fear of failure may provoke vehement pre-emptive reactions, and therefore evasive behavior towards anything that is remotely related to learning or schooling.

> **CASE HISTORY:** In elementary school, Konrad had difficulties learning languages, and was diagnosed with ADHD. He had immense problems with spelling in German, English and French. This prompted the teacher time and again to display Konrad's mistakes in front of the class. When Konrad was in his last school year, he could no longer endure the shaming and humiliations by the teacher. He stayed home without an excuse and started to use cannabis and cocaine. Konrad's mother became very concerned that her son would not receive his final certificate and would therefore not find an apprenticeship. The father used threats to motivate him to go back to school. A conflict developed between the parents, whereupon the mother sought advice in my family group. However, the assistance came too late; it was no longer possible to persuade Konrad to return to school.

FOLLOW-UP: When a social worker organized an apprenticeship for Konrad, he was happy with it, but he could not be moved to go to school even though he had a very insightful teacher. He developed stomach problems on school nights and would vomit every morning before going to school. All therapeutic efforts were in vain. They were perceived and rejected by him as pressure. Konrad could not be encouraged to go to school again. His school phobia was beyond repair.

Adolescence – endless quagmires

The impulsiveness of youngsters with ADHD accentuates in adolescence. If they show positive emotions, they quickly make friends, but if they are hurt, they immediately behave aggressively, and get rejected. Educators often have difficulties comprehending how these kids can show such aggression while also exhibiting great sensitivity and vulnerability to negative feedback. Because they lack understanding, educators leave the youngsters to fend for themselves with their extreme emotions. Their way of thinking runs along the lines of, "They are like mimosas. They expect to be handled with kid gloves but are rough and reckless with others, that won't do!" Further, adults also tend to adhere to the motto: "Don't do unto others what you would not have done unto yourself." This is a saying from adults about adults. But adolescents with ADHD are not grown-ups. They are not yet able to control their emotions. That's why they should still be given a so-called puppy license, a term which derives from animal psychology. Here, puppies are tolerated by their mothers and offered protection from adult aggression even when they "attack" them. The same should apply to human beings and their offspring.

> For parents and educators, the number one rule is: get your own emotions under control before you deal with ADHD adolescents.

- Endless discussions with adolescents with ADHD are not helpful.
- Parents and other educators often lose their self-control in the process. This may end in an emotional escalation, resulting in an educational impasse.
- Yielding occasionally, however, does not mean that principles have to be given up all together.
- Parents should grant their teenagers a certain amount of protection in confrontations.
- Pejorative or even derogatory attacks on teenagers harm their self-esteem.
- Teenagers must sometimes come out on top. This strengthens their self-esteem and is conducive to the development of their personality; parents don't always have to win the power struggle.

Adolescents with ADHD mature later and therefore need more time to adapt to social rules. Rules and values should routinely be enforced with mental strength and self-confidence. Punishment is not in the least bit helpful, it triggers aggression and resistance. Moreover, rules may be violated, yet breaking rules is part of puberty – yet teenagers should face up to the consequences.

Conflict management in adolescence

Teenagers with ADHD and ADD are easily offended. They react badly to criticism, especially when it is combined with hostile communication. It thus may lead to violent and aggressive confrontations (ADHD), or to complete withdrawal (ADD). The following rules should be kept in mind, so that conflicts don't get out of hand:

- Parents and educators must listen first and show empathy towards the adolescent's point of view.

- Only after listening should adults present their position clearly but without trying to persuade or convince.
- If teenagers react intensely, their emotions should be accepted without judgement.
- Emotionality and impulsivity cannot be argued away; it can only be calmed down.
- The spirit of adolescents' stubbornness should be regarded as an act of self-assertion as well as self-defense. One should thus continue to negotiate calmly, avoiding harmful power struggles.
- When defining conditions, adolescents should deliberately be granted some leeway. Most importantly, they must be allowed to try things out to gain experience, i.e. learning by doing.
- Refusals, unilateral decision-making, rejections, top-down commands and punishment are reactive educational practices that reinforce adolescents' oppositional demeanor.
- Leading by example, mental presence, acting with foresight and clear statements are all useful proactive tools for issuing instructions.
- The aim is to promote autonomy and responsibility and encourage the young to cooperate on an equal level.

Male pubescents with ADHD usually overcome their vulnerability with exaggerated posturing and aggression. Girls with ADHD or ADD often refuse to communicate with their parents or educators, withdrawing to their bedroom, discussing their problems with friends on Facebook, Twitter or in their diary, but reject relating to their parents. However, adolescents with ADHD can also show sudden flashes of reasonable behavior if not being hectored too much about principles and "normal" behavior.

AD(H)D and use of drugs

Teenagers do not want to be ordered around, neither by their parents nor other authority figures. Their top priority is to make their own decisions and to be independent.

Yet in cases where they display self-destructive behavior, one has to take a position. Many adolescents nowadays consume cannabis or other drugs to distance themselves from stressful circumstances in the family and at school. Sometimes they also consume because of peer pressure, or simply out of curiosity. Adolescents wish to and need to make their own experiences, which includes the consumption of cannabis and other drugs, sometimes to cross legal boundaries, but sometimes also to the point of self-destruction. The use of cannabis contributes to the risk of psychosis in young people with ADHD. Moffitt (2006) has shown that young people who consume cannabis can develop psychosis when there is a certain genetic disposition. I assume that this genetic disposition must be ADHD. Thus, the use of cannabis among young people with ADHD may indeed trigger schizophrenia. The consumption of cannabis in that case has a lasting, harmful effect on the development of the personality in these youngsters.

> Youngsters with ADHD and ADD are not only more susceptible to schizophrenia when they consume drugs, they also get more easily addicted than those without ADHD. They tend to use the drugs as self-medication and become hooked on them.

Cannabis – a risk factor for psychosis

Cannabis use among young people has increased dramatically over the past decade and a half. In a study by Wulf Rössler et al., an increased hospitalization rate of young people developing schizophrenia could be determined in recent years. The study shows that schizophrenia rates have tripled among 15- to 19-year-old cannabis users and has doubled among 20- to 25-year-old cannabis users. This increasing number of admissions of young people with schizophrenia into psychiatric hospitals has been linked by the authors to the increasing cannabis consumption and a higher concentration of tetrahydrocannabinol of indoor-grown cannabis plants.

In another study from 2005, young people who were diagnosed with schizophrenia for the first time were using cannabis regularly in more than 90% of cases, which is well above the average cannabis use of young people in general. This study therefore suggests that there must be a clear correlation between cannabis use and schizophrenia in young adults.

Stanley Zammit et al. (2007) examined 35 studies in a meta-analysis, in which tens of thousands of people were observed over a period of one to 27 years regarding the effects of cannabis use in relation to the development of mental illness. They found that the risk of psychosis was 40% higher in occasional cannabis users. In people who consumed cannabis weekly or even daily, the risk was increased by 50%. If, additionally, consumers came from psychologically stressed families, the risk of psychosis spiked even more, sometimes up to 200%.

In a follow-up study over a period of ten years, conducted by Jim van Os et al. (2011), it could also be determined that the consumption of cannabis significantly increased the risk of psychosis, regardless of age, gender, socio-economic levels, rural-urban differences, environmental factors, or childhood trauma. It could also be clearly shown that cannabis use was not self-treatment of a pre-existing psychosis. All individuals with pre-existing psychosis were excluded from the study. Cannabis use could therefore be clearly confirmed as a risk factor for the development of the persistent psychosis of schizophrenia.

Renowned scientists therefore consider it relatively plausible that cannabis use during puberty can lead to psychosis. This psychosis-inducing effect arises from the fact that cannabis disturbs the functioning of neurotransmitters in the brain such as dopamine. Through this interruption, the whole communication system in the brain, such as cognitive processing, short-term memory, learning ability and reaction time, is impaired. The influence of cannabis also causes social indifference, which

AD(H)D – Genetic Vulnerability

is called *amotivational syndrome*. Social learning is thus inhibited and the person therefore socially disadvantaged in everyday life.

My clinical observations of numerous therapy cases over many years have convinced me that cannabis use in adolescents is a clear risk factor for the development of schizophrenia. In some of my young patients, schizophrenia had started after having consumed cannabis just once; many others had used it regularly.

> **CASE HISTORY:** The parents of Roswita had divorced when she was a child. She grew up together with her older sister and her mother. Once she hit puberty, she felt drawn to a creative job and chose an apprenticeship in the arts. She entered into circles where cannabis was consumed regularly and also began to smoke it. At the same time, she had the strong wish to finish her high school degree but under the negative effects of cannabis, it was not feasible. At the same time, she had a love affair with a man who put her under pressure by massively harassing her. She developed delusional ideas with high anxiety and was admitted to a psychiatric hospital in an acute state of schizophrenia. On the ward, she was rebellious and the staff could not handle her. The ward doctor asked me for a consultation. I advised to call in the father and empower him in his father-daughter relationship.
>
> **COMMENTARY:** Roswita had experienced a stressful situation through her parents' divorce. There were two additional biographical stress factors: the use of cannabis and the imposed love affair. These three stress factors promoted the outbreak of psychosis.

Cannabis as a problem-solver

Cannabis use by young people is often referred to as self-medication as a means of problem-solving. A stressful family environment can be more bearable with the elucidative effect of cannabis. But in many cases a new problem arises when the hallucinogenic effects of cannabis enhances psychosis.

CASE HISTORY: As the youngest of four brothers, Alex had been affected most by the quarrels of his parents. Under the influence of alcohol, the father was repeatedly violent towards the mother. The children were on their mother's side, and fled with her to a shelter for victims of domestic violence. This angered the father even more. Alex dodged the daily drama at home from an early age and joined the homeless. He started to use cannabis and harder drugs. Not yet of legal age, he was sent to a correction home by the juvenile court. He went through several home placements until he was admitted to a drug withdrawal program. After the withdrawal, he developed acute paranoid schizophrenia and was hospitalized in a psychiatric ward for schizophrenia and addiction. However, he refused medication and didn't talk to the nurses or the doctors. Finally, they called in his father because he was the only person Alex would listen to. He accepted the father's advice to take medication.

COMMENTARY: Young people who tend to use drugs regularly during puberty are often exposed to prolonged stressful family constellations. They try to protect themselves from the emotional burden of the family through the shielding and euphoric effects of drugs. However, this coping strategy is an additional risk factor for the development of schizophrenia, adding to the already existing stressful family situation. Alex, as the youngest child, had to assume the role of mediator for his fighting parents. He felt responsible for the family atmosphere, but at the same time was most overburdened by it, which is why he fled from home.

Only when his father accepted his role as an authority figure and took care of Alex without being hindered by the marital dispute, did the son gain the necessary strength to become independent without feeling the need to mediate between his parents any longer.

AD(H)D – Genetic Vulnerability

Alex stayed in contact with his parents. During his regular visits with them, he consciously stayed out of the marital conflict. In other stressful entanglements with his neighbors, he became acutely psychotic two more times. He could, however, always be treated as an outpatient by family systems therapy.

> Cannabis use in adolescence as a problem-solving strategy in a stressful family environment ultimately becomes a decisive risk factor for the development of psychosis.

CASE HISTORY: Severin was the most sensitive of four siblings and reacted most strongly to the constant arguments between his parents. He began to use cannabis regularly as an adolescent. His mother and siblings were trying to stop him, yet to no avail. He was repeatedly admitted to a psychiatric hospital due to his acute psychotic state. After being discharged, he always went back to using cannabis with his friends. Severin developed paranoid schizophrenia with delusional ideas of persecution. He felt like someone was watching his every move and fought vehemently with officials at every opportunity.

COMMENTARY: Severin tried to shield himself from the disputes between his parents through cannabis use. To enjoy cannabis among his friends meant a nice alternative to the bad atmosphere at home, and to adult society in general. His relaxation method, which was meant to help him, nevertheless led to greater problems, as he repeatedly became psychotic. He was shouting in the middle of the night, swearing during the day, and was intimidating strangers on the street. The police often had to search for him and he was finally admitted for compulsory treatment in a psychiatric hospital. However, this reinforced his paranoid feelings that he was being persecuted by the entire world, and that society was against him. In his psychosis, he transposed his stressful situation from home to his environment in the form of ideas of persecution.

In the case of Severin, multiple risk factors thus triggered a renewed psychotic episode and induced the development of schizophrenia: innate ADHD as a genetic factor, environmental factors attributable to his parents' chronic conflicts, and cannabis use.

Guidelines for parents of adolescent cannabis users

Understandably, parents try to protect their young from the damaging effects of cannabis use. Therefore, they prohibit the consumption and control the abstinence of their teenagers. However, control measures such as bans, punishments and moralizing are counter-productive as concerns adolescent youngsters with ADHD. They rebel against it, which corresponds with their need for personal autonomy. Therefore, despite concerns and anxiety about the development of the adolescent, parents must learn to let them assume responsibility for their own health unconditionally. Even for parents of cannabis users who have already gone through an acute psychotic episode, the following rules apply:

- Step back from your caring role as a parent.
- Refrain from applying anxious control and punishment measures.
- Present your position on the use of cannabis as clearly and unambiguously as possible but do not try to convince.
- Do not declare your position on a regular basis, weekly or even daily. This results in a numbing effect through habituation, and in defensiveness on the part of the adolescents.
- Listen to the adolescents when arguing and respect their opinion.
- Enhance the adolescents' personal responsibility for their health.

If parents stick to these rules, the adolescents undergo a phase of trial and error and then learn to abstain from it, usually within one to two years, even if they have experienced a cannabis-induced psychosis.

Career choice – a decision-making process

Choosing a career is an important decision-making process in the life of each young person. For adolescents with ADHD, it is sometimes delayed and possibly more difficult because of their learning difficulties and their broad interests, and last but not least, because of their bad experiences in school. An unsuccessful career choice is an important stress factor we often find in the prelude to psychosis.

Career choices usually begin at puberty. For higher levels of education, such as university, the grades play a significant role. Bad grades reduce career opportunities. Moreover, too much pressure placed on children and their school achievements by the parents hinders the personality maturation of the child, particularly in youngsters with ADHD and additional learning disorders.

Missed learning through school absences can be made up for later on in life, but incomplete development of personality can only be corrected at great expense through long-term therapy and with a limited effect, if at all.

Sometimes, youngsters with ADHD also have career aspirations which parents react to with astonishment and with resistance, trying to talk their children out of their high-flying thoughts. I usually advise parents in such cases to take these special wishes seriously but to bet that reality will put a stop to them.

If adolescents with ADHD don't yet know what career to choose, their parents should patiently wait until the decision-making process is completed and they have made their own choice. A gap year, a meaningful new experience without affinity to any specific profession may be helpful in this respect. But pressure by the parents to hurry up may lead to an unfitting career choice, or to nothing at all as a result of the stubborn resistance of adolescents with ADHD.

The fact that adults with ADHD change their workplace more often than people without ADHD would also suggest that their career choice did not correspond to their wishes and was forced upon them at puberty.

Or they simply are bored with their job, and like to learn something new, which is also typical for people with ADHD.

ADHD and ADD – a genetic predisposition to mental illnesses

Today, frequent reference is made to comorbidity when adults with AD(H)D have an additional mental illness virtually added on to the symptoms of AD(H)D. Recent studies by P. Baud have shown that 70% of adults with AD(H)D were diagnosed with a further mental illness, such as eating disorders, depression, borderline syndrome, manic-depressive illness, or drug addiction and delinquency. This means that only about 30% of children with AD(H)D reach adulthood without developing an additional psychiatric disorder. This fact should make us alert to the issue of how preventive therapeutic measures could change this.

My hypothesis is that children with the AD(H)D genotype are generally vulnerable to developing different mental illnesses, not just schizophrenia, which is the theme of this book. The parenting style of the family and how schools deal with these children are crucial factors that influence the development of these various diseases arising in adolescence or later in life. The social behavior of children's environment, in my estimation, plays a decisive role in developing either an interesting and successful personality, or a psychiatric illness such as personality disorder, addiction, eating disorder, depression, or even schizophrenia and manic-depressive illness.

CASE HISTORY: Rosemarie was the scapegoat in her class. When she complained about it at home, her mother always took the side of the teachers, assuming her daughter had to learn to adapt.

After leaving school, Rosemarie refused any vocational training. She confined herself to her room and let no one come close to her. She aggressively rejected all attempts of help from her mother. The mother did not know what to do and had her committed to a psychiatric clinic, where she was diagnosed with psychosis. After leaving the hospital, Rosemarie continued to reject all attempts by her mother to contact her by telephone, letters or postcards.

COMMENTARY: Rosemarie was diagnosed with ADHD in childhood. Neither the teachers nor her mother, however, were instructed by professionals on how to deal with her ADHD to avoid her being at a disadvantage compared to the other children. Moreover, the teachers had no knowledge of ADHD. Only many years later, did Rosemarie's mother discuss her failure of her parenting practices in therapy, and felt greatly sorry for it. She had raised Rosemarie equally to her other siblings.

Rosemarie was hospitalized many times and failed to develop maturity in puberty, which could no longer be corrected. Rosemarie cut all ties with her parents as well as her therapists. She integrated neither professionally nor socially. She was leading the life of a chronic schizophrenia patient on the fringes of society, living off disability benefits.

I shall briefly outline some aspects which may arguably lead to various psychiatric illnesses in children with AD(H)D when they reach adulthood or even later on in their lives.

Drug addiction

Teenagers with ADHD protect themselves from any kind of stress, caused in particular by a patronizing and intrusive family environment, through self-medication often by means of consuming addictive substances. As reported by Hessler and Rice (2010), up to 50% of children with ADHD may develop drug addiction in adulthood as a result.

Antisocial personality disorder

A punitive, restrictive attitude towards male adolescents with ADHD may lead to antisocial personality disorder with delinquent behavior. They transgress the rigid limits of their parents, other educators and society in general, make their own rules within their peer group and create new norms out of their anti-social behavior.

Borderline personality disorder
Girls with ADHD whose individuality is restricted too much during puberty may develop a borderline personality disorder. They exhibit self-destructive behavior, or rebel by cutting themselves to dissipate emotional intensity and pain through physical pain. One female borderline patient was quoted as saying, "Only when blood flows, can I calm down".

Eating disorders
Anorexia and Bulimia are also typical illnesses among girls with ADHD who are not allowed to express their intense emotions within the family. Anorectic patients, almost starving themselves to death, tend to suppress feelings of anger.
Bulimic female patients who are socially restrained in their impulsivity act out their aggression through binge eating and vomiting in continuous self-destructive cycles. In very rare cases, impulsive girls with ADHD may also act out their emotionality in a delinquent manner, but this type of behavior is much more common in boys with ADHD.

Manic-depressive psychosis or bipolar disorder
Impulsivity and fierce temperaments in children with ADHD may lead to bipolar disorder if they are subject to too many strict rules within a fear-inducing, strict upbringing. During the manic phase of their illness, they suddenly let their temper run wild and ignore all social boundaries. During the depressive phase, however, they express remorse for the ways in which they acted during the manic phase.

Schizophrenia
Emotional over-involvement and invasive parental behavior towards

children with ADHD or ADD, as well as an ambivalent family environment, may lead to schizophrenia. These types of conduct can result in the build-up of an *emotional monster wave*, resulting in psychosis.

The previously mentioned studies of 2012 and 2017 by scientists from the Psychiatric Genomics Consortium, involving more than 60,000 patients, found common genetic risk factors in six different psychiatric diagnoses: attention deficit hyperactivity disorder, schizophrenia, manic-depressive psychosis or bipolar disorder, severe depression, autism, and eating disorders. The fact that the same risk factor of a certain gene locus could be determined in such various psychiatric diseases came as a great surprise in psychiatry – for me, however, it was a proof of my hypothesis.

> My hypothesis from decades of clinical observation and countless therapy cases: AD(H)D is a genetically inherited condition which – in 70% to 80% of cases – may lead to many different mental health problems in individuals as a result of unfavorable interactions with their environment – an epigenetic process.

Gene-environment interaction as a determining factor

Professionals in psychiatry nowadays generally accept the multifactorial hypothesis of schizophrenia, which means that several factors, interacting unfavorably with each other, are involved in the development of this illness. Innate genetic as well as environmental factors are both assumed to play a key role. Researchers of schizophrenia, however, have long been occupied with pure genetic research in twin and adoptive studies, which tended not to take into consideration environmental factors in terms of the interaction between the genetic factors, with a few exceptions. Only Tienari (1985) and Moffitt (2006) have examined the approach of gene-environment interaction in their psychiatric research.

In my clinical research, I have always focused on the gene-environment interaction. When considering hereditary factors such as ADHD and ADD, I always observed and analyzed the social influences of the affected individual's environment. This has provided me with extremely helpful insights into the development and the treatment of schizophrenia. This research approach should be used much more frequently in future schizophrenia studies. All the more because it could have a tremendous impact in terms of prevention. In many cases, one might alleviate, or even prevent, the development of mental illnesses. For this very reason, professionals in child care centers, kindergartens and schools should be trained in how to deal with children who have ADHD. Parents should be offered family therapy or educational counselling services for their difficult ADHD and ADD children without having to go through complicated diagnostic procedures.

Persons with ADHD are not only vulnerable to developing schizophrenia as dealt with in this book; they can also develop many other mental illnesses in case of an unfavorable gene-environment interaction. The fact that 70% to 80% of adults with ADHD receive a diagnosis of mental illness demonstrates that very clearly. Although modern brain research has proven that brain structures may change through environmental influences such as psychotherapy, psychiatry has not considered (adverse) social circumstances in the developmental of the illness in their basic research, nor has it used the expertise of systems therapy in the treatment of schizophrenia on a larger scale in recent years. To stress once more, ADHD and ADD are merely neurotypes of personality that are susceptible to developing psychiatric disorders. They should not be treated as a psychiatric diagnosis of mental illness, even though they are dealt with as such in the *Diagnostic and Statistical Manual of Mental Disorders* (DSM).

Children with ADHD or ADD are not necessarily predestined to become mentally ill; they may also develop into outstanding personalities under favorable circumstances. The ease with which they transgress borders opens up a wide range for creative thinking and action. Some become successful artists, scientists, entrepreneurs, politicians, adventurers, philosophers, religious founders, and much more.

Family Environment as a Risk Factor

Following the introduction of the genetic risk factor of ADHD, the following focuses on the family environment in more detail and presents various risk factors.

The "why" question

If a family member develops schizophrenia, the whole family suffers, and each family member feels somehow affected. Especially parents will almost invariably face such questions as:

Why has precisely this child developed schizophrenia?

Why did the other children in our family stay healthy?

What do the partnership issues have to do with our child's schizophrenia?

Does the family system even play a role at all in schizophrenia?

Couldn't schizophrenia be attributed solely to the genetic determination of the child in question?

There are no easy answers to these and similar questions. Throughout this chapter, we will work out different environmental factors from the perspective of family dynamics that might contribute to the development of the illness of schizophrenia.

How do family systems function?

Family systems are self-contained units which are functionally more or less cohesive. Its members are attached by degrees of kinship, hierarchical structures, and common values. They consist of social groups of genetically related and emotionally connected or even attached individuals, whose emotional processes are interwoven in tighter or loose links. The family members continuously adapt to each other but, at the same time, also influence each other. Each of them functions not only in isolation as an individual but also has an impact on the functioning of the entire system. Each biography is influenced by the family system and can influence, and even shape, the other family members based on its own emotional dynamics. At the same time, it is affected as well as influenced by the others. In addition, non-family factors from the broader social or political environment may affect everyone, and influence positively or negatively the whole family system. The neo-Darwinian concept of inclusive fitness applies very easily to the functioning and survival of families.

Common values of the family are implicitly or explicitly passed on in the family system as tradition to the next generation. Family systems have traditions that mediate a sense of cohesiveness and well-rehearsed patterns of behavioral interaction that contribute to the stability of the family functioning. Values and family traditions are creeds and rituals which are deeply imprinted on the emotional memory of each member and function as survival strategies for the family in the sense of inclusive fitness. They convey the collective identity, akin to a corporate identity in the world of business, which the family is proud of and which it upholds even under adverse conditions. These family values are also designed to ensure success and the survival of offspring. Passing these values on to the next generation represents the social inheritance of human behavior in addition to the genetic inheritance.

Families can also be considered highly complex communication networks with emotional, verbal and non-verbal interactive processes between the various family members. The emotional communication patterns within a family system are not linear and never one-dimensional; they are always circular. Emotional processes and certain behavioral patterns are reproduced over generations. Behavioral patterns that are no longer functional in the next generation – because they are not adjusted to the current circumstances – are often retained nevertheless.

In addition to family values and traditions, parents also pass on their secret wishes and dreams, the fulfillment of which they may have been denied during their lifespan. They therefore pass these on as an implicit or explicit task for the next generation to accomplish. This process is described in the professional terminology as *delegation*, or a projection process within the family system from one generation to the next. However, children also have the inherent duty to establish their own personality. If they are entirely delegated to fulfill the family obligation, they cannot become an independent person, and the generational cycle is therefore disrupted. As teenagers, they cannot detach themselves from the family system and live an independent life.

In families with schizophrenia, we can often observe disrupted detachment processes in the family system that extend over three or more generations. Where these detachment processes are impeded, they can grow progressively into *emotional monster waves* and manifest themselves in acute schizophrenic psychosis in one of the most vulnerable family members. The illness brings the failure of the family system to light. In this sense, I consider schizophrenia a final product of emotional process malfunction within a family system and not just as an impairment of biochemical neurotransmitter functions in the brain of one affected individual.

Family Constellations

The term *family-constellations* refers to special circumstances within the family system, which play a crucial role in the development of schizophrenia. Specific interaction patterns emerge from the observation of the course of events, which are significant both for the onset of this disorder and for its prognosis.

Emotional focus

Long-standing observations of individual cases and biographical analyses of schizophrenia patients and their families have, upon closer inspection, brought to the fore regular, typical family constellations and course of events which lead to an intensified emotional focus on, and involvement with, children who later develop schizophrenia.

A study by Zenon Cupa (1997) showed that factors which bring about an increased emotional and/or functional focus were significant for children who later developed schizophrenia, compared to children who were chosen at random from control families. However, what are these typical family constellations which lead to emotion-focused behavior, and thereby tie this very child increasingly into the projection process of the family?

> Characteristics that distinguish a child from its siblings in a positive or negative way may lead to increased emotional focus on that child by the entire family system.

Sibling positions

The sibling position is the first biographical distinction that may lead to a special form of focus on the child. Walter Toman (1976) studied and described in detail different sibling positions in an empirical study of students. He presented eight sibling positions, all of which lead to a specific role differentiation in the family system and bring with them certain personality traits. The following only quotes four of the eight sibling positions to describe the focusing process within family systems that are affected by schizophrenia: the sibling positions of the oldest, the middle, the youngest, and the only child.

The oldest child with structural responsibility

Every family usually focuses more anxiously on their first-born child. Later on, when other children are born – because of its position as the eldest – the child may be functionalized, becoming a so-called parentified child. Besides being a child, they are supposed to act as a role model as well as a parental substitute. Whenever the parents fail in their role because of absence, illness, or both, it may be expected to assume parental functions.

The oldest child is also expected to take on what I refer to as the *structural responsibility* for the entire family system in case parents are unable to perform their duties for extended periods of time. Such continuous functioning of a child in the service of the family is a burden and may impede the maturation of their own personality, perhaps even hinder that process altogether.

> **CASE HISTORY:** Anna was the eldest of eight siblings. Her father was a general practitioner who had little time for his family. Her mother was constantly overwhelmed by the many children she had to take care of, in addition to providing help in husband's office. Under these circumstances, Anna assumed her mother's role for her younger siblings, as one of her brothers recalled later. As a young woman, Anna developed schizophrenia.

COMMENTARY: As the oldest sibling, Anna had to provide structural responsibility for the family. She felt obliged to support her overburdened mother until her younger siblings left home. Stuck in the surrogate-mother role, she remained in a symbiotic relationship with her mother throughout her life, unable to detach from her family and lead an independent existence.

The middle child as an intermediary

In families with many children, the siblings sometimes split into two groups. However, if parents are not able to settle the sibling rivalry, one of the middle children takes on the role of mediator as a substitute for the parents. Middle children may be overwhelmed by this highly demanding balancing function they perform for the family, and some of them develop schizophrenia as a result of the emotional burden.

CASE HISTORY: Iris was the fourth of eight children. She was lively and a tomboy. Her behavior was often criticized by her mother, who blamed her for everything that went wrong in the family whenever she felt overwhelmed by the hustle and bustle. She even went so far as to call Iris a devil. This was shortly before she herself had to be admitted to a psychiatric hospital for mental health problems. When the priest in the village heard of this story, he removed Iris from the family and looked after her.

Ever since, Iris has felt guilty about the hospitalization of her mother. Years later – her parents had died long ago – inheritance disputes arose between the older and the younger group of siblings as a result of unsuccessful business deals by some of them. Iris, who had her own family, instantly felt responsible for mediating between her siblings but could not stand the emotional dispute. She developed psychosis and was admitted to a psychiatric hospital.

COMMENTARY: Many years later, Iris approached me for therapy upon her own request. She emphasized how much she was suffering even to this day whenever tension arose in the extended family system. She still felt the impulse of having to mediate between all her relatives – not only between her siblings but also between the cousins and their children as well as between nieces and nephews and their spouses. This is how much her former role in the family system influenced and molded her character.

The therapeutic task we worked on was to turn the focus on herself, and not to get involved, almost obsessively, in everybody else's problems with the obligation to solve them.

The youngest child with emotional responsibility

The youngest child is predestined to get involved in the dysfunctional nature of the family in other ways. They are faced with an emotional "fait accompli" when they are born, finding themselves in a family situation in which the older siblings have already taken on different roles and the framework conditions are largely defined. Their position as the youngest family member encourages the greatest dependency on the system. Moreover, they are usually more exposed to emotional vulnerability in times of strain and turbulence within the family system.

Unlike the oldest child who assumes structural responsibility in the event of parental failure, the youngest child automatically takes over the emotional responsibility for easing chronic tensions and conflicts in the family. They feel obliged to support the emotional wellbeing of the entire family system since they are also most dependent on a good family climate. Even though they are still too young to understand the family conflicts, they nevertheless promptly respond to any tense atmosphere and attempt to relax it instinctively. From a young age, children try to adapt and alleviate family tensions through their actions.

CASE HISTORY: Parents reported that Mike, their youngest son, as the only one of their three children, whenever they or his siblings were unhappy or sad, pulled up the corners of their mouths with his little fingers and told them: "Laugh, don't be sad!" As an adult, he maintained his role of restoring the emotional balance in the family and of cheering up his parents. The atmosphere in the family was often tense because of their oldest son's drug addiction. As an adolescent, Mike developed a manic-depressive psychosis, singing songs on the street with his guitar and collecting money, which was not exactly the type of behavior his parents and teachers were happy to accept. He was therefore hospitalized in a psychiatric clinic.

COMMENTARY: Youngest children, whenever the family system is under chronic tension which threatens their emotional home, must look for a survival strategy in their own interest, which, of course, also serves the family system well. They therefore adopt appeasement behaviors to remedy emotional issues in the relationship network of the family. This was what Mike had to do, but his older brother's drug addiction finally became too much of a burden, and he became depressed himself.

CASE HISTORY: George was the youngest of three siblings; he was also the most sensitive child. School came easy to him. A lively child at first, he became a taciturn teenager. When he reached adolescence, he began to consume hashish and quit his apprenticeship. His mother was desperate. She tried to bring him to his senses, arguing with him almost constantly. The disputes between the two escalated to the point that he became physically aggressive towards his mother. Under these circumstances, the father took charge and arranged for him to be admitted to a psychiatric hospital.

FOLLOW-UP AND COMMENTARY: During counselling sessions with George's parents, a profound conflict between them surfaced. The father was furious with his wife because of her constant interference in their children's issues. To avoid any disputes, he had withdrawn from family life a while ago. He did not want to deal with the friction between mother and son, since he had also experienced a very traumatic childhood with an abusive, violent father. His wife, on the other hand, was hurt by his withdrawal. She immediately burst into tears when the issue was discussed during therapy. George himself confirmed that his mother had often disappeared into her bedroom in tears, and that he had taken pity on her each time this happened.

The mother was greatly disappointed when George distanced himself from her as an adolescent. She could not understand why he suddenly rebelled against her, given that she had previously had a trustful relationship with him. Furthermore, she felt offended when I cautioned her against overinvolved parenting.

George, with his cheerful disposition as the youngest child, had kept his mother in a good mood for years, despite an ongoing marital conflict. However, when he wanted to go his own way in adolescence, the superficial domestic harmony broke down.

George's illness forced the father to get back in contact again with his wife over a common concern for their son. Their profound marital conflict was pushed to the back of their minds. In this sense, George and his illness helped his mother to actively involve his father again in the family affairs. Additionally, his illness forced his parents to begin their own therapeutic process, another typical task a person with schizophrenia often performs in the service of the family.

The parents decided to separate. George was released from his obligation and was considering taking up his vocational training again, while living together with his father.

The only child

Statistically, only children develop schizophrenia less frequently. However, in cases where they are raised by a single parent – who is regularly stretched to the limit and not in receipt of professional help or support from a new partner – they may slip into the role of a surrogate partner and thus experience development impairment.

CASE HISTORY: Ivan, an only child, was five years old when his mother divorced his father because of frequent violent disputes. After divorcing, his mother never formed another lasting relationship. She concentrated on raising her son along the lines of her own strict father. Ivan, a sensitive child, soon learned to read all his mother's needs and wishes from her lips. He barely knew his biological father and was afraid of having to spend the weekend with him.

Until adolescence, Ivan remained closely attached to his mother. He was unable to rebel. Though he had a few violent outbursts of anger, they immediately turned into nagging feelings of guilt. His mother, however, could only see his father's impulsiveness in him, which she absolutely abhorred and felt compelled to discipline. She dismissed his teenage outbursts as naughty childish behavior and tried to limit them as quickly as possible to get him under control again.

Ivan developed a testicular tumor as a young man. This alarmed him and suddenly changed his life. From now on, he wanted to take life into his own hands. Until then, he had conformed to his mother's expectations: school, studies, and part-time jobs. Now, his mother's headaches and her constant lamenting made him so angry that he "could have gone for her throat", as he put it. At times, his anger caused such wild upheavals in him that he was afraid of losing his mind. At the same time, he felt remorseful whenever he failed to call his mother every day, did not visit her regularly, or offer her his help. When he calmed down again, he regularly felt anxious about his emotional outbursts.

COMMENTARY: Ivan, an only child, always felt obliged to assist his mother as a surrogate partner in difficult situations. He had to be strong when she was weak. But in puberty, in his eyes, his mother was too weak to challenge him in the disputes that are characteristic of adolescence. Moreover, she was the only person of reference, and he could therefore not risk having her withdrawing her love and affection.

As a therapist, I was giving her support whenever she needed it. The son freed himself little by little from the obligation to take care of his mother and focused on his own life without feeling guilty any longer. The outbreak of psychosis was successfully prevented. He formed a long-term relationship with a woman and established himself in a professional career.

With my support, he dared to contact his father again, and even formed a warm relationship with him. He had to maintain distance to his mother, as her way of inducing feelings of guilt was still too powerful for him to bear.

Talent as a factor in emotional overfocus

After the sibling position, the respective talents of a child may also engender *focusing* by family members on that child. Children with a special gift, or a talent that is in the interest of the family, may become a target of emotional or functional focus, regardless of their sibling position. For that reason, they are more exposed to parental wishes than children who could never fulfill such expectations.

> Gifted children attract parental expectations and emotional focusing.

Even aunts, uncles, grandparents – in short, the entire family system – may impose particularly high demands on these children and participate in the powerful family projection process. They receive the mission to fulfill the potential of the family system – luminous professional figures to-be, they have to succeed.

CASE HISTORY: The grandmother of Argentina would have liked to become a musician, but the family circumstances did not allow for it. On her deathbed, Argentina's mother promised her that Argentina, who played the piano and had perfect pitch, would dedicate her life to music.

Argentina's mother, who played the violin, accepted the legacy of her mother and ensured that her daughter would go to a conservatory. The sheer stress of graduation, however, led Argentina to have an acute schizophrenic episode and she was hospitalized. After that, she faced the permanent dilemma of whether she should fulfill her grandmother's legacy or follow other interests. She became a chronic schizophrenia patient in need of permanent stationary care.

COMMENTARY: The biographical entanglement in the family system had been transferred from the grandmother through the mother to Argentina as a mission to be fulfilled. Argentina, the granddaughter, was duty-bound in two ways, namely to her grandmother's legacy and to her mother's promise, as well as loyalty to her. Mother and grandmother wanted Argentina to achieve greater things. Although she possessed perfect pitch, she became psychotic under the heavy pressure of the final exams as well as her family's expectations.

Gender as a positive factor in emotional focusing

Gender can also lead to focusing, and thereby become a stumbling block for children. A gender that is neither expected nor desired by the parents can trigger a negative focus when parental expectations are not met. Those children are inevitably regarded as a disappointment, which is a strain on their own development maturation.

CASE HISTORY: Sabrina was the elder of two girls, and the father's favorite child. She should have been a boy, and she also behaved like one. Indeed, she was a real tomboy, climbing trees, and always spent time with boys. Her father took her everywhere. He was proud of her, and liked to present her to his friends, relatives and acquaintances. But he also had great expectations of her. Having come from a humble background, he was ambitious. He hoped that his daughter would become successful in her professional career. Therefore, he was disappointed when she opted out of her apprenticeship because she couldn't get along with her boss.

Even as a child, but even more so as an adolescent, Sabrina opposed the wishes of her father; she was stubborn and knew her own mind. Her father, however, imagined a different path for his daughter and tried to exercise his authority to keep her under control. But he was unable to discipline Sabrina. He was also unable to get his wife to discipline Sabrina and make her conform to his wishes. After Sabrina had repeatedly stayed away overnight with friends, he had her admitted to a psychiatric hospital against her will. This was how he intended to break her stubbornness.

Upon her first admission, Sabrina was diagnosed with "adolescent identity crisis". After she was discharged, there were more heated arguments between Sabrina and her father, in which she smashed apartment furnishings and a glass door. There followed two further hospitalizations against her will. Upon her third admission, she was diagnosed with schizophrenia. In the clinic, she set her room on fire and destroyed all the furniture.

COMMENTARY: Sabrina's father was unable to handle his headstrong, rebellious daughter, her tenacious unyielding character, which she had most likely inherited from him. His lack of empathy and heavy-handed paternal guidance had disastrous consequences. She was continually on the run from her ambitious, rigid father, who was unable to change his parenting style and rise above his own perceptions. He even went so far as to wish his daughter dead, such was his desire to rid himself of his disappointment and her juvenile behavior. She broke off the relationship with him, and only resumed sporadic contact after the death of her mother. However, she continued to be affected by his criticism and negative attitude. She immediately felt under immense pressure and developed paranoid delusions of persecution whenever she perceived the slightest criticism or rejection from anybody in her environment.

Parental ambitions that turn into criticism and rejection in case of disappointment can often lead to suicide among young people with schizophrenia. They see death as the only way to escape from parental pressure and coercion as well as their own feelings of guilt. Sabrina survived with the help of intensive therapeutic support. She now lives on a disability pension, receives regular support from a therapist and has a job in a sheltered workshop, but remains estranged from her father.

Gender as a negative factor in emotional focusing

If a new baby ends up being a different gender to the one anticipated, it can also result in parents' focusing on their child, with greater expectations heaped on them. If a long-awaited and hoped-for baby girl is born to a family with only male offspring, or conversely, a baby boy arrives in a family with only female offspring, both receive increased attention as a result of their special gender position. However, if these children are unable to meet the higher expectations placed on them, the positive focus of the parents and the entire family system may turn negative, and finally, rejection sets in.

> **CASE HISTORY:** Andreas was born as the only son among four girls and was chosen by his father as his heir. It was his father's greatest wish that his son would choose the same academic profession. Moreover, during periods of depression, the father confided in his son that he was

the only reason he had for staying alive. He was his father's pride, his special child.

The parents had a long-simmering partner conflict, though outwardly, the mother maintained a harmonious family life. When Andreas reached puberty, he began to consume cannabis. This was an embarrassment for her, since she was active in local politics. She therefore sent him to a private school in another city. But to the great disappointment of his parents, he rather spent time with his friends, and did not get his high school diploma. His father's wishes were now thwarted, and Andreas became a problem child during puberty whose family focused on him in negative terms only. Andreas complained later that he had been without parental guidance at far too young an age. He developed schizophrenia when he was nineteen years old.

COMMENTARY: Many years later, right after his father had died, Andreas locked up his father's apartment. The result of this willful act, however, was that Andreas once more became the negative focus of the family. The sisters and his mother were angry at what he had done. They could not understand the symbolic process of locking up the family secrets and preventing them from being exposed. Be that as it may, Andreas was convinced of having to accomplish this self-imposed task at all costs. It was his last desperate tribute to his father as his loyal heir.

The black sheep

A black sheep in any group of people, including in the family, always has the task of absorbing shame and hardship for the entire system – in this case, the family system – even that of previous generations. It acts as a lightning rod of sorts, and simultaneously as a safeguard whenever something goes wrong. As such, it has a cleansing function for the family system.

Features in children which might remotely remind family members of a former outcast are like a red rag to a bull. Moreover, mother or fathers also tend to refer to the black sheep as a deterrent during the child's upbringing. The attempt at deterrence, however, has the opposite effect: it may provoke curiosity, affection, or even pity for the outcast family member. The social inheritance process of undesirable characteristics in one of the family members is thus enhanced through the family projection process, rather than erased.

> **CASE HISTORY:** Angela's maternal grandmother called her first husband a good-for-nothing, and a brute. He had been an unsuccessful artist whom she used, time and again, as a negative example during the upbringing of her daughter Sonja. During disputes, Angela's grandmother would call Sonja worthless and feckless, just like her own father, the black sheep in the family.
> When Angela's older brother began to consume drugs as an adolescent, Angela's mother Sonja was in fear of having another black sheep in the family and was afraid of being condemned for it by her own mother. Angela, Sonja's second child, was her only rescue from this trap because Angela was the grandmother's favorite grandchild. Yet in adolescence, Angela had a relationship with a man suffering drug-addiction who abused her and was also considered a black sheep in his own family. Angela began to smoke pot and became psychotic. Her mother had once again failed in the eyes of the grandmother, and Angela was placed in her custody because the former was convinced that she could provide her grandchild with more love than Angela's own mother.
> **COMMENTARY:** From a systemic point of view, the affection of the grandmother towards Angela served the hidden task of compensating for the naming and shaming of the grandfather as a black sheep and restoring the long-awaited domestic peace for the grandmother and the family system heretofore unattainable. Furthermore, Angela was extremely interested in her grandfather, the black sheep in the family, although

she had never met him. This unspoken task, reinstating harmony and honor imposed by the grandmother, even made Angela feel obliged to take care of her and her second husband until they died.

In therapy, Angela became increasingly aware of her behavior pattern. Whenever there were conflict situations between colleagues in her place of work, she would experience difficulties. She realized that she had the tendency to make those problems her own. However, when she was unable to solve them, she developed psychosis, and hence was dismissed from her job. Her integrating function, imposed on her by her grandmother, became her stumbling block.

Once she became aware of her role, she could change her behavior gradually. She no longer had to assume the mediator role, could hold on to her job, no longer became psychotic and stopped living off disability benefits.

The therapeutic child

Unfulfilled needs of the parents' family of origin may affect the first-born child as in the following family case.

> **CASE HISTORY:** Jacob was the oldest of four sons. He was a sensitive boy but also a headstrong one. He was closest to his mother, who had been suffering from an anxiety disorder since puberty. With his father, he had a rather distant relationship.
>
> In adolescence, he experimented with LSD, had a bad trip and experienced a psychotic episode, from which he never quite recovered. All therapeutic efforts were unsuccessful; he could not finish high school nor start an apprenticeship. He just did not feel able to cope with this life.
>
> Father and mother were health care professionals, thus used to solving problems, but in their own family, they were simply unable to succeed.

One day, when Jacob was desperate, he made a phone call to both parents, crying for help. His father's reaction was noncommittal, while the mother immediately wanted to come to his rescue but didn't know how. At last, she contacted me but by that time, Jacob had taken his life by lying on the tracks in front of an approaching train.

COMMENTARY: In therapy, Jacob's mother mentioned that she had always felt misunderstood and oppressed by her own father – yet he had provided structure and security. Her husband was the exact opposite of him. His attitude did not provide her with a sense of security. She bitterly complained about his lack of support; he always yielded in cases of conflict.

Since Jacob's birth, she had had a close relationship with her son. He was a sensitive child and became her closest confidant, offering understanding to her during all her worries. However, when Jacob reached adolescence, she was unable to cope with his pubescent experimenting behavior. Instead, she found a lover his age. The father also began an affair. Though both parents managed to satisfy their needs, they deprived their son of support and guidance during the precarious period of the detachment process in adolescence.

Jacob reacted to the situation of his parents' new relationships by avoiding all contact with their new partners. He left home in despair but had no place to go. As a talented photographer, he had taken shots of train tracks at junctions. They may have symbolized his fateful helplessness, leading to his suicide.

At Jacob's funeral, which I attended, it became clear to me how important he had been to all members of his extended family. Relatives and friends emphasized how much he had offered an empathetic ear to everyone. However, he was unable to overcome his problems.

The comforter child

Family circumstances around the birth of a child may also lead to an increased emotional focus on that child. The emotional stress in the system is passed on to the new-born through what is called a projection process. Regardless of their sibling position, gender and special characteristics or talents, the child takes on the function of providing the family with emotional comfort and support from the very moment they are born.

The family researcher Froma Walsh (1979) has found in an empirical study that patients with schizophrenia were born significantly more often around the time that several deaths had occurred within the family. In her study, it was the grandparents who had died at the time of birth of those who were later diagnosed with schizophrenia. Interestingly enough, the parents of these children had not consciously made the connection of the coincidence between the two events, the death of their own parents and the birth of their offspring. They only became aware of the coincidence of death and birth during the interview, which triggered strong grief reactions even decades later after the loss.

> Children who are born at a time of traumatic circumstances have the Herculean task of comforting the family system throughout their life; they become what we call *comforter children*.

The function of comforter children is thus coined by the coincidence of death and their own birth within a family. However, the emotional stress may also be caused by other traumatic events that are common sources of pain in a family system such as wars, accidents, social unrest or even unemployment at the time of birth. Those children retain their function of having to provide emotional comfort even as adults, since the task is inscribed in their emotional memory. Sometimes, the mission is even clearly expressed by family members.

CASE HISTORY: Annelies was born out of wedlock when two of her uncles and one aunt, her mother's siblings, died in a car accident. When I asked the grandmother about who had comforted her after the loss of her three children, she pointed without hesitation to Annelies, who was present, and said: "She was my sunshine, she consoled me." Annelies developed schizophrenia when she was eighteen years old. She had the delusion of being Jesus Christ and was firmly convinced that she had to bring "the light of life" to all people.

COMMENTARY: Annelies was a typical comforter child. She had to console her grandmother after the loss of her three children as well as her mother after losing her three siblings. It is not surprising she had the messiah complex.

The replacement child

Infants who are born after the death of an older sibling, after stillbirth, or even after several miscarriages are subject to intensified emotional focus. They are usually forced into the role of a replacement child and loaded with inflated expectations. This increased emotional attention and the high hopes may also prompt the risk of developing schizophrenia.

The death of a child is an enormous emotional stress for all parents; it casts a long shadow over the whole family. On the list of stress factors, it ranks at the top. Infants born under such circumstances cannot but absorb the mourning and parental sorrow in their emotional memory. They consequently adapt their behavior to the emotional needs of their family system from a very early age.

Often, replacement children even receive the name of the deceased sibling, which unequivocally expresses their mission. Replacement children make up for the loss and help parents overcome their grief. Parents often take particularly intensive care of these children, but they may also have absurdly high expectations of them, which include gratitude. Such children are in an impossible bind from the moment they are born, and from which they cannot escape.

CASE HISTORY: The Kern family lost their second child Armin at the age of five in a road accident. He had been run over by a truck while riding his tricycle. The pastor advised the parents to have another child as quickly as possible to heal their pain. The parents followed his advice and gave their new-born son the same name, Armin. He was cared for lovingly by his parents; nothing was to happen to him. Everything went smoothly until he reached puberty. He had problems in his apprenticeship but did not dare mention it to his parents. Fearing poor grades at school, he played truant. Moreover, he stayed away from work because he was afraid his boss would scold him for skipping school. For several weeks in a row, he pretended to go to school but went to the woods instead. When his parents were informed, a family crisis erupted.

The parents requested his older brother Hermann to break off his US trip and return home immediately to assist them. Overburdened by the demands of this task, and perhaps influenced by a series of suicides in the neighborhood, Hermann took his life shortly thereafter. Armin, in turn, was overwhelmed by feelings of guilt since the parents held him responsible for his brother's death. He was unable to bear their blame, became psychotic, and had to be hospitalized in a manic phase.

The parents were desperate. They reacted by retreating from, and finally rejecting, Armin altogether. They didn't want to have anything to do with him and cut off all contact. In another manic phase, he was ill-behaved, and spent all the money he had retroactively received from the disability benefits fund.

Some years later, Armin's condition stabilized under intensive care provided by the outpatient services. He even got married and had two children. But over time, problems developed with his wife and mother-in-law. They both complained that he neglected his fatherly duties. He became psychotic again, and his wife filed for divorce.

COMMENTARY: The priest and the parents had predetermined the role of Armin number two even before his conception. He had to compensate for the tragic loss of their child, his brother Armin number one. Until adolescence, Armin number two fulfilled his designated role as a replacement child to the full satisfaction of his parents. But once he reached puberty, he started to become a cause for worry rather than joy. Things turned out even worse. Hermann, whom they had called for help in panic was also pulled into the vicious cycle of forced loyalty. His suicide ultimately enclosed Armin number two within a guilt trap. His task to help his parents to overcome the death of their first Armin led him, the replacement child, astray in adolescence.

The comforter concept of a replacement child, which had been assured by the pastor, nevertheless worked for the parents in some small way. They could free themselves of their responsibility for the loss of their two children, as well as their guilty feelings about their replacement child Armin number two, whom they regarded as guilty and accused of negligence. He had to bear the brunt of all his family's mishaps. His parents died without reconciling with him. Armin number two became a chronic schizophrenia patient, living together with another chronic patient.

The planned child

Desperately awaited or planned children are also in a position of receiving heightened emotional attention. Adopted children may also belong in this category, since an adoption is usually decided by parents after many years of waiting for a child of their own.

CASE HISTORY: Sofia was a planned child. All the other siblings, a girl and two boys, were not planned. The relationship of the parents was fraught with conflict to an exceptional extent. The mother, a professional midwife, humiliated her husband at every opportunity in front of their children, and passed her negative attitude about men on to them. Sofia, the favorite child of her mother, also started to challenge her father when she reached adolescence. The parents divorced, but for financial reasons they remained living in the same house, and the disputes between them continued unabated.

COMMENTARY: Sofia as the only wanted child received emotionally focused attention in a dysfunctional family. The emotional pressure in the family became too great for her. Although Sofia was intelligent and had many talents, she had great difficulties deciding on a professional career. Her father could not understand that of all his children Sofia, being the most talented and the only planned child, had so much trouble finding her way in life. She was the one child out of the four siblings who developed schizophrenia in adolescence.

The disabled child

A congenital disability may also lead to increased parental focusing with heightened attention and care. In case partnership conflicts exist, they are often additionally projected onto that child via the emotional focus.

CASE HISTORY: Regula was the youngest of three siblings. She suffered from a genetic disorder which required frequent medical treatment. Nevertheless, Regula attended a regular school and was a happy child. But as an adolescent, she was driven into the position of an outsider by the intrigues of her best girlfriends at school. At home, however, she was the center of everyone's attention. The bullying at school reached such a point that Regula withdrew to an autistic state. No one could reach her anymore; not even her mother. The parents had to take her out of school and put her in an institution for mentally disabled children because no other institution was willing to accept her.

The mother gave her even more special attention, and her siblings were also ordered to look after Regula. Her father was rather critical of all these special efforts; he would have preferred more natural behavior towards his daughter. In the first joint family meeting, Regula was unresponsive, almost mute, despite all efforts on the part of the participants to communicate with her. Her behavior was typical for hebephrenia, a form of adolescent schizophrenia.

FOLLOW-UP AND COMMENTARY: In the therapeutic sessions with the parents, it became apparent that they had been stuck in their particular pattern of communication for years. Both gave the impression that nothing could be changed. The father felt neglected by his wife and withdrew from the relationship. The mother, on the other hand, complained that he showed too little understanding for her and their disabled daughter. Nevertheless, neither took steps towards a divorce. Instead, they found a common denominator in their concern for their ill daughter. They regularly went on holidays together with her. Regula's communication, reduced to a minimum, almost embodied the disconnected state of her parents' relationship. She kept them together through her illness.

Along the years with family systems therapy, she made progress, started to talk, and a quite cheerful, humorous young lady surfaced from behind the previously autistic state.

Early childhood disease as a factor in emotional focusing

Difficult births and life-threatening diseases in early childhood strain the mother-child relationship right from the beginning. Mothers develop a closer and, at the same time, more anxious relationship with these children, from which they often cannot free themselves, and that child receives increased emotional attention. If partnership problems exist, they are also loaded onto that child. Those children thus become confidants since they are closest to their mothers in emotional terms.

CASE HISTORY: Heinrich, the older of two brothers, suffered meningitis in infancy, which frightened his mother very much. Because of his illness, she gave him special attention, and a specific dependency relationship developed between the two. In adolescence, as Heinrich faced difficulties at school, she found a suitable placement for him abroad. She increased her efforts and intensified her own teaching up to the point of self-sacrifice to enable Heinrich to pursue an academic career. After high school, however, Heinrich caught up with friends, idling away, smoking pot. He had to be hospitalized several times in a psychotic state. Although he complained vehemently about his parents and rejected all contact with them, he repeatedly accepted their financial help or special support whenever he got himself into trouble. Intermittently, he lived in a neglected state in an apartment full of garbage, which was paid for by his mother for many years. One day, he left for Spain to live in his parents' vacation apartment until he was evicted by the condo-administration because he didn't stick to any of the rules.

COMMENTARY: In therapy, his mother expressed her long-cherished wish for an academic career, a goal she was not allowed to pursue as a young woman. To her husband, she referred disparagingly as uneducated and as a coarse person, though he was professor at a technical university. He came from a working-class family, while she had a middle-class background. They had heated arguments and insulted each other at any given moment.

When I suggested that she should continue her own academic education, she refused, insisting that her son's career came first. Her maternal duties hindered her own professional fulfillment, yet she never let go of her own dream of academia.

Heinrich, having been evicted from his parents' vacation apartment – meanwhile over fifty years old – went missing. His mother immediately wanted to involve Interpol to bring him home. She said that even though her feelings for him were long gone, she could not leave him to his fate in a foreign country without offering her help. For her own ambitions, it was now too late, and she had buried them once and for all.

A few years later, Heinrich remained missing, and could not be informed about his parents who had died within a very short time of each other.

Fatal adaptation

The following example shows a migrant family in which the most culturally adapted child, the adolescent girl, was functionalized as a cultural mediator, unable to leave her family in adolescence. When professional helpers with the best of intentions tried to support the young woman in pursuing her own individual path in life as a teenager, she became psychotic.

> **CASE HISTORY:** Celina, the pride of an immigrant Muslim family from the Middle East was good at school and socially well integrated, aiming for a higher education.
> Her older brother had more trouble integrating into western culture. As the only son of the family, he stuck to his traditional role as a male and objected to his sister's westernized attitude as a female. He repeatedly physically assaulted her if she refused to conform to his view of how a Muslim woman ought to behave.
> Celina turned to a social worker for help who found sheltered housing to protect her from her abusive brother. However, shortly after she had moved in, Celina's behavior changed suddenly. She was defacing her walls, scribbling all over her room, uttered things nobody understood. The emergency doctor had to be called; she was hospitalized in a psychotic state.

COMMENTARY: Celina, who had assumed a mediator role in her family, spoke fluent German. She enjoyed helping her parents as a translator in all official matters and became an indispensable link for her family, while clearly benefiting from the advantages and freedom she experienced as a female in the country of immigration.

Her older brother, however, could not accept it. He was traditional-minded and tried to make her behave according to the traditional customs of their home country. The well-intended support of the social worker who looked after Celina's rights and security in an abusive situation nevertheless ended in acute psychosis. Celina could not bear the loyalty conflict she experienced by leaving her parents. As a new sign of loyalty towards her family and their culture, she began to wear a headscarf for the first time in her life.

They cannot speak for themselves

The emotional focus of the family on specific children always leads to their taking on a functional role in the service of the family. Children who receive a designated function in early life usually retain this role beyond adolescence, and therefore cannot pursue their own path, or develop their personality. As teenagers, they struggle in vain to become independent. Irrespective of whether the expectations of the parents are positive or whether these children carried negative projections from the family system – they may have a disability, a special talent, a specific sibling position, the role of a substitute child, or even the role of a black sheep – they experience difficulties detaching themselves from home during adolescence.

The burden of a functionalized role, however, usually only becomes apparent when the detachment process from the family, as shown in the examples presented earlier, fails. Adolescence is the maturation phase when juveniles separate from the family and become adults. At this stage, dysfunctional families subtly undermine the children's drive for independence and self-determination, and the drama of psychosis emerges.

> Children who are subject to emotional focus remain stuck in their functional role in adolescence in order to compensate the disfunction of the family system, thus they cannot detach themselves to become independent adults.

Teenagers who cannot rebel against their parents openly because they must continue to fulfill their raison d'être in the service of the family build up tremendous anger and, at the same time, enormous feelings of guilt. This is usually the case in families with schizophrenia patients. Emotional turmoil thus leads to an *emotional monster wave*, a tsunami, which overrides all rational thinking and floods our cognitive capacities. Instead of a family row, which would release dammed-up emotions, psychosis breaks out. While the family cares for the sick child at that moment, the child's mission as a mediator persists. Moreover, the family members once again gather around the child with intensified care, their object of projection for all evil. Therefore, no real change can take place in the family system or in the psychotic family member if they don't receive help from the outside in the form of family systems therapy.

Pathogenic Family Interaction Patterns

The triangle

In the first few years of life, children are fully dependent on their parents or other primary caregivers, and originally have *undivided loyalty* towards them.

Parents or other primary caregivers who are involved in ongoing suppressed conflicts and are therefore unable to communicate with each other directly and openly over extended periods of time, significantly impede children's emotional and even cognitive development. Those children get drawn into a triangular relationship which hinders their emotional maturation from very early on.

Triangular relationships between father, mother and child can frequently be found in families with schizophrenia. This typical constellation exists long before the illness breaks out. Schizophrenia patients are almost without exception involved in a triangular relationship between their openly or secretly quarrelling parents and remain so even after the onset of the illness. Stuck in the service of their parents' relationship, they cannot detach from their functionalized role in adolescence in order to leave home and become independent.

The energy that juveniles usually muster during their maturation phase in adolescence is tied up in their parents' relationship. This investment of emotional energy, in concomitance with parental conflict, deters sensitive teenagers from rebelling. Rather than showing bad behavior toward their parents, as is usually the case for teenagers, they control their temper tantrums outwardly and undergo inward emotional upheavals instead. This is a key prerequisite for the *emotional monster wave* of acute psychosis.

The connection between chronic partnership conflicts and the development of schizophrenia during adolescence was confirmed in a study by Zenon Cupa (1997), supervised by me. In that survey, significantly more parents in the schizophrenia group indicated partnership conflicts than in the control group. This is remarkable considering the fact that parents of youngsters with schizophrenia usually suppress or deny their conflicts, a behavior that is known as *pseudo-mutuality*.

Mothers more often revealed conflicts with their partners, as well as with other relatives and social relationships. Fathers indicated more than three times as many conflicts with their relatives and significantly more conflicts with their teenagers affected by schizophrenia than fathers in the control group.

The accumulation of conflicts in families with schizophrenia is obviously not confined to the parents and the immediate nuclear family but also relates to the extended family system. This fact is probably due to hereditary increased reactivity and high sensitivity, most likely related to the ADHD neurotype, which runs in these families as a genetically determined *vulnerability factor*. Families with ADHD are known to have a heightened tendency toward conflict escalation.

Revolving-door conflict

Schizophrenia patients are continuously preoccupied with the dissonant relationship of their parents and gain their raison d'être, their pseudo-self, from their entanglement, almost obsessively managing the chronic parental tug-of-war. Caught in the emotional abyss of parental despair and anger, they cannot develop a self, nor can they feel a sense of self-worth; they don't know who they are, nor what they want.

Tied up in this triangular relationship, father, mother and patient are involved in a continuous revolving-door conflict. None of the three confronts and deals with the other directly: neither the parents with each other, nor the father or mother with the adolescent, nor does the adolescent stand up for his or her own interests with each parent one-on-one. All three of them are constantly mutually entangled. They seek assistance and support from one another instead of handling the original conflict bilaterally, thus keeping a triangular revolving-door relationship alive between the three of them.

Time and again, the parents pull the child into their partnership quagmire, and disqualify each other simultaneously in their roles as father and mother. They thereby place the patient, be it son or daughter, on a partnership level, using him or her as a substitute, and at the same time as a shield to avoid being directly confronted with each other in their incessant partnership rivalry.

The parental entanglement prevents the patient affected by schizophrenia from negotiating their detachment with each parent one-on-one. None of the three ultimately takes responsibility for the consequences of their action and interference, neither the parents within their relationship nor the adolescent in their detachment process from their mother and father.

> **CASE HISTORY:** Theodor had an acute psychotic episode during puberty and was placed in an institution for the chronically ill following his hospitalization. The father distanced himself from his son, while the mother continued to take care of him. Theodor visited his parents every weekend. On one of those weekends, his sister also dropped by with her children. While Theodor's father left, his mother complained that he would not even help her take care of their grandchildren. Theodor immediately replied, "But you still have me." Whenever problems between them arose, Theodor was immediately on her side like a little dog, defending her, or he would draw attention to himself, so that the father had to discipline him. "It has always been like this", the mother told me.

Theodor's mother suffered for years because of her husband's extramarital affair. She was unable, however, to file for divorce, fearing she would not survive on her own. Theodor was the one who tried to manage their conflictual relationship as an obsessed diplomat.

> Detachment conflicts, combined with incessant parental partnership rivalry, cause continuous emotional turmoil within the family system from which there is no escape for family members with schizophrenia.

Split loyalty

The offspring's *undivided loyalty* is primarily directed at both parents. This also applies to children caught in triangular relationships. However, if children are tied to parents who constantly bicker with each other, *split loyalty* sets in as a means of coping with both of their primary caregivers simultaneously. Yet having to maintain split loyalty causes emotional stress for them. Investigations by Guy Bodenmann (2006), a family researcher, showed that in the long run, quarrelling parents who stay together in a partnership have a more harmful impact on children than divorced parents.

CASE STUDY: Jim, a schizophrenia patient, complained about the atmosphere at home. He described the mood between his parents as so unbearably tense that he could hardly stand it. Every time he came home from school, he had the feeling that the ceiling might fall on his head at any moment. He developed schizophrenia as an adolescent and never went back home again. The parents divorced thereafter.
Split loyalty in children doesn't only occur towards their primary caregivers such as parents; it may also develop between two generations, between mother and grandmother, for example.

CASE HISTORY: Detlef, one of my schizophrenia patients, found himself in a triangle relationship between his mother and his paternal grandmother. He described vividly how he regularly felt torn between his grandmother and his mother. Whenever he was with his mother, he felt the urge to visit his grandmother, and when he was with his grandmother, he always missed his mother. It was like being homesick without having a home. Detlef developed schizophrenia in early adulthood and remained a chronic patient throughout his life.

The damaging effects of split loyalty usually first appear in adolescence, even more so when other stress factors such as an unhappy love affair or problems regarding the professional career choice join the mix.

CASE HISTORY: Loredana developed a psychotic crisis when she was rejected by her first love. In despair, she wanted to jump from the roof of her parent's home to escape her overwhelming emotions, as she told me later in therapy. This alerted the parents, and they asked for therapeutic help.

COMMENTARY: When Loredana described her childhood in more detail, it turned out that she had been following her parents' disagreements very closely since her school days. Whenever her mother confided in Loredana with the problems she had with her father, Loredana went to him to ask for his opinion on the same issue to get a more complete picture of the conflict. She wanted to do justice to both. Preoccupied with that task, she could no longer study, and her performance at school deteriorated. Loredana was so impaired in her cognitive development that she could not begin high school despite her intelligence. Her unhappy first love affair in connection with the emotional misfortune of her split loyalty made her fall into psychosis. Her parents decided to separate. The mother moved out, and Loredana remained with the father.

Soon after the separation of her parents, her split loyalty ended, and she could re-focus on her education. She now could take her life into her own hands. She passed her exams. Later, the parents resolved their permanent marital rift. The mother moved back in, and Loredana experienced living with her parents as supportive.

Split loyalties are a cause for stress in children and damage their emotional as well as cognitive maturation. Being trapped, they seek out options to convert the *split loyalty* into a *divided loyalty* that is less burdensome. This is, however, only possible if the quarrelling parents no longer live under the same roof, and the children don't need to maintain their loyalty towards them simultaneously but can instead remain in contact with father and mother on an alternative basis.

CASE HISTORY: The parents of five-year-old Konstantin were arguing regularly. One day, he said to his mother: "Why don't you separate from Daddy; I want to be alone with you, so we can live together happily. I can then visit Daddy whenever I feel like it."
COMMENTARY: The parents of Konstantin had drifted apart. The little boy was bothered about the endless parental arguments, which affected his emotional grounding. But the idea of a separation did not distress him at all; he even suggested it himself. He longed for a hassle-free environment, without having to always experience the destructive parental bickering. He wanted open access to both parents, separated in space and time, one by one, to avoid feeling a sense of divided loyalty.

Illness in the family's interest

According to system therapists, the illness of children often serves the basic need or wish of the family, keeping parents together, even if the destructive long-term malaise of an incessant marital discord leads children to an emotional impasse. The powerful impact of schizophrenia, which stifles them, may serve as a welcome distraction from the intended divorce. In the following case, the function of schizophrenia was to protect the parents from the failure of their marital relationship in public, from the acknowledgement of their faults as well as the naming and shaming in their close social environment.

CASE HISTORY: Boris developed schizophrenia when his mother seriously contemplated for the first time a divorce with the support of a therapist after many years of concealed marital conflict due to several extramarital affairs by her husband. However, the outbreak of the disease caused his mother to drop her plan. Moreover, the psychotic content of Boris' delusional system related entirely to his parents' divorce. Although his mother had not informed him of her intention, he had nevertheless sensed it.

COMMENTARY: One can interpret the story of Boris's family to the effect that his mother had a strong need for harmony, stemming from her family of origin. This meant that she suppressed any conflict in her partnership. One consequence was the denial of her husband's extramarital relationships. This inner need for harmony resulted in marital conflicts being dragged out for years without any suitable resolution.

At last, the mother was ready to divorce. Boris's psychosis, however, put paid to her plan. She was unable to go through with it and withdrew her decision. This corresponded well with her need for harmony and her loyalty towards her family of origin. The parents shared the care of their son over the following years. His illness had reunited them.

Many years later, when the parents finally decided to divorce anyway, a reversal in the disease process affecting Boris could be observed. At that time, the divorce came as a relief for him. He was never hospitalized again and pursued a regular job.

Triangulation persists after divorce

Parental divorce does not always end the conflict of *split loyalty* for the child in a triangular relationship; the triangle often persists. If both parents keep blaming the other for the failed partnership, and both don't own up to their part in the conflict, the schizophrenia patient remains entangled in the triangular relationship with the quarrelling parents, and the *split loyalty* persists, despite the divorce.

> **CASE HISTORY:** Ruth was the middle child of three siblings, and the only daughter. Her parents were from different backgrounds. The mother, a sensitive youngest child, came from a wealthy family and had been spoiled by her father. At the same, time, however, she feared his violent temper. The father came from a working-class family; he was used to a harsh upbringing.
>
> The mother suffered from a chronic physical illness that repeatedly led to hospitalizations. Her illness had most probably an important psychosomatic aspect which related to her chronic marital rivalry, while her husband regarded her illness mainly as an excuse to withdraw from him, to withdraw from her responsibility as a mother and housewife. For prolonged periods of time, he had to take care of the children alongside working with the help of a nanny. According to Ruth, the parents never fought openly. When her father was upset or angry, he often wouldn't talk for days.
>
> It bears mentioning that the mother, after many years of unhappy marriage, filed for divorce and secretly left with Ruth and her younger brother. Destructive legal battles followed for eight years. The bitter enmity went on even after both parents had entered new relationships. Both never missed an opportunity to complain and make condescending remarks about each other in the presence of Ruth, trying to gain the upper hand with the help of their daughter.

COMMENTARY: After her parents' separation, Ruth developed anorexia as a teenager, followed by schizophrenia few years later, after their divorce. She became repeatedly psychotic over the years, and the parents asked themselves why their daughter had to suffer so much. Yet the illness provided them with an opportunity to take care of their together. Thus, Ruth remained a mediator through her disease, a tragic victim of parental discord. In therapy, Ruth kept her split loyalty towards her parents a secret for a long time. Only after many years of therapy, she was able to make critical comments about them. For her thirtieth birthday, she purposely invited both parents, even though she knew that they still didn't want to meet or talk to each other. However, she had decided to give up her mediator role, and let the parents decide whether to attend her birthday party or not.

Strategies for dealing with split loyalty

To deal with *split loyalty,* some children also develop their own specific strategies. Loredana, for example, had always asked both parents' opinion about specific problems, trying to create fairness indirectly between the two. The following case history shows another strategy of a daughter dealing with the *split loyalty* between her parents.

CASE HISTORY: Martina, daughter of a migrant father and a Swiss mother, had always kept an accurate record of their ongoing struggles. In marital fights, she developed a strategy of agreeing alternately with her father and her mother. She applied an ingenious system to maintain impartiality during her estranged parents' times of discord. However, her system could not help make her parents stay together. They divorced when Martina had reached adulthood, assuming they had performed their task well, waiting up to that point. Neither did it work outside of her family; at the age of twenty-eight, she developed an acute schizophrenic episode during a conflict at work and was admitted to a psychiatric clinic. After discharge from hospital, Martina started therapy with me at her own request.

COMMENTARY: Martina's loyalty conflict originated from the ongoing leadership struggle between her parents. The mother felt superior to her husband, but still could not assert herself against him. She was only strong enough with her daughter in tow. The father, in turn, did not feel equal to his wife as an immigrant.

In therapy, it became apparent that Martina could not apply her ingenious system to the daily conflicts in her life. The strict record-keeping she had practiced came undone whenever personal conflicts cropped up in her environment. As an adult, Martina continued to have a protective attitude towards her mother. Whenever I asked her about the relationship with her mother, she could not say a word, let alone something negative, although at times she seemed to be quite annoyed with her. In these situations, she interrupted the conversation abruptly: "I don't want to talk about it."

During a new acute psychotic episode, it became obvious that she cared for her father, too. To everybody's surprise, she said that he was the only person she would take medication from, that only he was allowed to give it to her. When I asked her father, he immediately accepted her wish and acted accordingly. She empowered him in her critical phase of psychosis to assume leadership, a role his wife had never granted him. The psychotic crisis was overcome this time without another hospital admission.

On a later occasion, she told her boyfriend, with whom she had been living for several years, to ask her father for permission to marry her, thereby further strengthening her father's authority. Her boyfriend respected her request. Her father gave his consent, which had long been Martina's wish, and the two got married. Martina had defined a highly effective counterbalance in the covert, unequal parental dispute, therefore creating more security for herself and her own life. With this innovative method, she changed the split loyalty towards her parents successfully to a divided loyalty. After having married, she never became psychotic again, even though she went through some more crises in her life. At these moments, being assailed by doubts, she called me for a refresher session to manage her life again on her own.

Stressful Communication Styles

Communication styles have been analyzed by several researchers in order to characterize families with children diagnosed with schizophrenia. They have been used as a distinguishing measure in comparison with control families. It could be demonstrated in an adoptive study by Pekka Tienari (1985) that schizophrenia only broke out, even in genetically predisposed adopted children, when the adoptive family had dysfunctional features, which manifested themselves in pathological communication patterns.

> **CASE HISTORY:** Chantal attended genetic counselling for risk assessment because her brother suffered from schizophrenia. She was advised not to have children of her own, as the genetic risk seemed too high. Therefore, she adopted two babies who had no genetic predisposition for schizophrenia. Complying with the advice of the experts' risk assessment, she had done everything right, giving up her wish to have children of her own to avoid the illness of schizophrenia. Nevertheless, to her great disappointment, one of her adopted children developed schizophrenia in adolescence, which brought her to my family therapy session. She was devastated and wanted to know how this could happen.
>
> **COMMENTARY:** Chantal's story shows that even though the assumed genetic risk factor in her family was eliminated, as the genetic counselling center had asked for, environmental factors that had influenced the development of schizophrenia in Chantal's family had not been considered and were therefore not dealt with. Conflictual family patterns persisted unabated as environmental factors in her family system. The story confirms the result of the adoptive study by Pekka Tienari: environmental factors are crucial for the development of schizophrenia, even more so than genetic factors.

> Environmental factors are crucial for the development of schizophrenia, even more so than genetic factors, a significant epigenetic process, which should not be ignored.

High expressed emotions

The following section examines some of the stressful communication styles that seem to play a role as environmental factors in the development of the illness of schizophrenia.

From my clinical experience, typical characteristics of communication in families with schizophrenia are often slight impatience as regards the speed of physical actions, an urging tone of voice and an accelerated communication flow. The pitch is emotive, the voice sounds irritated and often has a critical undercurrent. All these features point to a person's heightened affective state of arousal. Most frequently, mothers of patients with schizophrenia present this style of communicating; they usually have a subtly irritated tone of voice. A trained ear will easily detect this when they register for therapy by phone.

This communication style can also be related to ADHD. Communication patterns of persons with ADHD have been analyzed and, interestingly enough, it was speculated that in the foreseeable future, it will be possible to diagnose ADHD solely by phonetically analyzing communication patterns. And indeed, people with ADHD can be recognized clinically by their typically emotional communication style. The *high expressed emotions* in families with schizophrenia are therefore comparable with the communication style of people with ADHD. This is yet another finding that confirms my hypothesis that families with ADHD and families with schizophrenia share the same genetically determined neurotype. The specific communication patterns of families with schizophrenia, already observed by the clinical researchers Wynne and Singer as early as 1976, are also in line with those of people with ADHD.

Leff and Vaughn were the first ones in 1985 who labeled this communication style *high expressed emotions* or *high EEs*. They observed this emotionally charged communication style in families with schizophrenia. The two researchers could demonstrate that the level of *high expressed emotions* correlated significantly with the rate of relapse of schizophrenia. The higher the negative emotional expressiveness of parents, the higher the relapse rate of patients.

Conversely, it could later be demonstrated that the relapse rate could be lowered, and the prognosis improved by the same percentage as through drug treatment with neuroleptics, if the negative emotional expressiveness of parents towards their patients could be reduced through psycho-educational training programs. This positive impact on the reduction of relapse rates of patients with schizophrenia was repeatedly confirmed in many further studies in Europe, the USA, and Australia, as Luc Ciompi mentions in the foreword of this book. However, relapses could never be prevented one hundred percent.

If this emotional style of communication is decisive in triggering relapses of schizophrenia, it might well be assumed that it also plays a role even in the pathogenesis of schizophrenia, since it increases the chances of an emotionally loaded climate in the family, and thus the risk of an *emotional tsunami* in particularly sensitive children as those with ADHD or ADD during adolescence.

Associative communication

An associative, non-linear style of communication is another feature which can be observed in families with schizophrenia. Topics are vented in many variations and additional details. Moreover, the focus is frequently shifted, so that the listener often has trouble following the thread of a conversation and gets lost easily.

This fragmented, unclear and directionless communication style was defined by Wynne and Singer as early as 1977 as a form of *communication deviance* (CD). They clearly linked this style of communication to the thought disorder that occurs in acute schizophrenia.

The easy distractibility, lack of focus or inability to keep a train of thought can once again be related to individuals with ADHD. Topics cannot be summarized neatly because the individual experiences too many distractions and associations. They often get sidetracked because of the many digressions they make, and bifurcations then follow their impulsive thinking. This specific speech and thought behavior pattern is typical of individuals with ADHD or ADD.

The associative style of communication is most pronounced during acute psychosis and is then referred to as an associative train of thought, which is a typical symptom of acute schizophrenia, one of Eugen Bleuler's *four As*.

Concealing communication

Indirect, evasive and secretive means of communicating, known as a *mystifying* communication style, is another typical feature of families with schizophrenia. They often "talk in a roundabout way", "beat around the bush", avoiding confrontational contents they don't want to express directly. Negative emotions are usually not communicated to the conflict partner. Deferred aggression and existing discrepancies in the family system, although they are clearly felt, are not called by their name and are usually even denied when asked about them directly. Anything vaguely discordant is generally dealt with through trivialization and appeasement through whitewashing.

Mishler and Wexler in 1975 described this indirect style of communication in families with schizophrenia as a way of exerting indirect control. Through this style of communication, parents seemingly intend to bring about behavioral change by inducing feelings of guilt, thus undermining the emotional intelligence of their offspring even in early childhood. Through this style of communication, the child develops a highly differentiated emotional perception, and the ability to skillfully read reality "between the lines". Furthermore, the child cultivates a "fine musical ear" for all nuances, undercurrents and dissonances in the parental communication patterns, and later on as adults in their social environment.

Owing to this emotional hyper-perception, schizophrenia patients have learned to draw inferences from their families' communication patterns. In later life, they often react immediately to affective inconsistencies in their environment whenever conflicts arise. This characteristic of reading the emotional climate can once more be related to ADHD or ADD, since high sensitivity is a typical quality of that very neurotype. Whenever a mother is asked which of her children is most sensitive to her emotional wellbeing, she will always point to the child with ADHD or ADD.

The double-bind

The *double-bind* communication style is another feature that has been observed in families with schizophrenia. The term, which was coined by Gregory Bateson in 1972, describes a form of expression in which contradictory messages or commands are communicated on different levels at the same time. Children are under the constant threat of punishment. Either way they lose. Furthermore, *double-bind* communication usually represents a relationship pitfall between the two quarreling parents, a so-called *split loyalty* trap:

- Children are constantly involved in the contradictory communication of both parents, and the inconsistency among them.
- They cannot address any inconsistencies, however, because of the loyalty conflict they are engulfed in concerning both parents.
- They cannot interpret the ambiguity of the double message and are

therefore exposed to the inherently contradictory *double-bind* communication of their parents.
- While exposed to this style of communication, children live in a state of incessant disorientation, both cognitively as well as affectively.
- They have to cope with *split loyalties* in relation to both parents, emotionally and communicatively, and are thus caught in an affective and cognitive *double-bind*.

Avoidance of conflicts – negation of perception – family group protection

Conflict avoidance through the negation of individual perception for the sake of family peace is another characteristic feature of family systems with members who suffer from schizophrenia. The *Color Conflict Method* of Holte et al (1987 and 1990) has demonstrated the strategy of negation of individual perception within schizophrenia families. In the experiment, parents and their children were presented with colors on individual computers and asked to confirm or deny the officially named color. If the family members – mainly the children – realized that their color descriptions did not match, they were in most cases unable to express the difference openly. The family only allowed affirmative feedback. When a family member nevertheless dared to point out their differences in color, the parents responded with an active disqualification. Such a reaction was not observed in the control group, nor in the control group with other psychiatric illnesses but not affected by schizophrenia. In both control groups, the family members could openly express disagreement over the colors. Only in families with schizophrenia were efforts made to deny the differing individual perception.

Schizophrenia patients, in turn, avoided conflict situations by responding with behavior that might be deemed incomprehensible and egocentric. The differences in perception between the schizophrenia patient and the other family members were clearly suppressed by the parents, and the patients immediately negated their individual perception as a result of what one may call blind loyalty towards their parents.

> The adaptive benefit of staying loyal to the family and remaining under the protection of the family system, represents the evolutionary strategy of kin-selection.

Family systems with high levels of anxiety live by an unspoken but real desire to stick together as a group. Family members are thus under pressure to remain emotionally loyal to the family group, otherwise they lose the protection. Cognizance of reality is thus suppressed by the emotional brain. Family systems that engage in such suppression of reality have been called centripetal families by Olson et al., a phenomenon which can nowadays be explained in neuropsychological terms.

Parenting Styles

Parenting styles – in addition to family constellations and communication styles – represent other influential environmental family-related factors which play a significant role in the pathogenesis of schizophrenia. Parenting styles pass on moral concepts and values to offspring in order to promote successful socialization in adult life, and thereby guaranteeing survival.

Parents are usually influenced in their parenting style by their own family of origin. If they felt that the parenting style they experienced at the hands of their own parents was adequate and just, they apply the same approach without giving it much further thought. If they suffered under their parents' instructional strategies during their upbringing, they will consciously apply a counter-strategy to their parents' approach, yet they often overshoot. Despite their best corrective efforts, the parenting style they experienced themselves usually asserts itself at some point in one way or another.

Mothers and fathers most often also have fundamentally different views on educational principles regarding the upbringing of their children. They may – or may not – substantially agree and go along with each other's approach. Moreover, it has to be kept in mind that the fundamental differences of the parents' own upbringing, especially with regard to their cultural, political and religious background, is always a balancing act, which has to be managed by them as an ongoing internal engagement of values.

Four distinct educational styles

In an empirical study, questions were asked about four different educational styles in families with schizophrenia as well as control families. In addition, the similarities and discrepancies in the maternal and paternal parenting practices were evaluated. The four different styles could be categorized as follows:

- **Education through punishment:** Parents educate their children in an authoritarian way and discourage unwanted behavior through punishment. Children are forced to submit to the orders of their parents, if necessary through power.
- **Education through auto-regulation:** Parents have an anti-authoritarian, laisser-aller attitude and leave the children mostly to themselves, as children of nature. From early childhood, they rely heavily on individuality, autonomy and self-responsibility.
- **Education through fear:** Parents exert emotional pressure on their children in case of disobedience through intimidation and withdrawal of love. They also appeal to the guilt feelings of their children in the attempt to bring about desired behaviors.
- **Education through cooperation:** Rules are applied instead of orders. Parents seek cooperation with their children by involving them in the decision-making process. The children are also encouraged to think and decide on their own if possible, and to communicate if they disagree.

For the first two educational styles, **parenting through punishment** or **parenting through auto-regulation**, the study revealed no significant differences between families with schizophrenia and the control group. These two approaches thus don't seem to represent factors related to the development of schizophrenia.

Education through fear, however, was reported significantly more often by families with schizophrenia than by those from the control group. Mothers, however, used parenting through fear more frequently than fathers in both groups. Mothers obviously tend to apply an affective-manipulative parenting style more often than fathers, using threats and fear, while fathers react more with punishment or consequences.

Parenting through fear and accusations occurred significantly more often in the families with schizophrenia. The state of parental emotional arousal for the sole purpose of disciplining seems to represent a risk factor for an intense emotional climate in the family environment, and thus increases the risk for the unfolding of an *emotional monster wave* in susceptible children with ADHD or ADD, promoting psychosis.

Parenting through cooperation seems to have been practiced more often by fathers as well as mothers in the control group as compared to the families with a history of schizophrenia. Cooperation is the most frequent and most accepted parental method in western cultures and is best adapted to today's living and political conditions in democratic countries. However, families with schizophrenia do not seem to be able to apply this approach. Be it the unrest in family systems with schizophrenia that forces these parents to apply a more anxiety-driven and fear-inducing parenting style, or the ADHD-child that contributes to this rather desperate educational style.

Kuipers (1979) and Day (1986) already concluded that the child-raising behavior of parents must be regarded as a clear risk factor in the development of schizophrenia. They described the corresponding parenting style as threatening, demoralizing, criticizing but, at the same time, also demanding in the sense of having high expectations. In addition, they also observed intrusive and cognitively confusing parental behavior in those families with schizophrenia. The impact of this threatening attitude of parenting through fear, blame and shame resurfaces most pronouncedly during acute schizophrenic episodes in the form of paranoia and persecutory delusions. Once again, one has to bear in mind that this typical parenting style is most likely to be related to the genetic factor of ADHD or ADD that runs in the family.

Conflicting parenting practices

A contradictory parenting culture between fathers and mothers appears to be another important family characteristic which presents a risk factor for promoting schizophrenia. Having incompatible attitudes in their common task of raising their children, with a widely differing educational style, is a definite source of conflict between the parents, and possibly also leads to ongoing conflictual issues in their relationship, which is yet another risk factor as described before.

> Discrepancies between paternal and maternal parenting practices is significantly increased in families with schizophrenia.

Children who are constantly exposed to their parents' contradictory educational approaches cannot form a congruent mental representation of reference and are thus unable to rely on either of them, emotionally or cognitively. One inevitable result is *split loyalty*. In order to assess the respective educational styles for cogency, they have to compare the contradictory signals of their father and their mother time and again. During patients' acute schizophrenic episodes, we can sometimes observe the cognitive dilemma they experience within their parents' conflicts, and even recognize that they are attempting to resolve it through delusional constructions.

> **CASE HISTORY:** Born after two older siblings, Alfonso was an unplanned third child. The mother was bound to the household chores and felt reminded on a daily basis of her subordinate role within her family of origin as an only girl among four brothers. Once again, she was suffocated by it.
> In adolescence, Alfonso's father was unemployed for two years. His wife, a daughter of a businessman, lost all respect for him. They were disagreeing with each other on personal matters as well as the handling of their son Alfonso. The father withdrew from the family, gave

up his paternal responsibilities and filed for divorce. This caused further anxiety in the mother, being completely on her own with her difficult teenage son.

Alfonso first developed anorexia, and then paranoid schizophrenia with grandiose delusions, preaching to his environment with great fervor to create a better world. In therapy, he became aggressive when I occasionally dared to contradict him.

COMMENTARY: The parents had relentlessly undermined each other, not only as partners, but also as parents and caregivers. This disqualifying behavior made it impossible for them to deal effectively with their teenage son. Alfonso designed his own world order as a problem-solving strategy to cope with his parents' mental confusion, to which everyone had to succumb, most of all his parents. As a replacement strategy for the disorder and contradiction within the family system, he aggressively intended to create order in the entire world with his delusional humanistic ideas. This can be interpreted as an attempt to heal the incorrigible rift within his family, as a result of which he had probably suffered greatly. One of his siblings became a satirical writer, the other one, his sister, became a minister.

Problem-solving strategies of parents

Behavioral patterns of fathers and mothers in critical situations have a major impact on their children's future coping strategies. Problem-solving behavior as well as parents' methods of coping with stress in crisis situations generally become learning models for children. They usually apply the same methods in similar situations later in life.

In a recent study, parents of children with schizophrenia and parents from a control group were asked about various problem-solving strategies and their behavior in stressful situations. The different behavioral patterns were subsequently categorized as:

- active – overactive problem-solving,
- passive – cautious problem-solving,
- avoiding – problem-solving by waiting it out.

Passive problem-solving behavior was declared significantly more often by fathers from families with schizophrenia than by fathers from the control group. This confirms the clinical experience of various schizophrenia experts that fathers of families with schizophrenia do not actively address impending problems within their families. They seem to behave passively when problems arise, and usually withdraw in conflict situations. Nevertheless, they undoubtedly acknowledge the conflicts and also suffer from them, otherwise they would not have specified conflicts three times more often than fathers in the control group in the study by Zenon Cupa (1997).

Avoidance behavior under stress was also more often registered in fathers of families with schizophrenia than in those in the control group.

These two findings are consistent with earlier clinical observations of other schizophrenia specialists. Theodore Lidz already concluded in 1965 – based on his family studies – that fathers of families with schizophrenia mostly played a passive role. In the families observed by him, fathers became outsiders and could no longer carry out their leadership role within the family. They were often inaccessible and assumed no responsibility. In Lidz's study, many of these fathers also had little professional and social success.

According to my clinical observations, fathers of families with schizophrenia could also be quite professionally successful. Their role in the family, however, was usually subordinate. This typical behavior has been described by Bowen as *functional helplessness*. Their passive problem-solving style obviously offers their families few coping strategies and guidance, and thus little safety. They are helpless in addressing emerging problems, and their insecurity penetrates the family system in crisis.

Mothers of families with schizophrenia reported a verbally overactive attitude under stress to a significantly greater extent than mothers in control families, a finding that other schizophrenia researchers also have reported. One might conclude that this type of behavior most probably plays an important role and constitutes an environmental factor in the development of the illness of schizophrenia.

Paternal withdrawal – lack of structure

Paternal withdrawal from everyday functions and educational responsibility has far-reaching negative consequences for emotionally vulnerable children. Theodore Lidz had observed this as early as 1965 in his family studies.

Fathers who withdraw during family conflict situations often rigidly entrench themselves in the role of an outsider. They occasionally comment with sarcastic criticism on the fights between the patient and the mother, only to retreat again thereafter. Towards therapists, they may even be quite critical and sarcastic, almost insulting. This type of degrading behavior, however, is more of a hindrance than a help in the therapeutic process and for the empowerment of the entire family system.

> **CASE HISTORY:** The father of two boys was very absorbed in his job and had little time for his family. The mother performed her tasks with great dedication until Pedro, the younger son, reached puberty. Overwhelmed as a mother of two teenage sons, she was desperately trying to get her husband's support but felt left alone and abandoned by him. She expressed her frustration by regularly reproaching her husband for his absence, complaining that he was neglecting his family duties, yet was unable to get him involved in the daily struggles of family life. She became depressed and turned to alcohol for comfort. The marriage ended in divorce, and the boys left home.

A few years later, as Pedro went travelling abroad alone, he suffered severe anxiety attacks and developed paranoid psychosis; he had to be admitted to a psychiatric clinic.

COMMENTARY: Pedro's father had lost his mother in early childhood. When he married, he presumed his wife could make up for his lack of maternal love. Right from the beginning, he delegated his part of parental responsibility entirely to her with the justification that she was closer to the boys anyway, and therefore better suited to taking care of them.

After the divorce, his relationship with Pedro, who still suffered from paranoid schizophrenia, did not improve – in fact, he expected his son to make the first step and contact him. Pedro, however, was unable to do so on account of his illness. Refusing all responsibility, the father left him to his mother and the medical professionals. At the same time, he complained about their incompetence and lack of involvement. The unmet emotional needs of Pedro's father, which he carried over from his childhood, prevented him from providing his son with paternal support. As a substitute for his father's empathy, Pedro turned to an imagined guru for daily instructions.

The mother's father was a patriarchal figure who set the tone at home but offered little support to her owing to his busy job. She silently expected her partner to offer her closeness and understanding, the paternal attention she had yearned for from her father. Her husband on his part expected maternal care from her, which he had missed out on as a result of his mother's early death. The unmet expectations of both, spilling over from their families of origin, collided head-on. The partnership issues could not be resolved. Pedro was left to himself during adolescence and was thus unable to establish a stable personality. She continued to stick to her overinvolved mother role, treating her son almost like a toddler. The father, seeking refuge in his ivory tower, remained aloof from his son, and remarried.

> Mothers' criticism of fathers' lack of involvement and fathers' sarcastic mocking of overinvolved mothers are usually a sign of unfulfilled expectations in both families of origin, and thus unresolved attachment problems.

Matriarchal leadership style – patriarchal dysfunction

A further question in our family study was whether mothers or fathers capitulated or asserted themselves in case of differences regarding parental leadership. Once more, significant differences between families with schizophrenia and the control families were found.

In families with schizophrenia, mothers asserted themselves significantly more often in case of disagreement while in the control group, the reverse was the case and fathers were increasingly more often taking the lead in disputes regarding the offspring's education.

We can therefore conclude that families with schizophrenia are characterized by a form of matriarchal dominance. This is consistent with the clinical observation of other schizophrenia researchers. They all have observed that the mothers in these families largely determine what happens, while the fathers are absent or inactive. This corresponds with the evasive, passive problem-solving behavior of fathers in families with schizophrenia, as explored above.

Yet how come that matriarchal dominance evolves in anxious family systems? Is matriarchal dominance in families which are primarily patriarchally organized already a first sign of systemic patriarchal dysfunction? Could this matriarchal takeover in families with schizophrenia be interpreted to the effect that these mothers only take the lead for lack of paternal presence, and not primarily as a result of wanting to be in charge? Is this systemic failure forcing mothers into both roles, the nurturer as well as provider of structure, if fathers are not available as a guiding force in the family? Or do mothers not get enough support from their extended family system?

Be that as it may, if mothers feel overwhelmed by their simultaneous caregiving as well as structuring tasks, they may become over-anxious, and thus emotionally overinvolved. They replace the lack of paternal leadership with fear-inducing, controlling and manipulative *instructional* strategies in dealing with their children. Later on, disadvantages of this educational pattern emerge as insecurity and anxiety in children who are most sensitive to the existential threat and most closely attached to the worries of their mother, contributing to the development of schizophrenia.

We should recall that children with ADHD and ADD are, indeed, highly sensitive to the emotional climate in family systems, and impulsive overreaction accompanied by aggression or withdrawal. And they are, as we have described before, often the subject of emotional focus by the system because of their special character traits, such as stubborn and obstinate behavior, exposing them to even further emotional pressure from the system.

Overinvolved mothers – helpless fathers

The family group I have been leading for over thirty years is attended almost exclusively by mothers. Their complaints usually concern fathers who are absent and uninvolved in raising their children. When confronting fathers of patients with schizophrenia with their wives' complaints, it turns out that they have no chance of meeting the expectations placed of them. In fact, they are being asked for assistance by their wives, but as soon as they get involved, they immediately face harsh criticism, "But not like this The admonishment prompts them to remove themselves once again from their responsibilities, abandon their adolescents and leave them entirely in the care of their mother. In reaction to their husbands' retreat, the mothers once more complain bitterly and voice harsh critique about the totally unreliable fathers – a vicious cycle.

In accusing and condemning the fathers of their offspring, mothers achieve exactly the opposite of what they intend: they lose paternal assistance, deprive their children of fatherly guidance, and destroy their male role model.

When analyzing fathers' and mothers' conflictual parenting behavior during their offspring's adolescence, it turns out that – upon questioning mothers' motivation more closely – they only wish to receive additional support for themselves in order to retain their maternal control, but no independent paternal support for the adolescents. Looking even deeper into their family of origin, it becomes apparent that what they wish for, in fact, is a protective and supportive figure who enforces their power when the youngsters start to slip from their grasp in puberty. They don't primarily want a father figure who engages with his offspring on his own terms, according to his values and judgement, but rather a figure who protects *them*, the mothers.

Interestingly enough, mothers of schizophrenia patients at first glance often convey to professionals exactly the opposite impression of a weak and desperate female. They appear strong and self-assured persons. Nevertheless, upon closer scrutiny, they are highly stressed and insecure individuals, hiding their emotional need for help behind a seemingly confident facade with overactive verbal communication.

Murray Bowen – one of the founders of family therapy and an outstanding researcher in schizophrenia – described this typical overactive verbal communication of mothers of patients with schizophrenia as *anxious mothers with a loud mouth*. Other schizophrenia researchers have described mothers as dissatisfied, suffering from chronic stress compared to mothers in control groups. Frieda Fromm-Reichmann (1948) coined the term *schizophrenogenic mother*. This term was later greatly discredited, because it ascribes guilt to the mothers, making them solely responsible for the unfolding of schizophrenia, which, of course, is not the case, as we have shown before on many occasions. Fathers, as well as the entire family system and the general environment, have to be included in the explanatory concept of the development of schizophrenia.

> Deeply ingrained patterns between anxious, overinvolved mothers and conflict-shy, passive fathers ensure the destructive cycles in family systems with schizophrenic offspring.

In our research concerning the issue of capitulating in conflictual situations, both parents in families with schizophrenia gave way under pressure more often than parents in the control group. Parents of schizophrenia patients are perceptibly less assertive towards their children than parents in the control group. The fathers, however, yielded less often under pressure than the mothers in both groups, which corresponds with male dominance behavior in general, and traditional authority figures in families in particular. Parental capitulation could thus also be related to the stubbornness of children with ADHD, who are indeed more difficult to manage than children without this behavioral disorder.

Competition of Instincts

Protective instinct overrules autonomy instinct

In puberty, the protected phase of childhood ends, and the crisis-ridden detachment phase begins. A key phrase aptly describes this transition period: "Puberty is when parents become difficult."

For parents, puberty often represents a crucial test of their relationship with their adolescents, and it is also a test of their partnership. For adolescents, it is a phase of transition and transformation towards an autonomous individual life with personal responsibility. The confrontation of two generations in coexistence stands for a major opportunity of conflict in the family system. This important phase of change from childhood towards adulthood also carries a certain risk for developing a variety of mental illnesses.

The interaction that goes on between the old and the young generation, between parents and their teenagers in the detachment conflict, may basically be described as a competition between two opposite instinctive demeanors:

- **The protective instinct of the parents,** which makes them keep their youngsters under control to protect them from all the evil in this world as well as from failure and disappointment in life. They are convinced they know for certain what is good for their children.
- **The autonomy instinct of adolescents,** which drives them to fight for elbow-room and make their own choices, battling fiercely against parental restrictions. They want to lead an independent, self-determined life, asserting their autonomy and freedom of action to make their own experience, and develop their personality and taste.

Anxious parents, led by their **protective instincts,** may hold on to their nurturing behavior longer than is appropriate, provoking the adolescents to fight for their autonomy all the more, and rebel against their parents' protective instincts. They violently reject any interference and want to get rid of their guidance. Under favorable circumstances, the **autonomy instinct** of the younger generation succeeds against the **protective instinct**, since the parents gradually realize that they lack the power to command obedience, allowing their teenagers natural exploratory behavior and personal responsibility; the maturing process then takes its natural course.

However, parents who cannot let go and are driven by an anxious care instinct, holding on beyond puberty into their children's adulthood, very often are not aware of their own unresolved detachment from the family of origin, which reveals a need to catch up with their limitations, experienced during their upbringing. Restrictions and punishments, still present in the back of their mind, nevertheless get passed on to their offspring. They implement blindly their parents' principles one-to-one, victimizing their own youngsters instead, without reflecting on their dependency-issues with their family of origin, although times have changed.

In general, the principal parental concern is for their children to have a better life than they had themselves. However, as soon as conflicts arise, they mostly fall back into the caregiving pattern of their traditional upbringing, which is affected by their own unresolved separation.

Another mode of reaction is the extreme opposite, which involves parents' relating to their teenagers in ways that contrast strongly with their own experience during puberty. However, unresolved detachment on the part of mothers and fathers cannot be resolved with generosity and leniency towards teenagers as a means of correcting missed opportunities in their own upbringing. Mothers who grant their teenagers unlimited freedom which they themselves were deprived of in their youth, easily feel insulted when their children rebel, and often interpret it as ingratitude towards them. They cannot see it as attempts by their children to gain their autonomy and enter adulthood and are personally hurt when they fight back. They feel like victims and place their emotions at the heart of the events. Unfortunately, this reaction by mothers most often provokes severe feelings of guilt in the adolescents.

The behavior of teenagers, however, is not the primary cause of mothers' suffering. Rather, they re-experience emotional trauma from their own adolescence. Memories of the painful separation phase, which they have not yet resolved, come back to haunt them. The emotional neediness of mothers, however, may also manifest itself in the intense empathy they have with their adolescents. This type of behavior is once again not very helpful since it may derail the already fragile emotional balance at a stroke.

> Mothers as well as fathers should be pillars of strength for their teenagers, and not on their own quest for love and understanding.

Avoidance of conflict by fathers

Fathers who cannot cope with the mood swings of their pubescent sons and daughters often react with harshness and sharp rebuff, holding on to their position of authority in confrontations with their teenage rebels. If they no longer feel accepted as the paternal authority, they abruptly distance themselves. They reject their youngsters with derogatory remarks and condemn their behavior as immature.

Rigid, authoritarian behavior on the part of fathers indicates unresolved detachment from their family of origin. The unconditional subordination to the patriarchal regime they are subjected to in their family of origin triggers fear in them if they cannot prevail against their recalcitrant youngsters. They are scared of disapproval and reprimands from their own parents. At the same time, representing values and moral principles of the past, they sense they might lose their standing as a father figure in the eyes of their teenagers if they don't always win in power fights.

Such fathers are weakened by their own subordinate behavior towards their families of origin. Their residual fear of confrontation with their own fathers means they have not acquired sufficient experience in handling conflicts with their teenagers. Sometimes, it's also hard for them to accept the fact that their children are granted more freedom of expression and are less limited in their movements than they could ever have imagined in their own adolescence.

For fathers, mothers and offspring, the act of unravelling an existing triangular relationship is almost as difficult as going through "the eye of a needle". All three are fighting within this triangular conflict for their own survival. However, it is the teenagers who suffer most since they are threatened in their personality development, and prevented from standing up for their autonomy, their own ideas and values.

> The problematic triangular relationship between father, mother and child inhibits youngsters in adolescence from finding their own identity.

The detachment conflict of adolescents may additionally be hindered by extraordinary circumstances in the family, such as:

- Mental or physical illness of a parent
- Disability or illness of a sibling
- Financial hardship due to prolonged unemployment of the breadwinner
- Chronic marital conflict
- Parental divorce
- Change in peer group due to the relocation of the family during vulnerable periods such as adolescence
- Single parent

- Death of an important reference person

During separation conflicts in puberty, youngsters are dependent on stable primary relationships as well as a supportive and resilient environment, even more so if they have performed a functionalized role before within the family system. If they are under the pressure to first and foremost attend to their parents' hidden need for support, and to appease their conflictual relationship as triangulated and functionalized adolescents, they are inclined to suppress their legitimate teenage rebellion out of consideration for their weakened family environment. Dysfunctional environmental conditions during puberty may therefore seriously jeopardize the youngsters' separation phase, rendering them unable to leave home and live their own life but oblige them to stay with the family of origin instead, sometimes even for life.

Puppy license by authority figures

During the separation conflict of puberty, teenagers need a steadfast parental counterpart, who is flexible, supportive, and also willing to learn at the same time. With a secure, unwavering opposite, they can engage in conflictual issues without fear of losing parental affection. Hence, they are fit to experience disagreements with their parents' core values as a maturation process of their own opinion-formation.

The phase of transition from childhood to adulthood entitles adolescents to protection from mothers, fathers and other authority figures such as teachers, comparable to the puppy license. They should never retaliate to the same extent as they are confronted and attacked by the teenagers. Adults should always bear in mind that they are more powerful than the young generation, and that the young first of all have to become able to assert themselves through their rebellious posturing. Teenagers should be treated by adults as equivalent, as per Jesper Juul's concept, but not as equal.

Malignant puberty

The term malignant puberty refers to a pubertal aberration which is typical of schizophrenia patients. It hinders the development towards adulthood. Young people who develop schizophrenia in the detachment phase during puberty often experience situations as described previously. They put their parents' needs first and feel subconsciously obliged to suppress their drive for autonomy. Children prone to developing schizophrenia – often children with ADHD or ADD – are particularly sensitive and therefore feel even more compelled to acquiesce to their parents' demands. They do not allow themselves to rebel for the sake of family peace, nor are they successful in fighting their own corner.

> **CASE HISTORY:** After many years of regular intrusive behavior by her mother, Evi, one of my schizophrenia patients, finally dared to fight back. However, her mother made fun of her daughter, trying to avoid any serious confrontation, calling her "Miss Sharp". The mother's brash behavior was intended to push her daughter back into subordination and dependency, which caused silent anger in Evi.

Teenagers who have developed schizophrenia are individuals who couldn't overcome the protective instincts of their parents. Adapting automatically to the anxiety of their family environment, they have been coerced into concealing their rebellious emotions, and thereby thrown into an emotional gridlock. This internal upheaval then triggers an *emotional monster wave*, psychosis as a consequence. Functionalized children have learned to adapt their lives to the family system from early childhood. The repression of their drive for autonomy robs them of the strength to stand up to their parents and fight for self-determination. Instead, they take refuge in internal rebellion and develop psychosis. They start to develop inexplicable behaviors, and enter a state of hyper arousal, agitation and irritability. Cognitively, they cease to be reasonable in their judgement, behave irrationally and develop paranoid interpretations of the people around them.

> Schizophrenia thus evolves from suppressed emotions in adolescence, which ultimately flood the cognitive network of the brain, rendering the patient mentally dysfunctional, so-called *crazy*, through acute psychosis.

Outsourced detachment conflict

Teenagers who undergo phases of *prolonged puberty* with acute psychosis are usually admitted to a psychiatric institution, forced to submit to the hospital hierarchy and the treatment programs of the institution. Parents thus avoid further confrontations with their teenagers, and the detachment conflicts get outsourced. However, young schizophrenia patients on their part usually see the clinic as an extension of parental control, and a new form of authoritarian oppression. Accordingly, they rebel against all medical advice and instructions, thereby resisting the pressure to conform to the clinic's treatment requirements. It should thus come as no surprise that all clinical-directed therapy programs of juvenile schizophrenia patients frequently do not have the desired therapeutic effect, as McGorry, a specialist on schizophrenia in young patients, has noted.

> **CASE HISTORY:** Patricia returned early from her stay in the French part of Switzerland because she became homesick. Her father didn't want her to hang around with friends and forced her to take a job as a nanny. She did as she was told but was extremely angry yet didn't say a word to him. However, from then on, she refused to shake hands with him. A

first, she developed anorexia. Later on, she became psychotic and had to be hospitalized.

Twenty-five years later, Patricia told her story in therapy. At that time, she had a delusional fear of knives, and was repeatedly tormented by the thought of turning violent against her parents, especially her father.

COMMENTARY: Patricia had been her father's darling. He spoiled her, nothing was too much for him. Such being the case, the father could not understand at all why his daughter suddenly refused to greet him. Yet he didn't visit her one-to-one, didn't enquire about her change of attitude, nor did he understand its meaning. He was entirely unaware of his all-encompassing yet supposedly well-meaning patriarchal caretaking which caused her internal anger and psychotic withdrawal during adolescence. He also did not confront her, but simply stopped paying attention to her, and attributed her alienation strictly to her illness.

For all those years, Patricia was unable to talk about her rancor. She could not stand up to her father and confront him. Instead, she fostered a delusion. However, she followed my advice to discuss the outrage and what had sparked her anger. To her great astonishment, her father listened attentively. Following this intimate exchange, she could shake hands with him again, and the paranoid fear of knives, which had been hounding her for twenty-five years, disappeared.

Suppressed temperament – emotional monster waves

The hot temper experienced by young people with ADHD – a major characteristic of the disorder – which cannot find expression within a strict upbringing may turn into powerful *emotional monster waves* during puberty or early adulthood. This state of mind is then psychiatrically diagnosed as manic depression or bipolar disease.

CASE HISTORY: Jeannette, the younger of two sisters, who had always been a dutiful, diligent student, delivered the best final exam in her class. Her maternal grandfather already envisioned her as a successful lawyer.

Shortly after starting law school, Jeannette suddenly developed severe anxiety symptoms. University seemed impersonal to her, and the contact among fellow students too anonymous. She felt lost and was terribly afraid of failing her first exam. She withdrew from friends and colleagues, tormented by panic. Retreating to her bedroom at her parents' house, she didn't dare to go out on her own and had to be accompanied by her parents everywhere.

Yet one day, Jeannette's mood suddenly flipped; she entered into a manic state. Now, she wanted to decide everything for herself, and not be told anything by her parents or anybody else. She ran away from home, stayed out with friends, spent a lot of money and gifted expensive items which she had just bought to anybody she met on the street. Her parents were shocked and reprimanded her, yet to no avail. They were desperate to bring her back under their control by reasoning endlessly with her. But Jeannette wouldn't listen to them. One day, her mother tried to prevent her from going out by using force. At that moment, Jeannette admitted herself to a psychiatric hospital to receive protection from her domineering parents, as she explained later. Shortly thereafter, her father contacted me as her therapist and informed me that he would appoint a legal guardian for his daughter, and get her admitted to a special psychiatric unit, where she could be treated adequately.

COMMENTARY: The father was an anxious person; he tried to protect his daughter from all threats posed by life. Her mother, on the other hand, was outgoing and sometimes dissatisfied with her overly reluctant and controlling husband.

The manic state was Jeannette's giant leap towards autonomy. Home and school had so far been her only social experience. Already groomed by her maternal grandfather to become a successful professional, she was like a staple between her active mother and her overprotective father. In fact, the parents' education represented a kind of straightjacket for her hot temper. Street life was her way of escaping parental condescension.

In late puberty, however, she developed manic psychosis and broke free from her family system. Yet Jeannette's parents could not understand her rebellious detachment attempts. They did not see what she was missing most: the need to get in touch with herself and the outside world. Quite the contrary, they saw the self-admission to a psychiatric ward not as a rescue attempt on her own behalf but rather as a concession to her mental illness and a permission for them to patronize her even more. Their goal was, in fact, not to protect her from injury but to protect themselves from disgrace by judicial means. After being discharged from hospital, Jeannette's lunge towards an autonomous existence had a positive outcome. She moved in with her boyfriend and found a job to her liking.

> Adolescents rebel in order to detach themselves from their parents' caretaking and become autonomous. If their natural urge to challenge is suppressed because the adolescent is a functionalized family member in service of the family system, they often only free themselves through psychosis with the power of an *emotional monster wave*, hopefully resetting and starting afresh thereafter with the help of therapy.

Mania – a big bang moment in the pursuit of autonomy

Teenagers' arduous efforts to achieve autonomy may also be obstructed by parents who refuse to take part in the therapeutic process. Out of loyalty to their parents, teenagers suppress their potential and turn their rebellious force inward in an emotional upheaval. From a systemic point of view, this desperate defiance through powerful *emotional monster waves* can be considered a *big bang moment in teenagers' pursuit of autonomy*, the ultimate drama of a hindered detachment process during adolescence.

This interpretation fits with parents' reporting that their sons and daughters diagnosed with schizophrenia did not rebel in puberty at all. However, if they were suddenly confronted with their children during their psychosis, they were stunned by the dammed-up aggression and often remarked: "This is not our child, our child would never be so mean, it must be the illness that makes them behave like this." Thereby, all aggressive behavior, which is an essential part of the maturation phase of puberty, is, without further reflection, associated with the illness. The parents regard all rebellious outbreaks merely as an expression of a disease. They do not comprehend that debating and reflecting present day issues is the name of the game with teenagers.

The slogan "better mad than bad", meaning that it is preferable for parents to have a sick child than a naughty one, accurately describes this parental paradigm that leads to schizophrenia. Teenaged schizophrenia patients are in a position of being functionalized and stuck in a position of forced as well as split loyalty in their family environment. Their perceived failure to solve both the inherent marital conflict in open debate, and to detach from the family of origin – adding to which, the family system does not allow them to rebel – results in all barriers breaking down, and the rancor turned inward suddenly erupts outwardly, manifesting in psychosis, combined with aggressive behavior or total withdrawal.

Such circumstances, in which the teenagers' drive for autonomy within the family system is constantly overruled, represent a pathogenic hindrance to their maturation process. The power of the *emotional monster wave* seems the only means of breaking the parents' dominance, yet often only for a short time. It is first and foremost a Pyrrhic victory.

Sometimes sensitive, functionalized children who experience psychosis can imagine no other way out of their internal confusion but by suicide. Their decision does not, in fact, represent a suicidal intent. It is simply a desperate attempt to escape the intolerable state of utter emotional enslavement, and a desire to end the inner turmoil. Suicide appears to them the only possible way of detaching.

Biographical Stress Factors

In addition to the genetically inherited vulnerability in combination with family constellation factors, individual biographical stress factors may occur, thus exceeding the emotional resilience to the point that psychosis breaks out in puberty.

The family constellation factors as well as personal stress factors in the immediate pre-phase of schizophrenia, are usually not registered by mental health professionals and thus not recognized as triggers of schizophrenia. Mental resilience – in contrast to physical sturdiness – cannot be clinically proven and easily measured, unlike bone density, for example. In case of schizophrenia, it is not possible to set a single standardized psychological resilience-scale as a benchmark. For this very reason, life-event studies, which explore traumatic experiences prior to the onset of acute psychosis, reveal no significant results in schizophrenia research.

However, analyzing family history as well as individual biographies, typical stress factors can most often be found preceding a first acute schizophrenic episode. Some of these biographical stress factors are listed below.

First love

An unhappy first love affair is a frequent biographical stress factor previous to the first outbreak of acute psychosis in young age. The process of self-discovery which accompanies courtship and sexual exploration is an intense emotional experience that is part of the personality maturation process.

> The first sexual relationship encounter represents a milestone for every human being, a chance as well as a risk factor at the same time.

CASE HISTORY: Susanna was attending the last year of high school. As a child, she had a close relationship with her father, with whom she shared the same athletic hobbies. However, as an adolescent, she did not think him sensitive enough. On several occasions, she felt overrun by him and distanced herself. He, on the other hand, felt offended by her behavior, and withdrew abruptly, thus depriving her of the paternal support he had previously provided for so many years.

At seventeen, she fell in love with a boy her age who seemed strong and confident but was not interested in her. However, she became involved in a delusional love affair, even though he was not her type, as she noted later. To gain some distance, she travelled abroad with a group of young people. While travelling, she was suddenly overwhelmed by an anxiety attack and felt persecuted. Susanna had to be returned to Switzerland, where she was admitted to a psychiatric hospital in an acute psychotic condition.

COMMENTARY: Susanna sought inner strength and protection in a delusional love as a replacement for the sudden loss of her father-daughter relationship. Away from home, her unhappy love affair couldn't offer her comfort or support, and she became psychotic.

The following story is another example of an unhappy love affair that ended in schizophrenia and ongoing sexual problems.

CASE HISTORY: Anton grew up with his mother and stepfather as an only child, but regularly visited his father and stepmother. In adolescence, he fell in love with a girl from a religious community who was living abroad. As he visited the girl spontaneously – her father realized his presence – he was told to leave the house immediately. Anton returned home to his mother, disturbed and confused. To take his mind off his unsuccessful visit, he wanted to go shopping with his mother's car, but she refused to give him the car key. In the ensuing fight, his mother called the emergency doctor in despair, and he underwent involuntary psychiatric hospitalization. He was diagnosed with schizophrenia.

FOLLOW-UP AND COMMENTARY: His first unsuccessful love affair seems to have changed Anton's life entirely. He became psychotic. During the course of his illness, he was unable to ever strike up a new relationship with a woman. Nevertheless, he was constantly on the lookout for a female partner but always in fear that his legal guardian would interfere, as the father of his first love had done. He also felt persecuted by the sound of his neighbors having sexual intercourse next door, and even had to move his bed into another room. Moreover, he was plagued by feelings of guilt whenever he masturbated. Only after he had convinced himself that female menstruation and male ejaculation were similarly natural, and his therapist confirmed that masturbation was neither unlawful nor forbidden, could he calm himself down. One day, years later, when he returned for further consultation, he suddenly stated: "I need a woman. I don't care what kind of woman; it could also be a prostitute." His desire remained unsatisfied. He was to suffer chronic schizophrenia.

Love delusion

Both male and female schizophrenia patients who cannot emotionally detach from their parents and have not found a suitable romantic partner, sometimes cultivate delusional love relationships that last a lifetime. Love delusions are imaginary love stories that help to stabilize their mental state, since they act as imagined gratification. They can be dealt with in therapy but cannot be corrected with antipsychotic medication.

CASE HISTORY: The father of Samuel had been brought up in a puritanical, religious family. For him, sexuality was only allowed as a means of procreation. When Samuel reached puberty, he had trouble identifying his gender role. He became psychotic and developed a delusional love relationship with a much older neighbor's daughter, though she was not interested in him. He harassed to the extent that her parents became alarmed and were thinking of calling the police and filing a restraining order against him.

FOLLOW-UP AND COMMENTARY: After his first unhappy love affair, Samuel was repeatedly admitted to a psychiatric hospital with paranoid psychosis. There, he fell in love with a female patient, twenty years his senior. Although she too was not interested in him, he constantly reproached himself for not having fathered a child with her. "The lost child", as he put it, haunted him henceforth. Despite being rejected by her, he believed that conceiving a child together was not only his but her cherished wish, too. In reality, however, this woman was extremely scared of him. She called the police whenever he appeared in her garden, and he was detained by the police for harassment several times.

From then on, "The lost child" was present in his mind on a metaphysical level and prevented him from leading a normal life. It was out of the question that he would take up a job before that child was conceived. He could not be dissuaded from his firm conviction. Years later, in his love delusion, he was still looking for another woman to help realize "The lost child". He himself was an unwanted latecomer in a partnership that had ended in divorce.

Intergenerational sexual issues

Unresolved sexual issues may even get projected onto offspring three generations later, distorted in an unhinged manner.

CASE HISTORY: Johannes' parents both came from religious families. Sexuality was a taboo. In his mother's parental home, sexuality was even downright demonized by her father who was a minister.

Johannes' father was also a minister. Since the sexual life between his parents was fraught with problems, the father began an affair with another minister's wife. The younger sister of Johannes had to comfort their mother every night for several years because she was so upset on account of her husband's affair. She additionally suffered from guilty feelings for having been raped as a young woman. This had fundamentally spoiled her sexual life throughout her marriage. Johannes, however, seemed not to care much about his father's adultery. He even saw an advantage in the affair. As he told me later in therapy, he gained a stepbrother, whom he liked. Nevertheless, he developed psychosis in puberty.

Johannes' hobby was "to research ministers", as he called it. He always read the parish journal. On weekends, he travelled to different parishes and churches to attend the sermons. He was informed of all changes, retirements and new appointments of ministers in each of the parishes.

FOLLOW-UP AND COMMENTARY: In therapy, which Johannes started only after many years of chronic schizophrenia, he alluded to women as dangerous. He thought they might rape him if he were to get too close to them. Each time he came to my office, he was extending his arm as far as possible and leaning back his upper body when I wanted to greet him by handshake. He was also careful to seat himself close to the door as an emergency exit.

During the weekends, which he usually spent with his parents, he only ever used a spoon at mealtimes, which angered his father. When I asked him for the reason, he mentioned that all family members used mostly forks and knives, that's why he would mainly eat with a spoon. As I tried to find out whether his habit was related to his fear of being infected by HIV, he silently agreed. He alluded to the fact that his father may have introduced the virus into the family through his extramarital relationship. Therefore, using knives and forks could contaminate him. He satisfied his own sexual urges with porn magazines, which he bought when nobody could observe him. Masturbation was a somewhat ambiguous matter to him as he was always plagued by remorse.

Johannes seemed to have accepted the extramarital relationship of his father without any moral qualms. Perhaps to relieve his father of the accusation of adultery, he was looking out for similar situations in other parishes; such was the basis of his research. His paranoia about contracting HIV nevertheless revealed that his father's sex life was not quite acceptable to him.

In line with the tradition of the Old Testament, he blamed women entirely for his father's adultery and saw them as seductresses, from whom he had to distance himself under all circumstances. During his weekend visits, he even kept distance from his mother, and refused to shake hands with her. Thus, he maintained his loyalty towards the father.

His mother admitted that she had mistreated him as an infant. She became pregnant before she was ready to become a mother, a fact she was unable to come to terms with. Owing to her sexual trauma, she had a strained relationship with her son from the very beginning and believed that he had been "contaminated" as a child by her frustration over her negative sexual experience, which she thought he had internalized. The personal history of his mother cast a long shadow over Johannes' conduct towards women.

Psychological problems – physical symptoms

Young men with unresolved sexual problems sometimes project these onto the groin and pubic area as physical symptoms of a psychotic phase.

These symptoms by proxy, as one might call them, are in most cases linked with physical illness.

> **CASE HISTORY:** Roberto gave his parents cause for concern when he was eighteen years old because of his conspicuous behavior. They first visited a center for drug-addicts, assuming he had a drug problem. When they failed to get help there, they were referred to a psychiatrist. By that time, Roberto was complaining of unclear symptoms in the genital area and therefore went to his family doctor, who then referred him to the urology department. Urethritis was diagnosed, and antibiotics were prescribed. However, it gradually became clear to the treating physicians that it was not a physical illness, and he was admitted to a psychiatric hospital for psychosis.
> **FOLLOW-UP:** After discharge, he refused to take his medication, and repeatedly had to be admitted to a psychiatric hospital, often in a physically neglected state. At the beginning of each new schizophrenic episode, he would always visit the urology department first for alleged urethritis. Years later, he developed testicular cancer.

Phantom pregnancy

Women who have never had a sexual partner in rare cases develop a delusional pregnancy out of their longing for motherhood. After a disappointing real or imagined love affair, their strong wish leads them to *imagine* they're experiencing *pregnancy*.

> **CASE HISTORY:** During her stay as an au-pair girl in French-speaking Switzerland, Rosa fell in love with the son of her host family. When he did not return her affection, she developed a phantom pregnancy, and held on to it for the following thirty-five years.

At the age of fifty, when she had to undergo a gynecological examination, her hymen was ruptured. The gynecologist wanted to reconstruct it, assuming Rosa wished to keep her virginity. To everybody's surprise, she reacted with anger. She didn't want her hymen to be restored since she still considered herself pregnant from her imagined lover. Under no circumstances was she ready to abandon the delusional fantasy of her false pregnancy. She held on to it for the rest of her life.

Sex as a tool of power

Young women may also use their sexuality in adolescence as a weapon to rebel against condescending parents, who may react with moral reprimands, or even by withdrawing love and showing rejection, since they consider female sexual activity in adolescence as a disgrace to the family. They fear that their honor may be tainted by their daughters' sexual activity.

CASE HISTORY: Elena's mother was admitted to a psychiatric hospital after her birth because of postpartum psychosis and stayed there for many years. Elena's father, in the meantime, filed for divorce, remarried and had three more children with Elena's stepmother. Yet his firstborn daughter remained his main concern; he felt deep pity for her since she had lost her mother so early. He was very protective of her and spoiled her all the more.
As a headstrong girl, however, she started to cause trouble for him as a teenager. To his dismay, she was hanging out with boys. She was very attractive and enjoyed partying with young males in the neighborhood, sometimes staying out late, drinking over the weekends. The father tried to restrain her but to no avail. There were many angry disputes between the two. But Elena did not succumb to her father's order. Finally, he lost his composure and referred her to a psychiatric hospital against her will. Doctors and staff were also unable to tame Elena as he

had hoped for. Disappointed by all, but mostly by his daughter's promiscuity, he broke off the relationship with her for good.

FOLLOW-UP: Elena continued to rebel. She didn't follow the rules of the institution, nor did she obey anyone in the hospital. As a therapeutic measure, she was transferred monthly to another ward because the staff were exhausted by her. Neither could the doctors mediate between father and daughter. For a while, the stepmother got involved and tried to maintain contact, but without success. Elena strictly refused to see her. She remained in the hospital for years as a chronic schizophrenia patient.

All these examples demonstrate that sexual problems can be important emotional stress factors in the preliminary phase of a first acute psychosis in adolescence. It may be an imagined first love affair, or delusional love and imagined pregnancy out of desperation for real love. A repressive, guilt-inducing attitude on the part of parents towards sexual exploration of their teenagers, as in Elena's case, may also be a stress factor leading to psychosis in young adulthood.

Unfortunately, the topic of sexuality is usually not addressed in therapy of young patients with schizophrenia. The dramatic symptoms of acute psychosis are so impressive that sexual problems are mostly left out and receive no therapeutic attention at all. A harmful first love experience, dammed-up sexual impulses due to a restrictive upbringing, or conspicuous sexual emancipation are therefore not recognized as triggering stress factors by professionals, although classic psychotherapy according to Freud has always placed special emphasis on the issue of sex. However, in the treatment of schizophrenia, only the acute psychotic symptoms are addressed, and the underlying biographical stress factors such as sexual problems are mostly neglected.

Young patients with schizophrenia are not able to talk about their sexual problems on their own initiative. They feel too ashamed. Thus, the mental stress factors caused by repressed sexuality or unfortunate sexual experiences remain undetected. From my long-term experience, young schizophrenia patients should always be questioned about their sex life, so they can receive help in overcoming the hurdle of shame, and talk about their sexual problems, thereby facilitating their maturation and entry into adulthood.

Failed career choices

A failed career choice is another typical stress factor in the preliminary phase of the first schizophrenic episode in adolescence or young adulthood. Fathers and mothers – consciously or unconsciously – may both exercise emotional pressure on their son or daughter with their expectations and thereby impede an independent, personal career choice made by their children in adolescence. Under parental pressure, insecure youngsters can't choose freely. Moreover, if they make a choice that turns out to be unsuitable, they often can't alter it because they are too afraid their parents might react disapprovingly. Instead of openly resisting their parents, they fail their exams, provoke dismissal by misbehaving, or they become psychotic. Under such circumstances, parents are forced to accept their youngsters' quitting and dropping out of their career, initially chosen under parental pressure.

> **CASE HISTORY:** Ronaldo was a gifted, intelligent boy. He wanted to go to university but was unsure of what to study. His father, an engineer, suggested law because he was convinced it would guarantee a secure income for him later in life. The mother, however, had a more artistic subject in mind for her sensitive young son. Yet Ronaldo followed his father's advice and went to law school, though he was never quite happy with it. He failed his final exam and became psychotic for the first time. After recovery, he tried a second time and passed. He even

continued his study to become an attorney but turned psychotic while trying to pass the bar exam, and again had to be hospitalized.

FOLLOW-UP AND INTERPRETATION: After being discharged from hospital, Ronaldo went travelling abroad to find himself, as he put it. However, being in a foreign country, he was unable to look after himself; he twice had his backpack, money and ID card stolen. On all these occasions, his parents had to get him out of trouble. Soon after returning home, he felt even more lost than before.

Out of desperation, his father secretly mixed antipsychotic medication into Ronaldo's drinks, wishing to help his son and make family life easier. When the father confessed this later, Ronaldo got extremely angry. He withdrew completely and avoided all contact with his parents. Active only at night, he took his mother's car to drive hundreds of miles every which way through the country.

Although the mother usually noticed this the next morning by checking the odometer, she did not dare to confront him. Some months later, having parked her car on a hillside late at night, he was run over by it and killed. Had he forgotten to pull the hand brake properly? We will never know.

COMMENTS: Commands and patronizing behavior, or the blind acceptance of everything he did, no questions asked, were the only paternal supportive methods Ronaldo had received. On the one hand was his father's request to get a job and be financially independent. At the same time, he patronized him by mixing the medication clandestinely into his drinks in order to change his behavior rather than confront with him with whatever conduct he didn't approve of. The mother on her part did not object to Ronaldo's nightly driving in her car. She had an indirect stake in his adventure-seeking avoidance behavior. But she later made the remark that she could never have denied him her car; she found that too harsh and would never have forgiven herself if she had done so. She thereby was an unwitting partner in Ronaldo's drive for autonomy – and weakened, even undermined, her husband's guiding principles. This parental behavior was confusing, which did not help Ronaldo find his way in life.

Sensitive teenagers may also be hampered in their independent career choice by chronic conflicts between their parents, plagued by fear of losing their affection if they would follow one parent's wish, losing the support of the other. This makes it emotionally impossible for them to form an independent opinion and exercise their choice. Thus, the only way to escape such a dilemma is to remain undecided. However, not only conflict between parents, but also conflict between parents and therapists, may hamper the decision-making process, as was the case with Joseph.

CASE HISTORY: Joseph's mother suffered chronic schizophrenia. His father, an engineer, insisted that his son get a good education. Joseph, a child with ADD and easily distracted was a loner and dreamer. When he finished his high school exam, he went to university, to the delight of his father. Soon thereafter, however, he felt overwhelmed by all the demands placed on him and became psychotic. A little later, he began vocational training in a technical field, which his father disapproved of. After one year, Joseph broke off the training and withdrew completely into an autistic state of mind. He was sharing an apartment with a colleague, and together they would consume cannabis on a regular basis. In a desolate physical and mental condition, he was admitted to a psychiatric hospital – he had become psychotic.

FOLLOW-UP AND COMMENTARY: After discharge, he was placed in a half-way house, and his choice of career was up for discussion once more. This led to disagreements between his father and the therapeutic staff. The father tried to persuade him to go back to university. He thought his son was intelligent enough to study. The therapists on their part recommended a less ambitious vocational training course. Joseph himself did not say anything; he left the decision up to his father and his therapists.

Due to the long-term illness of the mother, the family had always been in an extremely delicate situation. Without maternal protection, Joseph was exposed solely to his father's ambitions. As a substitute for maternal care and empathy, he was under the custody of mental health professionals. However, the disagreements between them and the father exposed Joseph to a loyalty conflict, rendering his career choice a difficult, almost impossible, task. After he had left the therapeutic community, Joseph remained in a sheltered workshop for several years, until he began to contemplate his own career choice. He registered in a professional IT training program with my support and also started as an intern in an IT firm, gradually socializing more often to leave behind his introverted way of life.

In Joseph's case, several stress factors had led up to the onset of schizophrenia: a mother suffering mental ill health, an inherited vulnerability factor of ADD, an ambitious father who subjected his son to emotional pressure, the use of cannabis, the conflict of loyalty between father and mental health professionals, and a failed career choice. However, with my long-term support as well as psychotropic medication he finally found his way.

Parental ambitions as stress factors

Emotional stress factors may also arise from parental ambitions. Sensitive children tend to adopt their parents' unfulfilled career ambitions even if those exceed their own predisposition. The parental projection process can cause tremendous stress in adolescents during their *career decision*-making phase.

> **CASE HISTORY:** Ilona's mother always had the dream that, one day, she would pass the final high school exam, which she had failed before, and attend university. She was unhappy about this her entire life.

> Daughter Ilona didn't like to study and had no wish to go into higher education. One day, however, she decided to enroll in evening classes. But it soon became too much for her, and she dropped out. Towards her parents and the therapist, however, she pretended for a while that she still went for academic training. The stress of lying, however, soon became unbearable – she became psychotic and was dismissed from her job.
>
> **COMMENTARY:** Her mother's unfulfilled ambitions accompanied Ilona like a shadow from which she could not free herself. Even in primary school, the mother had spared no effort to turn her little girl into a good student, but Ilona fought it vehemently. She wanted to go outside and play with her friends instead.
>
> Later, however, Ilona developed guilt feelings because of her failed academic performance and tried to make up for it. But the emotional distress was so great when she didn't succeed that only psychosis helped her hide the feelings of shame from her parents as well as from herself. Much later, she could openly admit that she had abandoned the evening school long ago.

An acute schizophrenic episode may cover up the dilemma of career choice temporarily, but the problem does not disappear for good, nor is it resolved for the patients or for the parents. Impressed by the illness, the parents hold back their ambitions temporarily, remove the pressure and assume a protective attitude towards the suffering youngster. However, once the acute psychosis has subsided, they usually resume leaning on their son or daughter in emotional terms. Yet they don't realize that they place great strain on their youngsters in order to satisfy their own parental ambitions. Adolescent schizophrenia patients on their part always wish to remain loyal to their parents, hoping to please them, instead of finding the courage to make individual choices. They don't want to disappoint them and are thus unable to address their choice of profession on their own.

Failed exams as a stress factor

A failed exam in a self-chosen profession which was not supported by the parents may also constitute a stress factor in the preliminary phase of acute psychosis.

> **CASE HISTORY:** Michael was the youngest of three siblings and still living with his parents at the age of twenty-four. After having failed his first exam, he was plunged into a deep existential crisis. Out of desperation, he slit his wrist in a suicidal attempt upstairs in his room while the parents chatted downstairs with their guests. They immediately hospitalized him.
>
> Michael felt very ashamed whenever he was asked about the scars on his arm and evaded the question. He could not understand how such a thing could have happened to him. The involuntary psychiatric hospitalization also troubled him deeply. He felt greatly stigmatized by it.
>
> **FOLLOW-UP AND COMMENTARY:** When Michael failed his first exam, he felt as if the ground had fallen out from underneath him. In therapy, I tried to find out whether he wanted to pursue his study, and if the choice of subject had in fact been his own. I also wanted to clarify whether he would be unsettled by his father's doubts. After having convinced me that he was fully committed to his studies, I supported him in his endeavor. At the same time, I motivated his father to support his son in finding his own apartment to gain more independence. Michael moved out and passed his final exam successfully a few years later.

Biographical Stress Factors for Women

Female postpartum psychosis

The birth of a child is a naturally stressful event for every woman, although a joyful moment nevertheless. The arrival of a new family member also engenders profound changes in the family system, which always has a lasting impact on the parents' partnership, sometimes leading to unpredictable and uncontrollable reactions in the nuclear family as well as in the family of origin.

Immediately after giving birth, mothers become aware of their overall responsibility for their newborn. Moreover, they are heavily dependent on additional support themselves from at least one other adult. In earlier times, the support system consisted of their own mother, the mother-in-law, a sister, an aunt, or other relatives from the extended family. Nowadays, new mothers usually expect support primarily from their husbands or partners. But they may not be available as a result of a demanding job, or they might not see the necessity of assistance. Yet new mothers who cannot rely on friends or caregivers such as professionals, and who are left alone with their new task, can feel desperate and scared. The danger of emotional overload is even greater if they are additionally burdened by family conflicts. The risk of postpartum psychosis is one of the typical, most dramatic acute forms of schizophrenia in new mothers.

Acute psychosis may occur immediately after the birth of the first child or may also happen after any subsequent births. Psychosis develops whenever they do not receive enough backing from their social environment and are therefore overwhelmed by the new challenge of being a mother to a newborn.

CASE HISTORY: Anna suffered under her controlling and interfering mother. Moreover, she was angry with her husband, reproaching him for not being able to arrive on time for the birth of her second child. Furthermore, she had an imagined love affair with her gynecologist who had delivered her second child as a stand-in. The moment she developed postpartum psychosis, she was referred to a psychiatrist by her gynecologist, which infuriated her. She did not regard herself as mentally ill; the referral was an insult to her. In her eyes, it was her husband who failed to fulfill his role to her satisfaction. The psychiatrist on his behalf thought a female psychiatrist might be of more help and passed her on to me.

FOLLOW-UP AND COMMENTARY: In our first session, Anna was extremely skeptical, even suspicious. Some of her thoughts bordered on paranoid delusions. She said she had been intentionally treated badly by her gynecologist and all other doctors. As it turned out later in therapy, she was first and foremost angry with her husband because he had been late for the birth of her second child. This negligence affected her so much that she wanted a third child by him to overcome her resentment, and indeed, she got pregnant again. This time, however, she wanted to give birth at home with the assistance of a midwife. As she went into labor, she had to go to the toilet to empty her bladder – and whoosh! – the newborn fell into the toilet. As the midwife had not yet arrived, and the husband was the only person present, he had to assume the role of the obstetrician.

In an emergency situation such as this, her husband could now demonstrate his support and compensate for his earlier neglect of her. He passed the challenge with flying colors. Anna was overjoyed. This time, her husband was in the right place, at the right time. She was to suffer no more psychotic episodes. Her faith in the doctors was restored. She even motivated other women with similar problems to seek psychiatric help in my office.

Excessive expectations set us up for disappointment

The overload of mothers at birth is often connected with an unresolved detachment from their own mothers. This type of psychic constellation leads new mothers to have excessive expectations, which are expressed in the form of high demands placed on their partners. Yet partners can never satisfy these unfulfilled needs, which date back to childhood and the family of origin.

Unresolved or incomplete detachment of fathers from their family of origin can also represent an obstacle if they are still loyally committed to their own parents. These fathers are incapable of offering the necessary support to mothers during childbirth and thereafter.

The following example applies to both of the above scenarios.

CASE HISTORY: It was a holiday acquaintance. For a long time, Peter maintained a relationship with Marianne only on weekends. Marianne was undecided as to whether she should marry him. She was strongly attached to her parents. Emigration was a momentous step she was fundamentally afraid of. Despite her feelings of doubt, she finally decided to marry Peter anyway.

After giving birth to her first and only child, she developed postpartum psychosis. In desperation, she sought support and security from her gynecologist in an almost obsessive manner. She would call him at inappropriate times, would appear at his practice unannounced to declare her love for him. She stalked him with her delusional love until he called the police and had her admitted to a psychiatric hospital. She had developed full-blown psychosis

Her parents came to her support for three months. However, this was not enough to make her feel secure in her new maternal role, far away from her homeland. She remained psychotic for quite a while, and her family doctor, who already considered her a chronic sufferer of schizophrenia, referred her to me for therapy.

HISTORY AND COMMENTARY: Marianne came for therapy alone at first and after some time, together with her husband. Later on, when her gynecologist died unexpectedly, she became acutely psychotic again, and was once more admitted to a psychiatric hospital by her family doctor. After discharge, she returned for outpatient therapy. She went through a long period of depression. Being constantly unhappy with her marriage, she finally decided to get a divorce. She moved into her own apartment in the same building with the support of her husband.

Unresolved issues within Peter's family played a crucial part in his choice of partnership. He had chosen Marianne as a tribute to his mother – who had suffered homesickness as an immigrant her entire life – giving his children the opportunity to learn his mother's language fluently. Yet the marriage to Marianne could never resolve the problems of Peter's mother. He had transplanted his mother's problem to his relationship with his wife.

Far from home and her parents, Marianne endured a similar fate to the one that had plagued Peter's mother. After the birth of her child, Marianne developed a delusional love relationship with her gynecologist to overcome her loneliness.

The divorce was the only way for her to escape her unmet expectations and her sense of entitlement to emotional support from her husband, who – still committed to his mother – was unable to satisfy Marianne's need. The divorce marked an end to her longing for security within her marriage, and also acceptance of her separation from her homeland. After the divorce, Marianne did not become psychotic for quite some time. She always maintained her job throughout all the turmoil, which gave her some independence. However, her unresolved attachment to her family of origin continued to exist.

To bear a child without the father's consent

A woman's desire to bear a child against the will of her husband or partner, the child's father, may also lead to an emotional overload and ultimately to psychosis.

> **CASE HISTORY:** When Kersten noticed that she was pregnant with her fourth child, she told her husband while making the beds. He responded: "For God's sake, not another one!" After giving birth, she developed postpartum psychosis and had to be admitted to a psychiatric clinic, where she was prescribed medication to help control her emotions. When this very child turned twenty, Kersten had another acute psychotic episode.
> At that time, she came to see me. She spoke about her distress, which she was still suppressing. She had never talked to anyone about this before. When I asked her whether she had ever mentioned it to her husband, she responded in the negative and added that she felt as if his "For God's sake" was still ringing in her ears as if it had been yesterday. She still bore a deep grudge against her husband and thought about it every day. I therefore instructed her to ventilate her grievance with her husband, which she did.
> **COMMENTARY:** The bitterness about her husband's exclamation was at the forefront of Kersten's mind. It had triggered anger, need and frustration; those feelings still sat deep. Kersten wanted her fourth child but was to a certain degree unable to take full responsibility without the consent of her husband.
> It was therefore fundamental that she process her trauma in therapy and get the deep-rooted frustration off her chest. Admitting that she still harbored tremendous anger towards her husband for his outcry, and sharing those feelings with him, calmed her down. Kersten did not become psychotic in the years that followed, and her trauma no longer resurged on a daily basis.

Mothers' separation anxiety

Family members or professionals sometimes prevent young, insecure mothers from exercising their roles by pushing them aside with their support, taking the lead, thereby putting them under enormous emotional stress up to the point that they suffer from separation anxiety from their newborn.

This may arise when young mothers are living with their husbands' in-laws. Under such circumstances, grandmothers often assume a dominant role in the child-rearing and prevent the young mothers from practicing motherhood. Living together in extended family systems, insecure mothers are easily matronized by powerful grandmothers.

In fear of a family conflict, these young mothers usually adapt to the situation, if reluctantly, since they are dependent on the system. However, feelings of resentment may build up. If they do not have the inner strength and courage to stand up to their own mothers or mothers-in-law in a self-assured manner, they run the risk of becoming psychotic.

CASE HISTORY: Alexia married a farmer's son and stayed with him and their three children at the farm of her in-laws. This living arrangement prompted internal conflicts for her because the mother-in-law intervened daily in her household as well as the upbringing of her children. Alexia felt that she was unable to satisfy her in any way. After the birth of her second child, she withdrew emotionally, became psychotic and had to be admitted to a psychiatric clinic. Despite regularly taking antipsychotic medication, she had a relapse after the birth of her third child and had to be hospitalized again.

FOLLOW-UP AND COMMENTARY: After discharge from hospital, the family arranged for a psychiatric nurse to provide support. She instructed the mother-in-law to abstain from interfering in the daily chores of her daughter-in-law. At the same time, the nurse supported Alexia as a mother and encouraged her to take up the daily tasks as a farmer's wife. From that point on, Alexia no longer required hospitalization. The children were fine. They no longer had to worry about their mother.

The child as a pawn between the generations

Grandmothers, whether they are on the maternal or paternal side, who are under the impression that they have missed something or done something wrong as mothers, may try to rectify their own past by taking charge of their grandchildren. Particularly maternal grandmothers may react with an abundance of affection towards the newborn. However, if they are repelled by their daughters, they can go as far as spreading rumors about the baby's not being taken care of properly by the mother. They may even threaten them with legal guardianship, thereby disenfranchising their daughters of their motherly role. This undoubtedly causes severe distress in these young mothers.

Sometimes, young women even become pregnant in order to break up their own mother-daughter relationship. If grandmothers aim to assume the caretaking role under such circumstances, more aggressive feelings build up in the young mothers, and the risk of their becoming psychotic is greater. Grandmothers then feel all the more entitled, if not outright obliged, to take custody of the newborn. Because child protection services generally get involved in such cases, young mothers are almost forced to assert themselves while facing these authorities. For the newborn, this entails being involved in a triangular relationship right from the very beginning between mother and grandmother or foster mother assigned by the child protection services – an unhealthy situation as described in the chapter *Triangle relationship*.

When child protection services remove children from mothers and place them with foster parents, mothers usually continue to bear children until they can keep one. A young woman who had six children by different men, had five of them taken away from her and placed in different families under the initiative of her own mother. She only succeeded in keeping the youngest with the support of a mother-child care institution. The relationship between that woman and her own mother, who had arranged the removal of the children it in cooperation with the child protection services, was highly conflictual and ambivalent. Their detachment process was locked in a stalemate. They had never gone through the separation conflict together but had broken off any direct contact with each other. Significantly, that grandmother had been sexually abused by her maternal grandfather during childhood.

Hyper-aroused mothers

During many years as a supervisor of pediatric nurses who practiced home visits for mothers after childbirth, I was repeatedly confronted with postpartum psychosis. The questions of the nurses always centered on the issue of how they should approach these hyper-aroused mothers without scaring them off. These psychotic young mothers immediately feared that their child could be taken away from them if they admitted to any weakness or insecurity and asked for help – a fear which is not always entirely unfounded, as the last example has shown. Therefore, mothers categorically warded off the visiting nurses during the initial contact. They made desperate attempts to make a strong impression as competent mothers who could master their task without further assistance.

Trying to maintain an intact façade while feeling complete despair is quite typical for women in the early stages of postpartum psychosis. By hiding their abysmal fear from their surroundings and even denying it when asked, they are neither able to ask for help nor are they willing to accept any if offered. Thus, the suffering of these young mothers often goes unnoticed for a quite some time, meaning that once their psychosis does eventually erupt, it often appears to be out of the blue.

However, experienced professionals can recognize psychotic mothers in their pre-psychotic state. They usually perform their maternal tasks in a state of emotional distress and in an almost mechanical manner. They detach fully from their feelings, and stereotypically obey their maternal instinct without any affective connection to their children.

Yet if young psychotic mothers are left to their own devices for any length of time and do not receive adequate assistance, they may display two forms of extreme behaviors, in particular. They either completely neglect their child, or they smother it with excessive care, which manifests itself in overly protective behavior. They no longer let the child out of sight and often constantly breastfeed. When the child is sleeping, they check every minute whether it is still breathing. This overprotective, controlling behavior serves as a kind of shield against their own fear of being bad mothers, and by the same token, confirms over and over again that they are indispensable, loving caretakers. The children are thereby subjected to total dependency on their mothers, and are compelled to respond and satisfy all their emotional needs. Babies learn this type of behavior pattern at a very early stage of life.

Danger of infanticide

Women's excessive sense of motherhood may even drive them to commit infanticide under extreme circumstances. They never kill their children because they want to harm them; they do it because they want to protect them from the suffering in life. They project their own fear of being hurt onto all the potential caregivers who might harm their children. Although they sense that they are unable to provide enough motherly care, they also do not want to leave their children in the hands of a foster mother or any other maternal replacement. These are the motivations that underlie infanticide. After killing their infant, the women usually try to commit suicide.

CASE HISTORY: Helga had two children with her husband, who had a drinking problem. After the birth of her first as well as her second child, she developed postpartum psychosis and was treated in a psychiatric clinic. With the second hospitalization, the child protection services got involved. They ordered a social worker to visit Helga once a week to check the wellbeing of her children. She found a household perfectly cared for, and the two children also seemed to be well looked after. Helga herself went for psychiatric outpatient treatment. In the eyes of the authorities, everything appeared to be going well until one day, the police received an emergency call. Helga had killed her two children and had attempted suicide.

COMMENTARY: The visits ordered by the child protection service were of no help to Helga; she simply felt watched. Under pressure from the authorities and feeling abandoned by her husband who was an alcoholic, she killed her children to forestall the removal of her children into care by the authorities.

Mental health professionals who are involved with postpartum psychosis should thus always consider the acute danger of infanticide. They must keep in mind that maternal instinct can lead frightened mothers to kill their children as soon as they sense that they may lose custody of them. Quick and comprehensive actions must therefore be taken by the authorities in cases of assumed child neglect in order to reduce the risk of infanticide. A less dangerous reaction on the part of mothers in fear of losing their children is to move them repeatedly to another district, hoping the authorities will lose track of them.

Unresolved Partnership Conflict

Middle-aged women who develop schizophrenia have a particularly poor prognosis, according to statistical data. This finding has consistently been linked to menopause and the decline of female hormones such as estrogens. At first glance, this interpretation seems plausible. The change of hormonal balance in women may well have a destabilizing effect on their psyche.

From a systemic point of view, however, other explanations can be posited. For many years, I had women in therapy who experienced their first psychotic episode in middle age. In all these cases, I could detect a state of extreme dissatisfaction with their relationship. Chronic frustration, deep-seated rancor as well as unspoken revolt had accumulated in their psyche over time to finally erupt in an *emotional monster wave* of psychosis.

Female self-realization

In relationships, women principally tend to adapt to their partners. This willingness to solve problems through adaptation is probably related to their inherent maternal role. As mothers, it is natural for them to adapt to the needs of their children. For the sake of family life, women are actively and consciously willing to sacrifice their personal needs and objectives over extended periods of time, especially during the developmental period of their offspring. Moreover, women often assume such an adaptive and supportive role not only with the children but also towards their husbands and partners if the career of the breadwinner requires them to do so. It thus comes as no surprise that they view their adaptive role as a natural duty, which fully coincides with their maternal role towards their partners as long as the children are not yet independent.

But once the children are grown up, the maternal role starts to take a backseat and women's desire for self-realization comes to the surface. They may not dare to stand up for their own needs, however, fearing conflict, or even fearing they might lose their partner altogether. Under such conditions, despite their innermost urges, they continue to adapt against their own will for the sake of family peace. This causes them tremendous mental distress that can ultimately lead to psychosis.

Men commonly tend to overlook the warning signals which arise when their partners are unhappy. And when they do notice them, they frequently avoid inquiring after the reason. Like most medical professionals, they are inclined to associate their wives' discontent with the mental disorder of depression, attributing it to the menopause and empty-nest syndrome.

Women who dare to attempt self-realization at that moment by applying for a job, for instance, are frequently hindered by their partners, who argue that the family is financially cared for and does not depend on an additional income. In case women decide to pursue an ambitious and expensive hobby, their partners mostly object to the extra costs. These women are therefore yet again left stranded with their rebellious feelings and resentment about their dependency on their husbands or partners.

Men who argue consciously or unconsciously against the self-realization of their wives have the hidden desire to maintain the status quo of maternal service most likely due to unresolved separation issues from their family of origin. At the same time, they defend their own powerful position as the sole breadwinner – a position of power they are reluctant to forfeit.

Women who lack the self-confidence to pursue their own goals without the support of their partners nevertheless still continue to harbor a desire for autonomy. This results in their reaching a motivational impasse in the sense that they don't know which way to go. Their inner compass abandons them. In vain, they lay special emphasis on their right to self-determination, constantly trying to motivate their partners to support their goals instead of motivating themselves. They frequently argue that for years, they bore the sole responsibility for the family as well as supporting their husbands' career while they attended additional training, but now it is their turn. However, despite all the logical reasoning and emotional pressure, partners usually fail to meet their wives' expectations. As a consequence, their silent aggression continues to accumulate in the depths of their psyche. If they also have an explosive temper, their inner rage ultimately erupts into an *emotional monster wave* – psychosis.

When they are admitted to the psychiatric hospital, they experience the exact opposite of self-realization. They are given – to complete their misery – a psychiatric diagnosis of acute schizophrenia, which disqualifies them socially as mentioned in the introduction of this book. Their desire for self-determination, obscured by their psychosis, is perceived by neither their husbands nor by the medical staff. They are now patronized not only by their husbands but also by the psychiatrists who determine with professional conviction what is and is not good for them.

Nobody realizes that their inner dissatisfaction is mainly directed towards their partners. In the psychiatric hospital, these discontented women are forced to submit to the routine of the medical system. The acute symptoms of psychosis are the focus of treatment, and the upheaval of their *emotional monster wave* is suppressed with medication. The underlying cause of the psychotic outbreak, however, remains unexplored. In their hopeless situation, deprived of any agency, the silent anger they harbor against their partners and medical staff is solely classified as extreme dysfunction. Although they receive twice the attention from their surroundings for a short time, their urgent need for independence is not acknowledged. Their desire for self-determination is by now completely crushed.

CASE HISTORY: Rosemary had a husband who cared for her, a child who brought her joy, and a modern home. Her temperament, however, did not match these well-ordered external circumstances. To the contrary, she felt imprisoned. She repeatedly suffered from psychotic episodes and behaved in a way that embarrassed her husband in public. Because of her eccentric behavior, she was picked up by the police and admitted to a psychiatric hospital several times. The treatment, however, was always unsuccessful. After futile attempts to keep her in line, her husband finally filed for divorce. Although she was now free to do what she wanted, she no longer had a child, a husband, nor a roof over her head; the father had received custody of their child.

COMMENTARY: Years later during therapy, Rosemary expressed her feelings of inner confinement in her married life. During all those years, no one had noticed her emotional state. i.e. her hidden needs, behind the diagnosis of schizophrenia. Attempts by her environment as well as the medical staff were solely directed at controlling her eccentric behavior with medication and behavior modification programs. Under traditional psychiatric terms, Rosemary was classified a chronic schizophrenia patient, and not a desperate woman struggling to find her own expression.

Divorce as an escape fantasy

During the acute psychotic phase, many women develop fantasies of divorce, and sometimes even act upon them with the help of a lawyer. After the psychosis has subsided, they mostly abandon their intentions. All the same, their deep dissatisfaction with their partnership continues to exist but remains unnoticed. The divorce fantasies are merely interpreted as an expression of the illness and thereby disqualified by their partners. Moreover, the withdrawal of the divorce intention is interpreted as a return to common sense, of treatment success, rather than simple acquiescence to their dependency on their partners. The divorce fantasies are registered as symptoms of schizophrenia and merely treated with medication. The disguised attempts at self-realization are not even taken into consideration and therefore never addressed.

Unresolved Partnership Conflict

CASE HISTORY: Verena, who was the youngest of three sisters, grew up with a father who was an entrepreneur. She was a spirited and fun-loving girl, and her father's favorite. She played the piano rather well and wanted to pursue a musical career. But her father objected; he considered music to be an unprofitable means of earning a livelihood. When she showed interest in his construction business, he didn't trust her to be able to manage it because she was a girl.

Verena went to a secretarial school while staying at her parents' house. Yet life under the tutelage of her parents soon became a strain for her. She desperately wanted to leave home, and a holiday acquaintance came to her rescue at this very moment; she married and moved abroad. When her sons reached adolescence, and her motherly duties were no longer in demand, she developed delusions of love for a man she had met by chance on the ski slopes during a winter holiday. She was convinced that this man would free her from her unsatisfactory marriage. During two other manic psychotic phases, she initiated a divorce via a lawyer. At this point, her husband arranged for an involuntary admission to a psychiatric clinic. After medical treatment, she returned home and dropped her intentions of divorcing him.

Years later, Verena returned from holiday in a deteriorated condition. When I asked what had upset her during the holiday, whether it had been her taciturn husband, she immediately replied: "Yes, very much so". However, she was unable to talk to him about it. Instead, she once again fell into a state of deep depression but her dissatisfaction with her partner remained unaltered.

COMMENTARY: Verena's unresolved separation conflict with her father, who was a controlling patriarch, ended in her running off with her first boyfriend and, subsequently, with her cutting herself off from her parental home by marrying the boyfriend, a random holiday acquaintance. Unable to handle the ongoing daily disputes with her parents and especially the process of detaching herself successfully from her father, she carried it into the relationship with her husband as chronic discontent. Her secret expectation of continuing an entertaining city life with various social contacts, as she had become accustomed to, was something her husband, a rather shy person, could not satisfy. He did not share her cultural interests but instead offered her a life in the countryside and tried to help her with the household chores. Verena, however, longed for more variety and entertainment. Life as a housewife became irrelevant as the children had moved out. Only during her manic phases did she dare to pursue an emancipated life. Not self-confident enough to find her own independent path, Verena always expected her husband's help in fulfilling her wishes. She was too afraid to live a life of her own.

Unresolved father-daughter attachments

Unresolved father-daughter relationship constellations produce an emotional condition leading to particular expectations that can never be met by a partner. The family therapist Ivan *Boszormenyi*-Nagy refers to these unconscious expectations as *entitlement*. This refers to genuine or alleged wrongs being avenged in the here and now. If a person's need for love and affection in childhood is not met during that time, the child – later as an adult – believes it is entitled to demand affection from his environment without having to ask for it. Overinvested daughters expect the same affection as adults as they received from their parents in childhood.

The biographies of women experiencing psychosis in middle age thus reveal two typical relationship constellations:

- The first constellation is characterized by absent fathers, which leads to a desire and a constant search for a strong father figure – partner or boss – later on in life.
- The second is characterized by indulgent fathers with an overprotec-

tive and, at times, domineering, infantilizing and controlling attitude towards their daughters.

Indulgent fathers

Studying the indulgent fathers' family of origin would most likely reveal a dependency problem in the paternal relationship system. Owing to a shortage of love and affection during their own childhood, they develop emotional dependence and crave affection even beyond puberty. These fathers compensate for their childhood hardship through affectionate devotion towards their daughters, but at the same time, ask for recognition and affirmative admiration in return. By remaining number one in their daughter's life, they reconstruct their mother-child bonding they missed out on. This type of need for affection could be observed in all the families throughout the three-generation history I observed.

> The father-daughter relationship described above is reminiscent of a Trojan Horse: from the outside, the affectionate behavior on the part of the fathers appears to be an unselfish and truly benign act of care towards their daughters. Yet, it may also serve the purpose of hiding the fathers' emotional hardship, a shortage of love and affection during their own childhood. From this point of view, it constitutes a patronizing act of exercising power over their daughters, weakening their personal development to become autonomous adults and infringing on their growth potential.

Abusive father-daughter relationships

One of the most extreme forms of a fatal father-daughter relationship is sexual abuse.

CASE HISTORY: In a family of five daughters, the father repeatedly abused four of them sexually, except for one, Emily. Despite resisting successfully, she was under the impression that her father didn't love her as much as her sisters. In puberty, this ambivalent, self-destructive attitude expressed itself in her father's blank refusal to accept Emily's dress sense. He criticized her miniskirt, her make-up, and made remarks that she would end in the gutter as a prostitute. Though she tried to win his approval, no matter what she did, she failed in her endeavors. The lack of fatherly love was a recurring theme in therapy for many years. It had greatly affected her self-esteem in adulthood; she suffered from recurrent bouts of severe depression, and even contemplated suicide.

COMMENTARY: The story of Emily shows the effect paternal abuse has on a female's personality development. This extreme form of molesting his daughters except for Emily led to a no-win situation for her regarding fatherly affection. She could not form a natural attachment to him. Even though she instinctively resisted her father's sexual approaches during childhood, she felt neglected by him at the same time. She paid dearly for her rejection, not being able to receive his support to develop self-esteem, self-reliance and independence. Her depression and suicidal thoughts mirrored her lack of paternal approval, a vivid example of trans-generational emotional deprivation turning into mental illness in the third generation.

Her father's emotional deficiencies, which have their roots in his own childhood, didn't allow him to express his fatherly approval of Emily during her childhood years. Though she successfully resisted his sexual advances, she nevertheless was subsumed into his problems and had to carry his dangerous burden into her own adulthood.

> An unmet need for affection in males during their childhood may undermine their daughters' female strength and autonomy.

The story of Sabrina described in the chapter *Gender as a stumbling block* is another example of how paternal abuse resulting from emotional deficiency can impede and infringe on a daughter's development. As a child, he spoiled her and proudly showed her off to his friends. However, when she reached puberty, his paternal expectations were at odds with her temperament and intellectual achievement. As a consequence, he abruptly cut his ties to her. He even dared to make the statement that he would rather have his daughter die than be frustrated by, and ashamed of, her in public.

> Females whose personality reflects the emotional shortfalls of their own fathers' families most likely transfer their unresolved attachment problem with their father to their partners, and from there to the most sensitive child.

Some daughters perceive their fathers' need for affection by virtue of their heightened sensitivity as well as empathy and try to satisfy them instinctively. Over the years, this relationship pattern of satisfying paternal emotional deficiency gets embedded in their personality. As adults, they are dependent on a father figure who has to be pleased, and as a reward, they expect the same indulgent behavior of their partners they were used to from their fathers, thereby remaining in the preferred father-daughter relationship.

Adaptive female behavior geared towards winning the favor of a father figure may indeed temporarily elicit praise and affection from partners as well as superiors. Yet under this type of father-daughter constellation, females may remain dependent on a father figure throughout their life.

Unless they receive therapeutic help to develop their personality, they are usually unable to gain autonomy. If they nevertheless stay in the relationship but don't get the expected support, they may react with anger and aggression, risking their partnership, or being fired from their job, and then suffer a *psychotic episode.*

> An indulgent father-daughter relationship tends to undermine female autonomy.

CASE HISTORY: Monika was the prettiest of five siblings and her father's lovebird. He treated her as his princess. She never had to do anything to earn his favor, as her husband put it later.

As a successful professional in a higher position – she had chosen a profession in the same field as her father – she was unexpectedly dismissed as a consequence of restructuring processes. She was so shocked, angry and devastated that she fell into psychosis. Her husband had her admitted to a psychiatric clinic several times, but the treatment did not bring about the expected improvement.

FOLLOW-UP AND COMMENTARY: After the layoff, Monika began to drink and neglected her household. She did not turn off the cooker before leaving the house, didn't lock the front door, and left the windows wide open. As her husband reprimanded her, she answered: "I need fresh air" – meaning freedom. In response to his insistent questions, she was evasive, denied everything, or said: "I know that you just want to get rid of me".

She boycotted any form of therapy. In desperation, her husband saw no other way out than appointing a legal guardian and filing for divorce. She was placed in an institution for chronically ill women. Once there she ran away, did not follow the rules, and went on walks in the middle of traffic. The institution no longer took responsibility for her and transferred her to a nursing home for the elderly. They assumed the diagnosis to be dementia.

Monika's behavior, however, concealed a secret that only surfaced when I asked her what had happened before her first psychosis. She replied bluntly: "My husband is a pervert. Over the years, I had to adapt to various sexual practices until they became unbearable to me, and I began to refuse him." Finally, this caused her tremendous feelings of guilt which she couldn't shake off. She feared punishment from her husband for her sexual refusal. Her repeated remarks, "I know that he just wants to get rid of me", must be interpreted in this sense. Her husband, however, thought she had always participated voluntarily; he never had to force her, he said.

Further therapy revealed that Monika's father, by spoiling her, actively stood in the way of her emotional detachment during puberty. She mentioned that she had got away with nearly everything without her father's objecting to it or confronting her. He was so permissive that she hated him for it.

Losing her job was a rude awakening for Monika. She had divorced her first husband, and in her second relationship, she lacked the courage required to confront her partner when performing sexual acts she did not enjoy. In her professional life, she could not bear the humiliation of being laid off. She had not expected that her boss, a symbolic father figure for her, would ever drop her.

> A good father-daughter relationship, though it might be an excellent starting point for a female's successful professional career, can later become a stumbling block when fathers keep their daughters in a position of dependency, thus undermining their autonomy.

Absent or neglectful fathers

Daughters who grow up with an absent or neglectful father may also be at a disadvantage. As adults, they expect their partners to compensate for the lack of paternal protection in childhood, and implicitly demand unconditional support from their partners as reimbursement.

> **CASE HISTORY:** Rebecca grew up in a family of eight children. Her father changed his job several times throughout his career. The family therefore had to move frequently. On the one hand, Rebecca felt uprooted; on the other, she learned to adapt to constantly changing circumstances. Following the example of her father, she became a professional woman with a job that enabled her to switch her place of work when she wanted.
>
> Upon marrying, however, she had decided to settle down. She gave up her job and had three children. When the youngest entered primary school, she suddenly became restless. It seemed as though her father, who had committed suicide shortly after her wedding, had taken control over her again. Nothing was good enough anymore. The house was too small, too many planes flew over the roof, and the village was too remote. She urged her husband to buy a larger house close to a city, which he did. But the project soon overwhelmed her capacity to cope, and she was in severe need of his help. He, however, expected support from her. He was convinced he had done what he possibly could, fulfilling her long-awaited wish; renovating a house was up to her, he thought.
>
> Rebecca in her view had always been supportive of her husband in all his undertakings. She had actively stood by him during disputes with his family, and now she expected him to be available when she desperately needed his help. She was unwilling to accept that he was absorbed by his full-time job and fell into a deep depression.
>
> Her husband had her admitted to a psychiatric clinic. After she was discharged, her mother was brought in for support, but Rebecca only wanted her husband. Her mother's assistance was to no avail. Over several months, she remained in bed in a regressed, psychotically

depressed state, crying for her husband's attendance and begging for his help. But he turned away from her; he could no longer bear her complaining. He himself had to cope with his own problems. He had no energy left to deal with his wife's demands and turned to another woman for support.

COMMENTARY: In puberty, Rebecca was never able to go through the normal process of conflicts of detachment. Her father's ambivalence, which caused this restless searching, had not allowed for this. This influence of her family system was reflected in her life. Even though she constantly longed for a secure and stable life, she couldn't settle down, thereby overtaxing her husband with her relentless demands, pushing him to the brink of collapse. Unable to meet her expectations, he had his own burden to carry from his family of origin. The conflict-riddled relationship was resolved through divorce.

Both women and men normally have their own unresolved issues with their families of origin, which they face again in the partnership. Thus, a war of needs may ensue between the two. They may fight as to who is more deserving of support from the other. However, in partnership, there is neither an answer nor a solution to this type of fight as to who has the "greater need", and who is entitled to more acknowledgement and support. It does not matter how much adjustment – in the sense of bartering – either partner brings into the relationship. It is never enough because the support provided can never compensate for the partner's deprivations experienced during their childhood. If people in partnerships are unable to free themselves from their intrinsic entanglement with their family of origin – with or without the help of therapy – divorce, psychosis, or both, may be the only way out. This was the case for *Rebecca*. The projected expectations that *Rebecca* and her husband brought into their relationship from their respective families ultimately led to the demise of their partnership. Only after divorce were they able to let go of their mutual demands and unfulfillable need for affection and support.

Women who are dissatisfied in their partnerships often don't realize that the person they should address – dead or alive – is their father or mother. However, *Rebecca* wasn't able to do that because of her father's suicide. Instead, she transferred her childhood dependency problems onto her husband and attempted to have her demands met with tears and accusations. Using emotional pressure only served to accelerate his withdrawal from the relationship. In her extreme desperation, due to her disappointed hopes, she developed an *emotional monster wave* – psychosis.

In the tug of war between spouses regarding their need for warmth and affirmation, husbands are usually the winners. They rarely develop psychosis but rather enter a new relationship to satisfy their needs, as Rebecca's husband had done.

> Middle-aged women who develop psychosis generally suffer from an unmet need for affection and support, dating back to their family of origin. This may lead to deep-seated anger towards their partner for not receiving the expected support they feel entitled to request.

Conflictual mother-daughter relations

Female psychosis in middle age, leading to conflicts within partnerships, however, may also be attributed in some cases to a long-term conflictual mother-daughter relationship in the family of origin.

> **CASE HISTORY:** Antoinette gave herself a break from her professional life because she wanted to have children. Unfortunately, she was unable to conceive. After two years of trying, she decided to return to work and forego having children. At that moment, she became pregnant. Although it no longer fit her plans, she nevertheless decided to stay at home to raise her child.

When her daughter reached puberty and had her own circle of friends, her husband encouraged Antoinette to look for a job. Yet she was ambivalent and couldn't decide which one to take. She remained at home and took an interest in her husband's work instead, but he was standoffish. He refused to answer her questions at the end of a tiring day, he didn't want to talk about his problems at work. Antoinette, however, insisted on participating in his professional life. She was so upset at his rejection – she was a temperamental woman – that she became psychotic during their summer vacation.

COMMENTARY: In therapy, she brought up unresolved relationship issues with her mother. Unravelling the past was a painful process. For several years, her mother had left little Antoinette in the care of a neighbor. Even though this had happened long ago, her mother still had guilt feelings that she had given Antoinette into another woman's care.

Her mother's feelings of guilt continued to linger on and disturbed her. She most probably also felt guilty that she had been unable to cope with her daughter's temperament at that time – and most likely was also jealous of the foster mother's successful handling of her. When her daughter developed a mental illness, she assumed that this had something to do with her having been a neglecting mother and was convinced that Antoinette would accuse her unconsciously of having left her to the neighbor.

Antoinette, however, didn't agree with her mother's interpretation, she felt completely misunderstood. She had a different perception of her situation, having had a happy childhood. She resented her mother's attempt to justify her actions, but the mother stubbornly stuck to it, insisting that the alleged deprivation Antoinette experienced in childhood was the reason for her psychosis. Because Antoinette rejected this interpretation, her mother broke off the relationship without further ado. On top of that, Antoinette's husband was more understanding of his mother-in-law than he was of Antoinette's own narrative; this made her all the more furious.

Threatened by her mother, deprived of her happy childhood memory in the care of her foster mother, Antoinette slipped into an existential crisis. Suddenly compelled to defend the happy years in the ongoing dispute with her mother's attempt to whitewash her guilt feelings, she risked losing her own narrative as well as the relationship with her husband. Her mother's unresolved attachment problems with her as a child almost drowned her existentially.

Finally, Antoinette could distance herself from her mother and found her own sense of self-knowledge without fretting over of the past. She divorced her husband and moved into her own apartment. After having worked through all these entanglements, she managed to build her own independent life.

Compromised female leadership

Families of entrepreneurs generally have a patriarchal structure. For that reason, leadership roles are generally reserved only for male offspring. Daughters, in contrast, are raised for jobs in the service sector, which can be a stumbling block for them later in their career choice as well as their partnership.

> **CASE HISTORY:** Ariane came from a family of entrepreneurs and was the eldest of four children. She was accustomed to obeying her father as the patriarch and adapted willingly to the conditions and circumstances of the family business. When she married a banker who was also involved in her father's business, Ariane had no trouble taking a backseat to her partner since she had children to care for. But as soon as the two sons moved out, she longed for a new task outside her home but certainly not one within the family business; she had different inter-

ests, she was more artistically gifted. Her husband, however, did not understand her dilemma. She began to have romantic fantasies about having an affair. One night, she unexpectedly left home and sought refuge at her neighbor's house. In the aftermath, her romantic fantasies evoked a paranoid fear of punishment that her husband would go after her, and she became psychotic.

FOLLOW-UP AND COMMENTARY: I also involved her husband in the therapy session. It soon became obvious how helpless he felt in dealing with his unhappy wife. He could neither comprehend Ariane's chronic discontent with her role as a housewife nor her desire for something new. In his eyes, Ariane appeared to have everything – successful sons, a secure existence, and a faithful, caring husband.

He was an amiable, gentle person with whom she could have discussed her problems. However, her husband's involvement in her father's business did not allow for this; she felt that discussing her problems openly would have harmed the family business. Out of loyalty to her father's business, she held back her inner rebellion until it exploded in an emotional monster wave – psychosis.

Over time, and with the help of therapy, Ariane learned to deal with her emotions and accepted her husband's position in the family business. She found an outlet for her creativity, designing and making her own dresses. She also attended cultural events on her own. She neither divorced her husband nor suffered from more psychotic episodes but voluntarily took medication because her strong temper still remained.

Women who develop psychosis in middle age often have a dependency problem as described. They are secretly longing for their father's acceptance. Since they are either financially dependent, or are only perceived as women in subordinate roles, they don't feel respected in their personality; their incomplete detachment expresses itself in the need for paternal acceptance. This may manifest itself as entitlement to support and recognition in partnership. However, if their sense of entitlement is not met, they may develop a psychiatric illness. If women under such circumstances are admitted to a psychiatric clinic, they are once more subject to a patriarchal system, which they experience as a violent assault on their personality. Feeling patronized and fighting against it with all their strength, it is therefore no surprise that middle-aged women have an unfavorable prognosis as observed in the statistical studies mentioned at the beginning of this chapter. However, if systemic therapeutic coaching, and not only medication, is offered to these women with psychosis in middle-age, they can become self-reliant and don't have to be condemned to chronic illness but rather can lead a healthy and contented life, integrated into society as demonstrated above by the examples of *Antoinette* and *Ariane*.

In some cases, psychosis in middle-aged women can also be triggered by conflicts in the workplace, and not in the spousal relationship. Women who were not allowed to face up to their fathers' authority, and thus never learned to deal with authority figures and issues, may be intimidated by having to make themselves heard by their superiors when problems arise in the hierarchical structure. Hindered from expressing their dissatisfaction, they suppress their anger and ultimately get flooded by their emotions in a *monster wave* of psychosis.

CASE HISTORY: Elisabeth worked as a nurse in a hospital. She was always prepared to go above and beyond her normal duties, which made her popular with patients and superiors. Nothing was too much for her. Her colleagues respected her as a competent and experienced professional woman.
However, there were chronic problems between her supervisor and the head of the department. Many of the staff made negative comments about the latter, yet she considered him the authority figure and accepted him the way he was. At the same time, she was unable to contradict her supervisor who was very critical of him.
One day, Elisabeth started to commit serious errors at work which elicited puzzlement on behalf of her colleagues since she had always been

so responsible and reliable. She had become psychotic. Her supervisor had to officially order her to stay at home for reasons of safety. Although in a psychotic state, Elisabeth wanted to continue her work out of her extreme sense of duty.

COMMENTARY: Elisabeth was a farmer's daughter and came from a patriarchal background. Conflictual issues were immediately suppressed at home in an authoritarian manner. As a professional woman, she became tremendously stressed whenever her supervisor or some of her colleagues criticized the management style of the head of the department. Even though she judged her supervisor, who was younger than her, to be completely incompetent, she was unable to assert herself and speak up in front of her. In the two following jobs, she developed psychosis twice under somewhat similar circumstances. In her relationship, however, she had no problems.

Losing hidden patronage

A further possible psychological stress factor for middle-aged women can be an unexpected resignation, retirement or replacement of a highly cherished old boss, acting as a father figure, to whom they had remained loyal all those years. Under the new management, they suddenly lose the expected support as well as the favors they came to enjoy. They therefore feel degraded, which can lead to an outbreak of psychosis.

CASE HISTORY: Adelheide had a longstanding job as a secretary in a government job. When her boss retired, he was replaced by a female. Many things changed. Adelheide felt lost and disoriented. Everything went wrong for her. She couldn't accept the change, nor orders from her female boss and finally had to be dismissed. Immediately thereafter, she became psychotic and was admitted to a psychiatric clinic.

After being discharged, she refused any form of therapy. She would only accept care from her husband at home. He tried hard to satisfy her needs but soon became increasingly desperate and sought advice for himself in my family group. When I asked him about his relationship, he mentioned that he had been discontented and unhappy for a while but did not want to abandon his sick wife. Nevertheless, a few months later, he decided to leave her and embarked on a new relationship. Many efforts on the part of home care nurses to activate Adelheide and free her of her passive victimhood were made, but all efforts were in vain. She became bedridden and wailed that she wanted her husband back, hanging on to the illusion that one day, he would return to her.

COMMENTARY: Adelheide's relationship with her husband functioned when she had a boss who gave her support, akin to a father figure. As soon as she lost his support, as a form of backup to her partner relationship, she had to rely entirely on her husband. However, he was unable or unwilling to muster all the encouragement and affection she demanded and opted out of the relationship. For a while, she hung on to her son for support but soon he withdrew, too. Querulous and complaining without end, she regressed to a chronic state of psychosis. Only in one short instance did she come out of her autistic shell, when she was invited to visit the nurse in her home where the nurse's husband would also be present. All of a sudden, she became talkative again. She had met another father figure, the nurse's husband, whom she was extremely eager to please in order to win his affection and acceptance.

In all the preceding examples, dependency on a father figure could be detected in the biographies of these women experiencing psychosis in middle-age. This made them vulnerable whenever they lost their functioning father figure, be it in the workplace or in their family situation. Without exception, their constant stress factor was chronic dissatisfaction in their partnership, and the inability to achieve self-realization without support from their husbands or bosses because of unresolved detachment issues from the family of origin. Where they are also in possession of a passionate, impulsive temperament – typical for ADHD or ADD – the chances of developing psychosis are much greater. They develop a *monster wave* when their need for affection is not met, and the expression of their emotions is suppressed as a result of their strict upbringing. If they are not hot-tempered, they may react with psychotic depression and withdrawal. Yet they all lack the strength to live an independent life, continuing to suffer in unhappy relationships, locked in anger and frustration. They turn psychotic ever so often whenever their emotions have once again intensified. All these circumstances lead to a poor prognosis for middle-aged women with schizophrenia.

The term "melancholia" derives from the Greek μέλαινα χολή (melaina kholé), which refers to a major depression. According to Hippocrates and subsequent tradition, melancholia was caused by an excess of "black bile", from Ancient Greek μέλας (*melas*), "dark, black", and χολή (*kholé*), "bile""; meaning "Galbladder secret". The ancient Greeks related a "thickening of bile" to inwardly directed anger, which, in turn, leads to a deep depression. The most extended treatment of melancholia comes from Robert Burton, whose *Anatomy of Melancholy* (1621) treats the subject from both a literary and a medical perspective. Burton wrote in the 17th century that music and dance were critical in treating mental illness, especially melancholia.

This is exactly what happens to the emotional state of middle-aged women who are unhappy but cannot express their anger and frustration. Their inwardly directed aggression causes depression and finally emerges an *emotional monster wave,* turning into a manic or schizophrenic psychosis. The preliminary phase of a psychotic episode is quite often a deep depression, as in the case history of *Rebecca*.

Independent women who are also professionals have better strategies. They assert themselves without the support of a father figure when they undergo significant changes, be it in private relationships or at work. They seek new partners just as men do in similar circumstances. They don't suffer from empty-nest syndrome after their children have grown up; instead they feel free to pursue new adventures and projects with or without the support of their husbands – despite the hormonal changes experienced during menopause.

Biographical Stress Factors for Men

Men and psychosis

Men are not subjected to the same emotional stress factors that women experience in partnerships. They play a secondary role in childcare by nature, as well as by longstanding social tradition, which is only now gradually changing. If dissatisfied in their partnership, they have a wide range of strategies available to them; they can easily invest more time in their career and are almost always expected to do so. Additionally, men have plenty of opportunities to take a break from family life, such as business trips, weekend excursions with colleagues, or activities in various clubs and political parties to avoid aggravating circumstances stemming from emotional stresses at home. They may also start new relationships or have one-night stands. However, this behavior does not trigger an *emotional monster wave* such as schizophrenia, because men don't tend towards cumulative negative emotions. Instead, their behavior leads to the opposite: an emotional discharge. The result is that middle-aged men rarely develop psychosis because of partnership conflicts.

Male dependency problems stemming from the mother-son relationship usually don't surface in partnership conflicts because women are prone to concealing the emotional deficits of their partners. Owing to their nature, they almost unnoticeably become substitute mothers whenever they perceive a certain neediness in their male partners, resulting from unresolved attachment problems. Males show symptoms of distress only when females withdraw sexually and emotionally, or when women deny their motherly role. Furthermore, men's ego might feel threatened if females take a lover and file for divorce. However, they are not inclined to respond with an *emotional monster wave* directed inwardly or a depression, like females do, but rather with outwardly directed aggressive threats, a typical dopamine response. They assert their male pride, which has been violated by the conduct of their female partners, and in the worst case, they plan revenge or threaten suicide. Under such circumstances, women usually back off and make a U-turn. They abandon their intentions to gain independence through divorce, stay in the relationship, and resume their adaptive female role again, out of fear of their partners' aggressive reactions.

Women who refuse to be intimidated by their partner's threats and stand by their decision to separate, or even pursue a new relationship, inflict a deep narcissistic wound on the male psyche, which they often perceive as a severe existential insult that even entitles them to use violence and physical punishment, sometimes leading to dangerous irrational acts. They commit suicide, an inwardly directed acute fight reaction, or in extreme cases, commit murder-suicide, killing their female partner and the children, committing suicide afterwards.

Psychiatrically speaking, this represents acute psychosis of short duration, a psychotic fight reaction. Irrational acts like these are a combination of feelings such as panic, anger and revenge. These are primitive stress responses, accompanied by cognitive dissociation. The brain, when in such a highly excited state, cuts off from its conscious cognitive control and even interrupts memory function to some degree.

Aggressive panic reactions in males, triggered by females' intention to separate, always conceal a personal blow to masculinity. But the intense reaction also contains a deep, uncontrollable fear of abandonment by a mother figure. Such reactions always indicate an incomplete *detachment process* of the mother-son relationship.

Male dependency problems, stemming from the mother-son relationship, most often don't surface in partnership conflicts. They rather erupt in emotional psychosis of short duration such as *rampage*, which can be interpreted as a fight-reaction of personally offended males. This short-lived psychotic state is preceded by long-term, heightened emotional stress such as continued insults and humiliation of the individual concerned. These negative interactions are not necessarily recognized by the social surroundings as such. Triggers leading to the emotional fight reaction are often only noticed retrospectively.

Rampage is thus an accumulated psychic injury, acted out in an acute aggressive outburst; it is sometimes a premeditated fight reaction after a series of injuries to the personal ideal of masculinity. Extreme emotional distress and despair are transformed into aggression directed at one or more deliberately chosen individuals, sometimes also at random bystanders. Offenders may also take revenge on individual representative of institutions, religious or political groups which, in their eyes, had grievously wronged them. Many of these tragic stories can be read in the daily news.

Male postpartum psychosis

In rare cases, the birth of a child can also trigger psychosis in fathers. However, this is not discussed in the professional literature, and is usually not associated with the birth of their child. Moreover, it is not referred to as postpartum psychosis but rather as conventional schizophrenia in adult men. No reference is made to the stress caused in men by the pregnancy of their partners and the birth of their child.

During their wives' or partners' pregnancy, men already feel neglected. Abandoned by the soon-to-be-mom's emotional withdrawal and the expected arrival of their child, they often start an affair with another woman, thereby compensating for the loss of affection by their pregnant partners. However, if an extramarital affair is not acceptable to them, and they do not seek professional support instead, they may be at risk of developing psychosis as a result of the stress of the birth of their child that affects them more deeply than they admit to themselves, or to others.

CASE HISTORY: Ron was one of the youngest children of a large family. His mother was overwhelmed with her chores, an older sister therefore took the role of a substitute mother. When Ron married, his young wife became pregnant soon after. Yet Ron felt it was far too soon for him. He did not want to have children so quickly, it was absolutely unexpected and unwished-for. He had decided to invest in his career first and was very concerned about not earning enough to support his family. The pregnancy bothered him to the extent that he became psychotic and required psychiatric treatment.

COMMENTARY: Ron's emotional distress persisted even after the birth of his second child. His wife had to bear most of the emotional burden of raising a family. The lack of parental care Ron had experienced in his large family of origin had fatal repercussions. As tragic events unfolded, his second son also became psychotic as a young adult after he had failed in his professional career and took his own life.

Men who develop psychosis during the pregnancy of their wives or partners, or immediately after the birth, are usually confronted with negative memories from their own childhood. Previous childhood deprivations are reactivated, and their neediness on account of the negligence they experienced at the hands of their own parents suddenly resurfaces. Yet most men are probably unaware of the lack of parental care they experienced, as well as their strong ties and loyalty to their family of origin. This prevents them from openly addressing their emotional shortcomings during childhood. They cannot express their unfulfilled expectations to their partners and mothers of their children. These on their part often criticize their husbands for being jealous of their own child.

Fathers may also become psychotic in the wake of guilt feelings when they have sought comfort in an extramarital affair at the time their child was born.

CASE HISTORY: Gerard had just started to set up his own business when his wife got pregnant for the third time. He was so overwhelmed by this situation that he absconded to New York with another woman. In his various phone calls to his wife, she no longer recognized him; he had become psychotic. Later, the relationship ended in divorce.

As a result of unresolved separation issues from their family of origin, men may be unable to resume the role of supportive father right after birth. Far from providing a helping hand to the new mothers, these men need and expect support for themselves. However, if these mothers are unable to emotionally support them in addition to caring for their child, they are thus left to fend for themselves. Mothers, however, usually have difficulties understanding their partner's distress and instinctively dismiss it simply as weakness.

CASE HISTORY: Max was liked as a professional, he was considered a friendly and sensitive man. However, in private he appeared more insecure. His wife Dorli was an extremely resilient and energetic person. She did not realize that Max became psychotic following the births of all three of their children.

COMMENTARY: Max was used to receiving a sympathetic ear from his mother whenever he was troubled but did not receive the same treatment from his wife Dorli. She showed no understanding for him and his emotional state and could therefore not take his feelings of anguish into consideration. At the time of birth, Dorli turned her complete attention to the newborn. The helpless and agitated state of her husband at the birth of their three children was completely alien and incomprehensible to her. Each time, Max felt lost and slipped into psychosis, which required professional treatment.

In the past, professional support was habitually provided only to childbearing mothers. Fathers were generally not included in the professional support system. Nowadays, however, the roles of mothers and fathers are viewed as more equal, and fathers are also perceived as needing support during and after the birth of their child. Public services for families with newborn children therefore offer coaching and support for both parents. In some places, counselling is even offered to fathers in special men's groups. All these public services are there to ensure that adequate childcare is provided right from birth, in line with contemporary views on the importance of child-rearing by mothers and fathers.

Masculinity and job achievement

Unfair treatment in the workplace is probably one of the strongest threats to masculinity that can lead to acute psychosis in men.

> **CASE HISTORY:** Helmut had served his company faithfully for forty years. He was active in the field service around the world. For the sake of his job, he had put up with many hardships and inconveniences. But one day, he noticed that for financial reasons, his company had used his successful sales figures to manipulate the bookkeeping. He became so upset that he suffered a heart attack. After he had recovered and returned to work, he was promptly dismissed without further comment. Helmut was at a loss. He was deeply hurt and, at the same time, furious with his superiors. He left the office in a trance, completely beside himself with rage. All of a sudden, he envisioned himself killing his superiors and then committing suicide. At the last minute, he realized that he was about to lose control of himself. He immediately went to see his family doctor and admitted himself to a psychiatric clinic. After discharge, the family doctor sent him to me for therapy.

A man's emotional dependency on a mother or father figure becomes apparent when he doesn't receive gratitude or acceptance, either from his partner or in the workplace from his superiors, as was the case with

Helmut. The absence of hedonic gratification – i.e. receiving approval and appraisal from the outside world – reveals how much the self-image is dependent either on a nurturing mother figure or a superior at work as an appreciative father figure. This dependent personality structure of men has also been demonstrated in a study. Widowed or divorced men who don't enter a new partnership have a shorter life expectancy than women in the same situation. Men who live on their own are obviously less capable of taking care of themselves alone in life than women. Men seem to experience more of an existential threat when they divorce and remain single than women in similar situations.

> Personal insults in the workplace, or jealousy and fearing the loss of a partner's love, are the two typical stress factors that may precede acute psychosis in middle-aged men.

Suicide – the only way out

Some men with schizophrenia ultimately free themselves from their suffering by committing suicide. This aggressive and irreversible solution to mental illness is more common in men than in women.

> **CASE HISTORY:** Christophoros was a child with ADHD. In school, he was unable to perform as well as his father expected. For his mother, he was a problem child she cared for with special attention. She herself was not particularly satisfied with her own life; she was chronically depressed.
> Christophoros developed schizophrenia as a young adult and could not lead an independent life. He remained dependent on his parents. When the situation became intolerable, the father had him admitted to a psychiatric clinic. After discharge, he was placed in an institution for disabled persons, where he performed simple manual work, although

he had an outstanding creative talent. He studied impressionist and expressionist art in his free time and had produced many expressionist paintings. His social worker had even organized an exhibition for him. He was enthusiastic about his success, and therefore looked forward to a place in another residential community where his talent would be more appreciated.

Christophoros was delighted about this new possibility but at the same time became scared and eventually experienced another psychotic episode. For fear he might harm himself, he was readmitted to the same psychiatric clinic. Shortly afterwards, he hanged himself in his room in the clinic.

COMMENTARY: Throughout his life, Christophoros was patronized by his surroundings, first by his parents and then by mental health professionals. He carried the suffering of his depressive mother as a legacy, in addition to his own problems. They had been particularly close to each other since his childhood. He was never allowed to lead an independent life. The only way out of his emotional imprisonment was suicide.

Men who have suffered serious emotional injuries during childhood, and who neither had room nor support for their personal development, may first react with autistic withdrawal, but ultimately may also end their misery through suicide. Potential resilience factors are a supportive environment at work and a caring partner. Both could prevent the development of psychosis. If neither of them is present, psychosis and suicide are quite likely, as related in the case history.

CASE HISTORY: Vladimir was a mathematician. He worked in an engineering office, where he was responsible for accounting. After his divorce, he led a solitary life without a new partner. He neglected his apartment as well as his personal hygiene. During therapy sessions, he hinted at how much his mother had hurt him and how deeply ashamed he had felt because of her. He described his childhood simply as crappy and mentioned that his parents hadn't taught him suitable strategies for coping with life. He received little support from his absent father. As far as Vladimir could remember, his father was a stubborn man.

In our therapy sessions, Vladimir tried to define his mental pain, dating from his childhood and from his life as a lonely divorcee, using meticulous mathematical graphs. Each week, he would bring them to the therapy session, and lay them out on the floor to explain them to me. This was his way of mastering his emotions.

At times, Vladimir felt he was being followed by evil invaders of his particular way of life. He desperately walled himself off from them, as he put it. He gradually developed a partial paralysis of his legs as a psychosomatic disorder. He could only walk with a cane. In the office, he felt his way forward along the walls. Vladimir, quite literally, seemed to be going nowhere in his life.

THERAPY AND FOLLOW-UP: I admitted Vladimir to a clinic for neurological rehabilitation because of his partial paralysis, since he had refused a voluntary admission to a psychiatric clinic, and I didn't want to force him against his will. After treatment, which should have alleviated his psychosomatic paralysis but didn't bring about progress, he returned to his old apartment – littered with garbage – in a disillusioned state of mind. Out of fear of being dismissed from his job, and unable to see a way out of his predicament, he committed suicide by throwing himself from the 12th floor of his apartment block. On a hot summer's day – which was, incidentally, my birthday – the police had me identify his body; it was a sad farewell to Vladimir.

When his superiors and various colleagues discussed his tragic death at a meeting they had invited me to, it was revealed that he had been greatly appreciated as an employee. As a foreigner, he had always given helpful advice to other employees from overseas. Apart from his physical disability, which had slowed him down, nobody had ever noticed his desperate situation, his inner suffering and hopelessness.

He gradually withdrew into an isolated, self-contained world. To prevent himself from getting hurt, he had developed a paranoid worldview that prompted him to shut others out. Only with great mental effort was he able to maintain his inner balance at the cost of considerable limitations. He clung to mathematical graphs, a delusion that was meant to protect him from further trauma and total collapse.

Statistically, men who develop schizophrenia in middle age have a more favorable prognosis than women. In men, the stress factors do not primarily stem from their partner relationship. As mentioned above, men are subject to different relationship dynamics than women. For middle-aged men, more frequent factors that trigger psychosis are high professional ambitions combined with a lack of recognition, such as demotion or dismissal from work.

Dissatisfied mothers casting a shadow

Middle-aged men who develop psychosis when they are unsuccessful in their professional career sometimes carry with them the baggage of a dissatisfied mother who projects all her ambitions onto one of her children.

CASE HISTORY: Franziskus was the second son in a family of eight children; the oldest child, a brother, had committed suicide in his twenties. Franziskus was an outsider in his family because he rebelled against the strict religious upbringing by his mother. He blamed their religious, guilt-inducing education for his brother's suicide. His school career went smoothly at first until he failed his admission exam to high school. Originally, Franziskus had planned to pursue an academic career but was now forced to take up an apprenticeship. Once he had finished his apprenticeship, he saw another chance to fulfill his desired goal of higher education but failed again.

As a form of compensation, Franziskus entered local politics, supported in his political ambitions by a girlfriend; he was not elected, however. At that point, he invested all the energy he could muster in his job to demonstrate his extraordinary commitment, as well as his skills, to his boss but overstretched his capacity. He had a psychotic breakdown and was admitted to a psychiatric clinic. In the following months, his girlfriend left him, his wife moved out and filed for divorce. Moreover, he was dismissed from his job. After discharge, he found new employment. Once again, he worked hard to gain recognition from his superior by overextending himself. He fell into a manic psychosis and had to be re-hospitalized. His superior confirmed in a meeting that Franziskus had indeed worked twice as hard as other employees before his breakdown.

During his manic phase, Franziskus always came up with the same story. He referred to his mother as a warship that sunk everything that came across her bow. After some years, he had become a chronic schizophrenia patient, yet he saw himself as a highly successful designer of major projects as part of his delusion. He was never able to work again.

COMMENTARY: The mother of Franziskus had never been satisfied with her family situation. She projected her dissatisfaction onto her son, who perceived her constant criticism as aggressive frustration. In fact, he was the copy of her alter ego, who wanted more than was possible. Even in adult life, his mother's aggressive emotional state remained a permanent threat to him. Franziskus had internalized her threatened self-esteem and attempted to redeem it through professional success. He encoded her permanent dissatisfaction in the monumental picture of a warship that sunk everything, including his own ambitions. Even the additional support of another woman didn't get him out of this trap. Quite the contrary, in his mother's eyes, he had broken a taboo by pursuing an extramarital relationship, something she had also done but successfully concealed from her family. She had secretly pursued her love affair for years and had then sought exoneration from a preacher. His mother remained critical of Franziskus throughout his life, even after he had fallen ill. Because of her motherly rejection, he still continued to seek her approval. He went back to live with her after his divorce, and regularly had her do his laundry.

The source of his mother's persistent frustration, which was neither satisfied by family life nor by her secret love affair, remained entrenched in Franziskus, who was loyal to her his entire life.

Helpful interventions by employers

Schizophrenia may be prevented if no time is lost between the onset of early symptoms of impending cognitive deterioration caused by stressful circumstances and the start of helpful systemic therapeutic intervention. The individual with impending or even acute psychosis, however, is not able to ask for help. It is therefore absolutely vital that the social environment notice the symptoms and a third party organize professional support as soon as possible for the soon-to-be patient.

Employers, supervisors or co-workers can take on this job. The vulnerable individual with early-onset psychosis has to be reassured, however, that they will not be dismissed from the job, and thus don't have to conceal their ailing mental state. If approached in private, the person can be calmly persuaded to request therapeutic help, and a first appointment with a therapist may even be arranged together.

> **CASE HISTORY:** Marco could no longer concentrate at work; his mind was a jumble of thoughts. As he was afraid of being unable to conceal his debilitating mental condition, he put in considerable overtime to make up for his sluggish performance. Yet no matter how much effort and time he put in, his performance steadily deteriorated.

Marco was so terrified of "going mad" that he could no longer sleep at night. While daydreaming, he saw his wife in a black dress and became scared that something bad had happened to his children. Marco's supervisor noticed his poor condition and suggested he seek therapeutic help. He immediately agreed and received an emergency appointment with me.

COMMENTARY: Being overworked and experiencing marital conflict, Marco's two network systems had become shaky at the same time: the relationship and the job. He slipped into an existential crisis with high anxiety and became psychotic. During the acute stage, I prescribed him neuroleptics. Then I started to explore his family history as well as his job situation. We discussed and developed strategies for restructuring his work situation to prevent from overburdening himself again. As for his marital conflict, he decided to get a divorce. Both measures brought him relief. He kept his job and did not suffer any further psychotic episode. Moreover, he could stop taking medication after a short time.

Employment despite schizophrenia

Successful psychiatric treatment is highly dependent on a benevolent mindset on the part of employers, as the example of John Forbes Nash Jr. shows, who had long-term psychiatric treatment before he received the Nobel Prize (1994). Superiors who demonstrate understanding of, and appreciation for, their employees when they are temporarily unproductive as a result of their psychosis, may offer favorable conditions for remaining employed despite this illness. The expertise and skills of these highly intelligent and creative employees with schizophrenia does not disappear with the psychotic episode, quite in contrast to earlier beliefs.

CASE HISTORY: Herbert, the father of one of my patients suffering addiction, was a physicist. He held a senior position in a scientific institute and had undergone several schizophrenic episodes during his employment. After the successful treatment of his occasional psychotic relapses, he could always return to his job. Once he had overcome the acute schizophrenic phase, he regained full cognitive function each time. He remained a valued and appreciated employee in the institution until his retirement.

Stress Factors in Old Age

Unfulfilled expectations

The majority of individuals who develop their first schizophrenic episode in old age have not made peace with their life. They are dissatisfied with what they have achieved and unhappy about what they have missed out on. Many of them never gained a foothold, and their life just went awry. Others have done amazingly well, yet they expected more out of life than they were given, remaining unhappy and thus unable to find inner peace as life comes to an end.

Their discontent can usually be traced back to several unfortunate circumstances during their lifetime, finally evoking inner rebellion in old age. Such individuals have remained in a tense state throughout the course of their life, secretly hoping that one day, something would change for the better. But things stayed the same, and their hidden desire for happiness went unfulfilled. They suddenly become conscious of all the failures at important life junctions, and disappointment comes to the fore. Such people are unaware that they could have shaped their own destiny, but at this point in life it seems too late. The deep regret which comes to the surface then erupts in an *emotional monster wave* – psychosis in later life.

Unrealized potential

Individuals who nurse a grudge and are convinced that they could have done more if fate hadn't stood in their way realize what is lacking as life draws to a close. They become painfully aware of missed opportunities, and with a finishing stroke, they try to make up for their lost dreams. In a world of delusional psychosis, they finally allow themselves to reach a state of fulfillment in a fantasy world or try to whitewash the shortcomings in their real life.

CASE HISTORY: Elena was raised in the Christian faith and believed in life-long partnership. However, fate had other plans. She was the daughter of her father's second wife who died when she was in her twenties. This left her mother, who had suffered a stroke and was bedridden, in her care. Elena most probably had ambitions for a higher education but as a teenager, she was obliged to take a job to support her family after her father had suffered financial hardship during the great depression. Although she loved her job, family obligations made her stay home during the second world war.

Her husband had a very busy job and therefore little time for her and the family. After his premature death, Elena refused to seek a new partner because of her religious convictions, even though she repeatedly told her children that she could also have married a different man when she was young. In old age, she began to have delusions, and was visited by a companion with whom she had a conversation every afternoon.

COMMENTARY: Elena's remark that she could also have married another man was most probably related to her husband's early death. Being under emotional strain and feeling lonely, she still struggled with her religious belief and was questioning her fate. Had she chosen the right man with whom to enjoy old age? Her husband had died 30 years earlier, but her belief in life-long partnership did not allow her to choose a new one, instead it left her in stare of ambivalence.

As an escape from her dilemma, Elena formed an imaginative relationship through psychosis in her old age. While in distress, she invented a fantasy figure for companionship with whom she spent a few hours in the afternoon for the rest of her years.

Missed opportunities

Individuals with psychosis in old age can also project the struggles that shaped their lives, such as hidden desires and unfulfilled expectations, onto their family members or the caregivers around them by way of paranoid delusions.

The closest caregivers are usually the victims of their projections. Homecare nurses, for example, are often accused of theft, which is a method of concealing forgetfulness. Elderly individuals frequently are neither willing nor able to admit that they themselves have misplaced the object in question. Therefore, they project their problems onto relatives such as their daughter- or son-in-law with whom they have a conflictual relationship. For the accused ones, this is extremely insulting, in fact it is downright abusive. They are drawn into a conflict and blamed for something that has nothing to do with them. Most often, they cut off all contact as a response. However, if they do defend themselves and refute the accusations, it is immediately interpreted as a sign of guilt by the paranoid person. Under such circumstances, the conflict escalates, and the relationship is finally terminated for good. The delusions of old-age psychosis, however, continue.

For relatives and homecare nurses who look after psycho-geriatric patients, my advice is to always ask for the biography of the patients and inquire about causes of general discontent at particular points in their life. Getting to know their patients is gaining a better understanding of the pathological behavior. All of a sudden, the delusional thoughts and accusations appear in a completely different light. One may be able to rationalize them to some degree by bearing in mind their life history, and the patient's behavior therefore becomes more bearable.

Caregivers who became entangled in their patients' conflicts and were forced to break off all contact to protect themselves may resume the task of providing professional care. At that point, once no longer perturbed by their patients' difficulties, the latter don't have to be left alone with their suffering but rather benefit from adequate professional distance.

> **CASE HISTORY:** A young homecare nurse who visited an elderly woman daily was accused by her of having stolen her favorite night gown. The nurse was so outraged and hurt by this accusation that she was no longer willing to look after the woman.
>
> **COMMENTARY:** The patient's illusionary accusation, seen in a broader sense, can be interpreted as a lament for lost youth. The young nurse probably reminded the elderly patient of her life as a young woman, which she looked back upon with melancholy; she had been forced to endure great hardship because of her familial situation and the circumstances during the second world war. We can consider this accusation of theft a form of suppressed envy of the young nurse. The patient's projection showed her pain and anger that she was never able to enjoy life to the extent this young woman was able to.

Delusional sexuality

In some cases, repressed sexual needs and unmet desires, which may still be active even in old age, are suddenly revealed in encrypted forms of delusion.

> **CASE HISTORY:** Miss Bertie was in an advanced age and required psychiatric home care. On one of my visits, I noticed that she had moved her mattress and her bedding into the kitchen. She looked alarmed. When I asked her why she had done this, she told me that she felt persecuted by men. They would stab her mattress through her wooden bedroom floor from the apartment below while she was sleeping. She implied that the concrete kitchen floor would offer her more protection

than the wooden floor in her bedroom. She felt safer sleeping on concrete in the kitchen. She always kept the kitchen door locked.

COMMENTARY: As it turned out, Miss Bertie had never had a sexual relationship in her entire life. Her sexual desires, which she secretly harbored but rejected at the same time, were projected as paranoia onto her neighbors. In her delusional fantasies, male sexuality was expressed as a phallic symbol through a knife. Sleeping on the concrete kitchen floor was supposed to prevent penetration.

Sexual trauma projected onto the third generation

By way of social inheritance, sexual trauma can even be projected onto the third generation within the family system.

CASE HISTORY: A grandmother expressed one day her firm conviction that her granddaughters, the two girls of her youngest daughter Tamara, had been sexually abused by their father. Although nobody believed her, she could not be dissuaded from her belief. Tamara was forced to take her two girls to a child protection service to have her mother's allegations of sexual abuse investigated. She wanted to handle this delicate matter in a clear and objective manner. Many surveys and evaluations were conducted but none yielded evidence of sexual abuse. Because of a lack of evidence, the case was closed by the authorities. However, the grandmother continued to stick to her belief, thus creating a situation of permanent unrest and suspicion in the family.

At that time, Tamara's older sister decided to come for a therapy session together with her to get my advice. She wanted to know how she should handle this unpleasant family story and help Tamara at the same time. The interview revealed that her older brother was a problem child with ADHD, and the older sister was seen by the mother as the rebel in the family. Tamara, the youngest, was her mother's confidant, she had a particularly close relationship with her, and assisted her through various hardships.

A year or so later, at her 70th birthday party, the grandmother unexpectedly wanted to tell the assembled family her life story. Everyone had heard fragments of her extremely difficult childhood, but nobody had ever heard her talk about her life in such a coherent manner at an official family gathering. As children, she and her sister had to relocate to Switzerland without their parents because of the second world war. As she told her story, she repeatedly asked everyone present whether the insight into her difficult past was too burdensome, but everybody encouraged her to continue.

Listening carefully, Tamara suddenly realized that the sexual abuse was probably buried in her mother's past. In all likelihood, it had been her who had been sexually abused as a child by a catholic priest. However, she was unable to talk about it because she didn't want to contaminate the reputation of her own family of origin.

At another family meeting, the grandmother once again alluded to the sexual abuse of her granddaughters by their father. This time, the grandchildren defended themselves without assistance from their mother. Tamara then urged her mother to talk about what she had experienced as a child. However, her mother immediately fell silent. After this event, for the first time, Tamara truly felt detached from her mother. She could face her with more serenity and without developing feelings of guilt or anger. As a side effect of her new-found self-assurance, she was able to lose weight after trying in vain for the last twenty years.

COMMENTARY: This is a classic example of a three-generational unresolved attachment. The grandmother, who felt obliged to remain loyal to her family of origin, took all conceivable measures to deflect from the traumatic events of sexual abuse in her childhood. The inner child in her put all emotional energy into preserving the image of her family system. The taboo of sexual abuse in her childhood could not be spoken

about. However, she revealed her childhood trauma by passing it on to her granddaughters and accusing her son-in-law of sexual abuse. She thereby endangered Tamara's partnership and, at the same time, created a stumbling block for her granddaughters as well as their father-daughter relationship.

From a systemic perspective, the grandmother's secret of sexual abuse, which she projected onto her son-in-law, can be seen as a desperate call for help to achieve justice for herself, but at the same time, preserving the honor and dignity of her family of origin. The grandmother had carried the sexual taboo for decades until she had found a suitable object for projection in her son-in-law, who was an introverted and taciturn man, a marked contrast to her own family, which was highly communicative.

By working through the family narrative of three generations, Tamara was finally able to detach herself without cutting off her relationship with her family of origin altogether. The grandmother, in turn, preserved both her own honor and that of her family of origin by writing her memoirs.

One year later, Tamara and her husband nevertheless got divorced. In this respect, one could say that the dark cloud of the grandmother's family of origin reached further than one generation and was stronger than Tamara's partnership.

One can further speculate that Tamara's divorce, among other things, served to redeem the grandmother's unresolved childhood trauma and provided legitimacy to her using her son-in-law as an object of projection. In this sense, tribute was paid to the grandmother's family, thereby the son-in-law was sacrificed in a partnership conflict, though not convicted for an act he had been accused of but had not committed. In this sense, he had fulfilled his function as a "friendly helper" in Tamara's maternal family of origin. Moreover, Tamara's ex-husband could no longer be used as an object of projection by the grandmother after the divorce, and thereby could remain in his role as a father to his two girls.

At the end of her therapy, Tamara stated that she could never have detached herself from her mother without the help of her husband. This, as well as the sacrifice of their relationship, was the tribute to be paid for disentangling her own unresolved symbiotic mother-daughter relationship. Fortunately, the third generation was not harmed, although the grandchildren had been drawn deeply into the unresolved family history. The divorce no longer threatened the daughters' relationship with their father; their relationship became well established. The grandmother's accusations against her granddaughters' father was therefore not able to harm the father-daughter relationship, and the third generation was freed from the dark cloud of the grandmother's childhood trauma.

Significantly, the granddaughters broke off their relationship with their grandmother, a decision Tamara respected. They categorically separated themselves from the all-pervading trauma that had extended over three generations within the family system. Moreover, they could preserve their relationship with both parents despite their divorce and pursue their own lives.

The Brain and Adaptation Strategies

An evolutionary approach to the human brain as a social organ, which is constantly adapting to its environment, may render the illness of schizophrenia generally easier to understand. To that effect, I will be using Paul MacLean's model of the *triune brain* in order to provide insight into the maladaptive, chronic over-functioning of the brain, eventually leading to dysfunction and outbreak of acute psychosis.

Of all organs, the brain performs the main and most active adaptive functions towards the social environment of an individual and is thus most developed in social species such as primates. It consists of an enormously complex and extensive network of hundreds of billions of nerve cells, which can connect and disconnect in hundreds of trillions of ways. In principle, this connectivity of the nerve cells is retained over an entire lifetime. Cognitive, emotional, and sensory experiences are perceived, processed, linked, and stored within the brain as imprints, called memory. New environmental influences can overwrite previous ones, and thereby induce a reorganization of the brain, which subsequently affects how new experiences are processed. These imprints can be retrieved via short-term or long-term memory function under new but similar conditions, a process called learning.

The brain is thus constantly undergoing reorganization, adaptation and learning processes, which result in increasing complexity and thereby improved adaptability. This morphological and functional remodeling is referred to as *plasticity*. The brain's adaptive capacity in a changing environment continuously optimizes the survival strategies of our social species, which is the essence of evolution.

Paul MacLean's evolutionary *triune brain* model, which dates back to the 1960s, makes the different functions – and consequently also the dysfunctions – in schizophrenia generally more comprehensible and accessible for treatment. This model divides the brain into three different functionally and structurally definable areas. These three brain structures, which developed during different stages of evolution, are clearly distinguishable from each other but are also intertwined and work together holistically most of the time.

MacLean's triune brain

The three brain structures outlined by Paul MacLean are derived predominantly from the evolutionary ladder of the species: the reptiles who lay eggs and don't bear live offspring; the mammals who give birth to living offspring who are nutritionally dependent on a lactation from their mothers; and the primates, which are animals immediately capable of manipulating objects and live in family groups.

1. Reptilian Complex: This part of the brain consists of the brainstem and the motor cerebellum. From an evolutionary perspective, it is the oldest part of the brain, called *reptilian complex* because it was already well developed in the species of reptiles. It is responsible for all autonomic functions and automated motor skills. All instinctive automated motor sequences and the corresponding internal functioning of the organs are controlled by this part of the brain.

2. Limbic System: This part of the brain developed with the species of mammals. It is responsible for bonding behavior, which is essential for the survival of the offspring of all mammals. In humans, all emotional energy and motivation for thinking and acting also originates here. The limbic system is a quick emotional processor that sorts out all sensory stimuli and decides whether an object, a situation, or a person is liked or disliked, approved or disapproved of. The system thus controls affection as well as aversion, sympathy and antipathy. Moreover, it is responsible for the regulation of our general mood and emotional state and therefore has an overall integrating function for all thinking and behavior. It is responsible for maintaining our affective balance.

Since the limbic system has evolved in mammals over the course of evolution, its function was to guarantee the bonding between mother and child during the lactation period, a behavior that is essential for the survival of all mammals. It is also responsible for learning behavior, which first takes place in the parent-child relationship. Later in life, it plays an important role in social bonding within a family, clan or a larger social group.

The limbic system, located in the middle of the brain, is organized in a circular fashion, thus the name *limbic system*. It can be accelerated when stimulated, and emotions are thereby aggravated. This always happens under stress. I refer to the circular process of neuronal acceleration as the *turbo effect,* which may eventually lead to an *emotional monster wave,* thus disturbing the other two parts of the brain.

3. Cerebrum: This part of the brain evolved in primates and hominids. It is the most recent evolutionary acquisition of the brain. It is particularly highly developed in Homo sapiens. The main weight gain is due to the enormous development of the cortex which consists of a tremendous amount of brain folds of relatively thin layers. Interestingly, the cerebrum originally evolved into the forebrain from the archaic *olfactory bulb,* which was responsible for the sense of smell. The main functions of the cerebrum are the processing of stimuli intake – called perception – the storage of data, analyzing them for patterns, and conceptualizing new thoughts as well as concepts of action for future behavioral plans in new situations. Furthermore, this part of the brain enables self-perception as well as self-reflection.

The frontal lobe of the cerebrum is where planning, imagination and visionary thinking takes place. It is directly stimulated by brain pathways coming from the limbic system over the prefrontal cortex. These pathways operate via *dopamine receptors*. Interestingly enough, intuitive visionary thinking, often referred to as "following your nose", refers to the sense of smell, i.e. the archaic *olfactory bulb,* the original function of this part of the brain.

The reptilian complex, the limbic system and the cerebrum, as defined by MacLean, are intertwined and cooperate closely, hence the term *triune brain*. These three separately functioning systems of the brain act as a coordinated whole; they control as well as disrupt each other. Control, however, is not hierarchical in the sense that the most highly developed part of the brain, the cerebrum, always takes the lead over the other (evolutionarily older) parts. Instead, the question of which system governs at any given moment is determined by the function most needed for survival based on the respective situation.

Although the cerebrum has the ability to consciously analyze situations and control well-designed behavior patterns, it is not always top of the hierarchy when it comes to ensuring survival. If the situation requires urgent action in the face of acute danger, there is no time for pros and cons in the decision-making process of the cerebrum to determine the best strategy. In severely dangerous circumstances, the reptilian brain with its automatic reflexes of fight, flight or freeze reaction, as well as the limbic system with its holistic situational awareness and intuitive decision-making about acceptance or aversion, are better equipped for rapid problem-solving, so called adaptation strategies. Under such circumstances, the reptilian complex and the limbic system are much quicker to react than the rationally controlled cerebrum and are thus more efficient and effective.

In acute psychotic episodes, as well as in chronic schizophrenia, the dysfunction of the brain unfolds in the limbic system, reptilian complex and cerebrum in a specific maladaptive way.

Each outbreak of an acute psychotic episode is usually preceded by prolonged periods of emotional stress, which keeps the limbic system in a constantly heightened state of excitement, also called *hyperarousal*. Individuals who have experienced psychotic episodes or are in the preliminary stages of acute schizophrenia, often speak of their fear of spinning out of control and losing their mind. This phrase aptly describes the *turbo effect* of the limbic system as it plays out in the preliminary stages of an acute schizophrenic or manic episode.

During a psychotic episode, dysfunction in the brain occurs on several levels. Some of these dysfunctions can nowadays be visualized with modern imaging techniques. In an acute schizophrenic state, the *turbo effect* of the limbic system hyper-stimulates the pre-frontal cortex, resulting in a dysfunction of the cerebrum. This over-functioning of the pre-frontal cortex is referred to as *hyperfrontality*. It triggers the abnormal flood of thoughts from the cortex during the acute schizophrenic episode. This hyperactivity of the pre-frontal cortex can be visualized in a PET scan or a functional MRI.

The *turbo effect* of the limbic system, which is perceived as extreme anxiety on an emotional level, drives the reptilian brain into a state of increased vigilance called *hyperarousal,* which leads to hyperactivity and sleeplessness. The reptilian brain thus initiates compulsively ritualized fear-aversion behavior, which is frequently observed as obsessive-compulsive behavior before the onset of acute schizophrenia. Such compulsory ritualized behavior can indeed help to calm down the anxiety for a short time and thereby decrease the state of arousal, protecting the frontal lobe from emotional system overflow, thus preventing the collapse of the cerebrum's cognitive functions through flooding. But this obsessive behavior as a means of suppressing fear only works for a certain time. If the limbic system continues to be in a state of hyperarousal, an *emotional monster wave* arises, the cerebrum is flooded by impulses, and finally breaks down in its higher cognitive function owing to the overstimulation through the prefrontal cortex.

In later stages of schizophrenia, the hyperactivity of the prefrontal cortex, the *hyperfrontality,* recedes. It even changes to an underactive state, referred to as *hypofrontality*. This low activity is due to lack of stimulation because of withdrawal and social isolation as well as the long-term effects of neuroleptics, which all dim the dopaminergic systems of the brain, of which there are many located in the prefrontal cortex, connecting the limbic system with the cortex.

> **CASE HISTORY:** Margrit had undergone several psychotic episodes with manic features. Before each psychotic breakdown, she would always show obsessive compulsive disorder. When leaving the house, she would repeatedly have to return to check whether the windows were closed, the oven was off, and the lights were out. If her husband helped her to clean up over the weekend, she removed every single item from the waste container to ensure he had not thrown away anything of importance.
>
> During full-blown psychosis, however, she discarded all conventions and rules. One afternoon, when her neighbor had left his keys in his car, she even drove off with it to visit her imaginary lover.
>
> **COMMENTARY:** In the pre-psychotic phase, Margrit had always demonstrated obsessive compulsive behavior. As soon as her anxiety-reducing, obsessive ritual was no longer able to keep the turbo effect of the limbic system in check, the prefrontal cortex of the cerebrum was flooded with impulses from the limbic system, which resulted in system overload and a breakdown of the cognitive function of rational control. She was thus no longer able to act rationally and slipped into a state of manic psychosis. The emotional driver behind all this was her deep dissatisfaction and anger with her husband who did not communicate with her enough. She was a very social woman, having grown up in a lively city, but was now living in the countryside, which made her feel desperately isolated.

In the later stages of schizophrenia, cognition often gets reconstructed, albeit in accordance with the person's own delusional logic, as seen in *Margrit's* visit to her imaginary lover. This kind of cognition is always adapted to the person's emotional needs. Luc Compi describes it in his concept of *affect-logic*, a logic that no longer adheres to the rules of common sense of ordinary people but follows the emotional needs and logic of the respective individual.

This restructuring of cognition, the conceptualization of delusions, having ideas of reference, having delusions of persecution or of grandeur, hearing voices, can all be understood as mental adaptation strategies of the brain, in this case the cerebrum, which is geared toward keeping the person's emotional system somewhat in balance through complicated mental construction.

Auditory hallucinations are a typical symptom of schizophrenia. These false perceptions are most probably elicited in Broca's motor speech area, where conceptual thinking arises as preparation for planned communication, thus stimulating Wernicke's area of sensory hearing. Both areas are closely connected and located in the left cerebral hemisphere and represent the brain area responsible for language. Delusional thoughts are, most likely, conceptualized in the motor speech area, and are combined with a certain level of emotional intensity perceived as voices in Wernicke's sensory area.

Auditory hallucinations are, then, adaptive strategies by means of intensive mental conceptualization. In schizophrenia, the cognitive adaptation process through conceptual mental problem-solving strategies is obviously so intense that one's own thoughts are perceived as voices from external sources which in reality don't exist. The brain creates these auditory stimuli within its own language center. It is a self-activity of the brain, which is comparable to dreaming.

Schizophrenia patients are thus no longer able to compare their own internal perceptions with the reality of the outside world and correct it accordingly; their emotions determine their cognition as well as their perception. Their misperception can no longer be corrected by them through external stimuli from the real world, nor by another person such as a therapist, who attempts to introduce elements of reality. Instead, they vehemently defend their delusional ideas against any attempt at correction from their social environment. Their delusions are part of their cognitive adaptation strategy, designed to restore emotional balance. They will not let anyone interfere with their strategy since they do not have a better one for returning to a state of calmness.

> Hearing voices can be interpreted as an internal dialogue, originating from unresolved conflicts, intense anger, a bad conscience or fear of punishment for one's own aggression.

The phenomenon of hearing voices most likely occurs in an intense state of internal ambivalence and turmoil, from which these people are trying to escape via cognitive reconceptualization. Despite intense treatment with high dosages of neuroleptics, these symptoms often persist as long as no effective strategies for disentangling the conflict are found.

CASE HISTORY: Anatina, an attractive woman, married as a teenager, and gave birth to a mentally disabled daughter. As time went on, she started to dream of another life. Her lover to-be, a diplomat, she picked from the daily paper. She went through many psychotic episodes, divorced her husband, who came from a different cultural background, and continued her delusional love affair as a means of gaining emotional comfort. Anatina had expected a luxurious life, comparable to the one she had experienced as a child living next to a neighbor with a luxurious villa. She was very disappointed and dissatisfied with her husband for being unable to offer her such a life.

FOLLOW-UP: After several years of psychotherapy, I could clarify the subject of her the delusional ideas. Gradually, she could accept that her diplomat lover offered only an illusionary escape from what she perceived as her miserable reality, and we could even start to laugh about it together. She no longer went through manic phases and intermittent psychiatric hospitalization. She remarried her husband, accepted him the way he was, and could enjoy their modest life. She needed no more neuroleptic medication.

The brain – the social organ

All stimuli coming from the outside world get processed in the brain through perception. As a reaction, emotions, thoughts and behavior patterns are evoked thereafter. The emotional condition we call mood, the state of alertness known as level of arousal, the thought process as well as behavior patterns are all controlled by the brain. The mood, state of arousal, and the memory of previous experiences constantly influence new perceptions and influence human behavior.

In a state of high arousal, external stimuli are more likely to be perceived as dangerous and thus elicit stress reactions, such as fight or flight, much more easily than in a lesser state of arousal. When in a happy and cheerful mood, the brain processes stimuli differently than in a depressive mood. All behavior and thinking patterns are regularly tainted by a specific prevailing mood. Everything looks black and hopeless if somebody is in a depressed mood, and all things appear bright when one is happy.

Mood is located in the emotional middle part of the brain, the limbic system, from which direct pathways go to the *pituitary gland*. The pituitary gland, which steers the entire hormonal system, is thus directly connected with the limbic system. The limbic system, however, does not only control the current mood itself but also influences the long-term mood via hormones through the pituitary gland. The hormones on their part have a long-term effect on mood, on the psychic energy as well as on the entire physical condition.

The neuronal adaptation processes of the brain are rapid, occurring via the neurotransmitter system between the different neurons and their synapses. In contrast, the adaptation of hormones via the pituitary gland, and all the dependent hormonal systems, is slow but more long-term. Hormones exert their effect over longer periods of time via long-term release into the blood stream. They are long lasting, in contrast to the neuronal system of the brain, which cannot maintain a steady state over longer periods of time because it continuously has to regenerate.

As mentioned before, the brain as a social organ determines how we perceive our environment and interact with it. On the other hand, our social environment perceives us and interacts with us according to how we behave and react.

The brain as our social and historical organ determines how we perceive and interact with our environment. Our environment perceives us according to our behavior and responds accordingly. As social species, we are constantly influenced by our environment while having an influence on it ourselves, an interminable feedback loop.

The brain – the most adaptive organ

Schizophrenia is a disorder that takes place in the brain. Yet despite all our knowledge of neuroscience and modern imaging techniques, the exact dysfunction of the brain during this illness can still be interpreted and understood only to a limited extent.

According to Selye's stress theory, an organism enters into a state of stress when its adaptive functions are exhausted and therefore begin to fail. This is the very moment when the adaptive response turns into a dysfunction, and the disease develops. Selye's stress concept, originally developed for somatic and psychosomatic diseases, can readily be applied to psychiatric diseases such as schizophrenia.

As can be deduced from the various case studies mentioned previously, it is my hypothesis that the destabilization that leads to acute psychosis most often occurs after a prolonged period of emotional stress. Emotions build up in the central, circularly arranged brain region, the limbic system, and escalate into an *emotional monster wave* with intense feelings of anxiety. This monster wave stimulates the prefrontal cortex via dopaminergic pathways, leading to an uncontrolled production of thoughts, a type of brainstorming called *flooding of thought process* or *flight of thought*. At the same time, it also activates the reptilian brain, which leads to hyperarousal and hypervigilance expressed in motor restlessness and an inability to sleep.

However, brain activity, remaining in a state of hyperarousal and hypervigilance for a prolonged period of time, gradually exhausts the cerebral function. The higher cognitive functions begin to fail and finally break down completely. This explains why in an acute schizophrenic state, even highly intelligent people are no longer able to interpret abstract meanings of proverbs but turn to a very concrete interpretation, demonstrating the breakdown of their higher cognitive function during acute schizophrenia. Higher cognitive functions such as abstract thought processing are no longer available. For that reason, schizophrenia is called a *thought disorder*.

Individuals going through psychosis often describe their state of mind with such expressions as "My mind was going crazy", or "I lost my mind". This aptly describes the dysfunction of the cognitive performance of the brain at that very moment of acute psychosis.

Once the higher functions of the brain have failed, as occurs in the acute stage of schizophrenia, the three primitive stress reflexes *fight*, *flight* or *freeze* take over. These stress reflexes can be observed on behavioral as well as cognitive mental levels in schizophrenia patients.

Memory function

A further important function of the brain, which plays a long-term role in adaptation, is memory. In memory, experiences can be filed and retrieved again at a later date in order to be applied as a more effective processing and adaptation to new similar situations. This function of the brain is called learning. The processing and integration of different content of memory into knowledge, called cognition, is one of the highest adaptive functions of the human brain. Memories with access to consciousness are stored in the cerebral cortex as images and thoughts. Emotional and physical experiences even from the preverbal phase of a child, although not consciously accessible through words, are nevertheless stored in the limbic system as physical and emotional memories or even images and smells. However, they can come into consciousness as a result of specific triggers, which remind us of the original circumstances regarding where and when the emotional imprinting took place. The limbic system is the gatekeeper of incoming stimuli and thus the emotional motivator for learning. It judges quickly whether something should be accepted as valuable or repelled as dangerous. It decides what gets stored and retrieved again from storage under certain conditions.

> Learning is continuously optimizing cognitive and behavioral adaptation to an ever-changing environment.

Information stored in the long-term memory of the cerebrum over the course of a lifetime can be consciously retrieved. However, memories which trigger strong negative emotions, involving unpleasant feelings or relating to a taboo, are withheld from consciousness by the emotional brain. In psychiatry, this process of suppressing memory is referred to as denial and repression. Under certain circumstances, however, repressed memory content may suddenly surface into consciousness, thereby flooding the brain with intense emotionally laden images. Emotional and physical traumatization which could not be communicated verbally heretofore, suddenly enters the emotional memory. Even though children were unable to master language and higher cognition at the time of traumatization, their brain can still remember these traumatic events in adult life. Under specific trigger conditions, images, emotions and smell may enter into consciousness and be communicated verbally at that point.

Schizophrenia – intellectual high-performance

Let us recap briefly the functioning of the *triune brain* for better understanding of its dysfunction in schizophrenia, or any psychotic state. The cerebrum, the largest part of the human brain is the cerebral cortex, or simply called cortex, contains a seemingly infinite number of folds in a relatively thin layer. This part of the brain has massively evolved over the course of evolution, increased by one kilogram, distinguishing the human brain from all other primate brains. The prefrontal cortex of the cerebrum is where the planning, and preparation for action – called anticipation – takes place. Having visions and setting visionary goals originates in this part of the brain, motivated and energized by impulses coming from the limbic system.

Thanks to the human brain's enormous memory and processor function, it can retrieve and recombine an infinite number of stored experiences and use them strategically as needed by projecting them as imagined behavior patterns into the future. Moreover, these futuristic plans for action are constantly screened for their adaptive value in new situations, which bring to mind earlier experiences.

The human brain can thus design and simulate adaptive patterns in advance of actual situations. Primates, our closest relatives in the animal kingdom, already show some capacity for anticipation. But memory function of anticipation is much further developed in the human brain. High intellectual achievements such as those of world chess champion Bobby Fischer, physicist Albert Einstein or John Nash are telling samples.

However, as surprising as it might seem, this highly developed cerebral function is, at the same time, responsible for the development of schizophrenia. Under constant stress and pressure, the cognitive capacity of adaptation in the cerebrum is driven to its extreme by the *emotional monster wave* of the limbic system. John Nash, a mathematician famous in the fields of game theory, differential geometry, and partial differential equations is a good example of such a transition from high mental performance to the outbreak of schizophrenia. In 1959, he was about to receive a full professorship at MIT when the first signs of psychosis became apparent as his first child was born. In May of that same year, he was diagnosed with paranoid schizophrenia. Thirty-five years later, in 1994, despite his illness, from which he had meanwhile decided to recover, he was awarded the Nobel Prize in Economics for his game theory.

Behavior Patterns in Schizophrenia

Flight reaction

In the hyper excited stage of acute schizophrenic psychosis, brain activity produces a variety of thoughts, which are all simultaneously released into consciousness. This process is referred to as a *flight of ideas*. Individuals in such a state switch from one train of thought to the next, introducing thoughts in ever-faster succession, fragmenting them to bits and pieces, which cannot even be understood by the individuals themselves – let alone their counterpart – because the bits of thought are connected indiscriminately and no longer follow the logic of the linear rules of language and logical thinking.

The cognitive phenomenon of an accelerated thought process, however, is not confined exclusively to acute schizophrenia. Anybody's brain may get into this type of thought pattern in an extremely stressful situation; the brain's activity has entered a state of increased arousal at that stage. One can no longer think straight but rather jumps from one subject to another, and thoughts penetrate consciousness uncontrollably.

Individuals who have been involved in accidents often describe retrospectively a *flight of ideas,* a pattern of racing thoughts. Once the shock has subsided, accident victims recall having processed innumerable thoughts and memories in their mind within a fraction of a second. At breakneck speed, their entire life was played back to them. The phenomenon of racing thoughts is the brain's automatic reaction to extreme and stressful situations. This experience of thought processing at lightning pace can very well be compared to the flight of ideas during an acute schizophrenic episode. In both situations, brain activity is in a heightened state of arousal and immediately reactivates a plethora of memories, which leads to the accelerated production of thoughts. Individuals with acute schizophrenia as well as victims of accidents demonstrate the same type of adaptive response of the brain under extreme stress.

> Brain activity in a heightened state of arousal is an attempt to search for quick-fix problem-solving strategies on a cognitive level.

Unexpected external events such as an accident triggers acute psychological stress in victims. In the case of schizophrenia patients, however, the stress is induced by the family system or special environmental conditions over a longer period of time. Family-related stress factors are usually – in contrast to accident-related stress factors – of long-term duration; they even build up over generations through the family projection process until they are released in an *emotional monster wave*.

> **CASE HISTORY:** Kathrin was deeply rattled because her marriage was falling apart. Divorce, a taboo in her family of origin, was not an option for her. Under no circumstances did she want to burden her mother with the news of a divorce. However, she saw no way out of her unsatisfactory marriage. She felt that her partner neither understood nor supported her in raising their two sons. She was also furious with him because he had had several extramarital affairs over the years.
> Kathrin was an emotional woman. For a long time, she tried to suppress her anger and disappointment with alcohol but when she quit her drinking habit, her emotions suddenly surged. She would wander around for days and nights, seeking out friends and neighbors for support. She had turned psychotic. After medical treatment, Kathrin calmed down and could describe how, in her psychotic phase, she had been unable to control her thoughts and irrational behavior; her entire life had been played back in her mind at breakneck speed.

Whether this type of brain activity is elicited by sudden stress caused, for example, by accidents, or emotional stress that builds up in family systems over years, the accelerated thought process can be described by individuals in both types of situations. Thus, the *cognitive flight reaction* is typical for accident victims as well as people going through acute schizophrenic psychosis.

Schizophrenia sufferers frequently show a *physical flight reaction* whenever problems or conflicts arise in their environment. They force their partners to change their place of residence with the argument that they can no longer stand their neighborhood, even disregarding their children's schooling or their friends and family relationships. When partners resist this problem-solving flight reaction or avoidance strategy, anxiety builds up. They become highly distressed when the urge to move is ignored. If partners don't relent, they may face another outbreak of acute schizophrenic psychosis.

Behavior avoidance

Absenteeism and frequent job changes are another mode of escape or avoidance response by patients with schizophrenia. This type of problem-solving often manifests itself at work. Schizophrenia patients shy away from even the smallest of disagreements on account of their increased sensitivity. Their fear of conflict, which their superiors are usually unaware of, makes them avoid going to work.

> **CASE HISTORY:** Karoly was a chronic schizophrenia patient who worked in a sheltered workshop. One day, he announced that he was unable to go to work because he saw strange flashes in his eyes. He used this symptom to explain his absence.
> **COMMENTARY:** I asked him if he felt mistreated at work. Hesitating at first, Karoly then replied somewhat reluctantly that he had felt bullied by his colleagues the day before. I expressed empathy for him and

was understanding of his situation. As I mentioned Karoly's concerns to his superior, he was astonished and told me that Karoly had never complained about anything. His behavior at work had been normal, and he had given no hint as to why he had stayed away from work. His colleagues, too, had not the slightest idea. They linked his absenteeism solely with his illness. After I had discussed the situation with his supervisor, and also talked to Karoly about it, he returned to work the next day; his symptoms had disappeared.

Schizophrenia patients may also respond with a flight reaction when they anticipate a reprimand from their therapists and stay away from the next session. Plagued by feelings of guilt and, at the same time, fearing a punitive response for not having taken their medication, or not gone to work as demanded, some discontinue therapy altogether.

> The habitual flight response of people with schizophrenia is most probably related to their genetically determined sensitivity resulting from their ADHD or ADD. However, it can also be related to a fear-inducing parenting style experienced during their upbringing, as well as to current stress factors in their environment, which leads to a system overload.

Individuals with schizophrenia perceive the slightest nuances and emotional inconsistencies in relationships around them as threatening – even if these have nothing to do with them. Owing to their ADHD or ADD neurotype, with its tendency to *system overflow*, they immediately feel a strong urge to escape any potentially difficult situation. They are poorly equipped to dissociate themselves emotionally in conflict situations, partly because they generally have not learned to apply suitable conflict resolution strategies. Conflicts within their family were usually not handled properly but rather suppressed and denied, as demonstrated in the color plate experiment by Holte with families with schizophrenia.

The following example of a schizophrenia patient demonstrates his fear of receiving unsatisfactory grades, leading to avoidance behavior with delusional ideas.

CASE HISTORY: Rolf, who was diagnosed with paranoid schizophrenia, attempted his final exams, which he had already postponed twice after prolonged psychiatric treatment. Things went quite well initially, until he was about to pass an exam for which he had insufficiently prepared himself. Shortly before the deadline, he came up with the idea that a bomb was hidden in the exam room, and he was the only one who knew about it. He wanted to avoid this deadly situation at all cost and refused to sit the exam.

FOLLOW-UP: Short of time because his examination was imminent, I interpreted his delusions on the phone as a fear of receiving an unsatisfactory grade. The bomb seemed to be the most severe, life-threatening punishment for being poorly prepared, as well as an appropriate excuse to stay away. I encouraged him to sit the exam despite everything and pointed out that he still had a good chance of passing even with an unsatisfactory grade. Rolf accepted my interpretation and followed my advice. He calmed down and sat the exam, and indeed received an unsatisfactory grade. Throughout his other exams, Rolf phoned me again and told me about a dream in which he had successfully performed heart surgery. Three months later, Rolf successfully passed his final exams.

COMMENTARY: Rolf could neither accept getting a bad grade nor could he face the prospect of failing. He concealed the extreme threat of impending shame about not having studied enough in his delusional daydream. With my therapeutic support, however, he overcame his barrier and passed his examinations despite an unsatisfactory grade. His second dream – performing heart surgery to great success – proved how skillfully and fearlessly he confronted these enormous emotional obstacles without suffering a relapse of his illness.

In my view, schizophrenia patients have genetically inherited heightened sensitivity as a result of ADHD or ADD. Conflictual issues are therefore the main reason why they break off relationships within their social environment. They also forego new relationships for fear of getting hurt. Even the slightest disagreement during therapy sessions may cause them to break off the therapeutic relationship, thereby interrupting any long-term treatment process, complicating successful therapeutic learning and personal development. Thus, they become isolated in their own world and end up as chronic patients with a withdrawn, autistic state of mind. For some, suicide appears to be the only way out. All these factors contribute to a poor therapeutic outcome, namely that only one third of all cases improve and resume a normal life.

Freeze reaction

The *freeze reaction* is one of the three stress reactions, a symptom that can be observed in extreme forms of acute schizophrenia. During a freeze reaction, the entire thought process and all motor activity stalls completely. This is a sign of extremely overstrained brain function yet without loss of consciousness.

This total inhibition of thought and movement in an acute schizophrenic state is called *catatonia*. Catatonic behavior thus belongs to the three primitive stress reflexes: *flight, fight, and freeze*. A person who suffers a catatonic state – a freeze reaction – is experiencing a mental shock and literally paralyzed by fear. At that moment, the symptoms are not limited to the thought process; the brain's entire functional network is blocked.

However, the freeze reaction does not include a disturbed consciousness. On the contrary, the consciousness is on heightened alertness, *hypervigilance*. In this state of mind, the person perceives vividly all goings-on around them but is unable to communicate or move. This catatonic state is a toxic form of acute schizophrenia. In extreme cases, a dangerous inflammatory swelling of the entire brain results, a cerebral *edema*, which may lead to death if immediate measures such as cortisone injections or electroshock are not taken. ECT reduces the over-excitement of the brain by switching off all synapses via a generalized depolarization. Cortisone is an anti-stress hormone, which reduces the inflammatory reaction of the brain.

It has to be emphasized that a freeze reaction is not confined solely to a person with schizophrenia. This type of stress reaction can happen to anybody who is exposed to a sudden frightening event such as a robbery or violent assault: the limbs become heavy like lead, one feels frozen and paralyzed by fear, making the call for help seem all but impossible. In one way or another, we are familiar with sudden experiences of blackout during exams, for example, when all we have learned is temporarily lost and cannot be retrieved from our memory. We refer to this as a stuporous state of shock. In psychiatry, this state of mind is called *schizophrenic stupor* or *catatonia*.

In the animal world, the freeze reaction fulfills an important function. This stress reflex is a successful survival strategy for many creatures who have natural predators. Many hunters in the animal kingdom primarily respond to movement and track only moving objects. As soon as movement ceases, they abandon the object. Trailed animals no longer appear as prey, thereby causing predators to lose interest in them. In cats, this can be observed with a moving ball of wool. As soon as the ball stops moving, the cat loses interest in it because it no longer imitates or reminds the cat of the movement of a mouse.

The archaic stress-survival reflex seems to still exist in homo sapiens, though the authentic function of the freeze reaction has lost its adaptive value in most situations of our modern urban life. Students are unable to protect themselves from unsatisfactory grades and failure by means of a freeze reaction. Under certain conditions, however, when schizophrenia patients activate this archaic instinct, they may delay the emotional intrusion of their families for a while. But contrary to predators' reaction in the animal world, the complete withdrawal of schizophrenia patients usually mobilizes all the family's available means to get their maladapted member come out of their retreat. Nonetheless, these well-intentioned interventions of family members and professionals alike only reinforce the freeze reaction of schizophrenia patients.

From flight to fight reaction

Statistically speaking, individuals with schizophrenia are no more prone to violent behavior than the average member of the population. Nevertheless, it is widely assumed in public that individuals with schizophrenia are more dangerous than the average citizen.

Persons with schizophrenia first and foremost adopt a flight reaction; whenever possible, they look for an escape strategy or avoidance behavior when facing stressful situations. However, they switch from flight to fight and pose a risk when they find the escape route cut off, or their flight reaction is physically hindered, as is the case on locked wards of psychiatric clinics.

The phenomenon of locked doors combined with the sudden awareness of losing control may already trigger an anxiety reaction, leading to a panic attack. Physical restraints which limit their mobility, be it real or imagined, can indeed elicit an aggressive response in people with psychosis.

Courtesy distance

Professional caregivers as well as family members who do not remain at arm's length and respect the flight distance – termed courtesy distance in human psychology – are often quite dumbfounded when patients in a state of hyperarousal unexpectedly react with a fight response and become acutely aggressive.

> **CASE HISTORY:** In an acute state of schizophrenia, Jussi had smashed a drinking glass while venting his anger. The head nurse immediately reacted by picking up the broken pieces, unaware that he had bent down too close to the patient and invaded his private space. He was attacked by Jussi, not bearing in mind the unwritten rule to respect the important courtesy distance. The nurse was unable to extricate himself from Jussi's fight reaction and had to call for help.
> On yet another occasion, Jussi had unexpectedly slapped the doctor on duty because he, too, had not respected the patient's courtesy distance.

Barring the physical escape routes by locking the ward, however, is not the only way of preventing schizophrenia patients from acting on flight reactions. Professionals as well as family members quite often attempt to argue with schizophrenia sufferers, since they are convinced that the power of reasoning could dissuade them from delusional thinking or socially incompatible behavior. Yet they fail to realize that delusional thinking is essentially a cognitive escape strategy for schizophrenia patients that provides temporary relief from emotional pressure. Hospital staff and family members feel snubbed and are utterly surprised when they are suddenly confronted with the patient's aggressive reactions. Their usual response comes in the form of a complaint such as: "I just wanted to bring him back to his senses." However, reasoning with people affected by schizophrenia does not lower but rather raise their anxiety level. Reasoning does not calm them down; on the contrary, it destroys the highly precarious, delusional balancing act of their emotional state. When dealing with schizophrenia patients, it may therefore help to show respect towards their narrative of events and their family system as a face-saving strategy. The aim is social compatibility, and not stating the objective truth.

Cooperation is worth striving for in the context of therapy with families of individuals with schizophrenia. Social compatibility is more important for a successful therapeutic alliance than objective truth.

Better mad than bad

The avoidance of conflict and the suppression of aggression are typical adaptive strategies in families of individuals with schizophrenia. Arising problems are swept under the carpet, or even transferred to the next generation. Multifaceted problems, accumulated over several generations, are no longer recognizable as such in the end. To keep the ailing system in place, however, the pseudo family peace must be maintained under any circumstances, even at the high cost of sacrificing a child.

Parents who raise their children to suppress aggression in order to avoid conflicts, prevent them from acquiring competent problem-solving strategies to overcome conflictual situations in life. Children who develop schizophrenia in adolescence are most likely those members who – under the premise of avoiding conflict – suppress their own needs above all else. This is a typical condition under which an emotional tsunami, a *monster wave,* can develop in adolescence and lead to psychosis.

The dictum *better mad than bad* succinctly describes the dilemma faced by children affected by schizophrenia when dealing with their families' conflictual situations. The inherent rule of these families requires them to adapt to the powerful forces of conflict suppression within the system to secure the endangered family cohesion and disguise the fact that the family peace is at risk.

The rule of *conflict suppression* plays a particularly fatal role during puberty. Children who develop schizophrenia constantly endeavor to prevent their parents from being exposed to aggression. They go as far as suppressing even the slightest sign of aggression to protect their families from the stigma of imperfection. They keep a lid on their aggression, thereby avoiding disputes, but at the same time, they miss out on their chance to fight for autonomy. They seek an escape in delusions, developing a psychotic episode. Juvenile rebels in these families are thus immediately classified as *mad* when they misbehave.

> Psychosis usually obscures parental conflict and prevents detachment issues of the adolescent from being brought forward and resolved, instead all negative emotions of the affected family member are inwardly concealed and conceptually projected outwards onto strangers in form of delusional ideas.

For many parents of schizophrenia sufferers, nothing is worse than the damage being done to the reputation of their family system. It seems that a *mad* – in the sense of crazy – child is easier to bear and seemingly less defamatory than a mis-behaving *bad* child who ruins the family image and prestige.

The drama of madness in acute psychosis, however, not only conceals the painful and troubling separation conflict, but also all ongoing parental conflicts within the family. It thereby fulfills an important adaptive function within the entire family system, helping to maintain the family's cohesion.

> Families of individuals with schizophrenia quite often mention, sometimes even with pride, that their child never went through puberty.

Delusions to Avoid Painful Reality

Delusional processing of sensory inputs from the environment – also referred to as ideas of reference – and sensory hallucination, such as hearing voices, are the most noticeable symptoms of the cognitive disorder in schizophrenia. These symptoms usually only develop after a longer duration of the illness but, in some cases, may already occur during the initial acute schizophrenic episode.

Delusions are cognitive problem-solving strategies detached from reality. Using their imagination, the person tries to maintain psychic stability to prevent the ego from collapsing. Illusions and delusions can be understood as fantasy solutions to maintain the *pseudo-personality* as well as the cohesion of the family. These pathological symptoms are complicated mental acrobatics, protecting the family's name from humiliation or shame. At the same time, delusions provide the patients with the desperately needed emotional balance within their dysfunctional family system by keeping up a pseudo self-image.

Delusions, moreover, reveal the highly precarious secrets related to taboo subjects in the family, which have to be suppressed and cannot be directly addressed. Over time, this unsatisfactory emotional state of unresolved problems in the partnership as well as the families of origin can no longer be ignored by the sensitive schizophrenia patients. Attempting to accomplish their unachievable mission as *obsessed diplomats* while also concealing the family secrets, they are under continuous pressure on a cognitive meta-level to find problem-solving strategies to bridge this schism.

> Delusions can be referred to as creative self-deceptions for the sake of achieving family cohesion. They are attempts on a mental level at fulfilling the unachievable mission as *obsessed diplomats* to conceal the family secrets and taboos.

Delusions of reference

Delusions of reference most often occur in people who live in social isolation most of the time. Their loneliness, for which they feel ashamed, is projected onto their surroundings. A woman with schizophrenia, living a remote existence, had the strong belief that her former psychiatrist, with whom she had fallen in love, was talking to her via TV on the daily talk show.

In the following story, disappointment resulting from unfulfilled expectations was projected in the form of hate and envy onto a friend.

CASE HISTORY: Ralph grew up with a depressed mother and an older brother who created a lot of difficulties for his mother. As a reaction to his brother's behavioral problems and his depressed mother, he tried to be as inconspicuous as possible. He did not want to give his mother any additional concerns and adopted a cool demeanor that made him appear more self-assured than he was. In school he played the clown. Stressed by his first unhappy love during puberty, he turned to cannabis, and, later on, problems arose at work. Ralph soon became psychotic and developed delusions. He was convinced that his colleague robbed him of his thoughts and firmly believed that he was at his mercy. When his colleague was confronted with Ralph's delusions, he was shocked and tried to refute them. However, Ralph became very aggressive and accused him of lying. In his delusional state, he even suspected his colleague's cousin of wanting to scratch out his eyes. He had to pre-empt him, he said. Shocked and horrified by Ralph's criminal intent, the colleague immediately broke off all contact with him.

COMMENTARY: Ralph was probably jealous of his colleague's popularity with women and his success at work. He felt resentment building up inside and reacted as though having suffered a blow to his ego. Yet unconsciously, he aspired to be as successful as his colleague but could not live up to it. He kept his nagging feelings of inadequacy and self-doubt at bay, instead projecting aggressive, delusional hate constructs onto his colleague and his cousin in the form of malevolent intentions.

Ralph was unable to make his own decisions. Although he didn't like his job, he had not the faintest idea of what else he could do. He always acceded to what others proposed to him, just as he had earlier conformed to his family and its environment. Later on, he turned to cocaine to enjoy moments of pleasure but shortly after consumption, he immediately felt remorseful and guilt-ridden, especially when face-to-face with his parents.

Delusions of grandeur

As mentioned previously, individuals with schizophrenia have often spent their entire lives helping to maintain their family's cohesion and cover-up parental conflict until they are admitted to a psychiatric hospital by their parents. At that point, the parents have given up on their teenager's behavior and put them in professional care to have them treated for psychosis.

Feeling depleted because their functional role within the family has become obsolete, schizophrenia sufferers attempt to find an honorable way of compensating for no longer being the handlers of their family's emotional ego mass, a term coined by Murray Bowen, referring to the family system, which functions as a collective body. At that point, they may turn to megalomania, which is characterized by an exaggerated self-perception. Having developed a proxy personality in their family, they may easily copy famous people's identity to perform as a *persona*. They adopt a *pseudo identity* in their delusion and make renewed attempts to satisfy the unfulfilled wishes and desires of their discontented parents who have given up on them in total exasperation. Some patients, receiving treatment for mental illness on a psychiatric ward, imagine they are outstanding personalities with divine inspirations, or made significant inventions or discoveries to save the world.

CASE HISTORY: Kevin most probably was a child with ADD and learning disabilities in languages who never quite felt accepted at school. His mother always had to help him with his homework. Yet Kevin had other above-average abilities, especially in spatial perception and visualization. In fact, he wished to study physics but ended up in a sheltered workshop for psychiatric patients. One day, he began to work on the formation of black holes. Night after night, he filled page after page with calculations and curves, and programmed computer simulations to find out about the origin of the world. He even tried to find loopholes in Einstein's theory of relativity. During therapy sessions, Kevin often demonstrated his mathematical achievements to me, but at the end of every discourse, he immediately apologized for taking up my time.

COMMENTARY: Kevin's mother was a resolute person. She would have liked to go to university but could not finalize her ambitious dreams. She was therefore all the more disappointed when she realized that Kevin had learning difficulties together with ADD. She used all means available to her to help him overcome his deficits. No effort was too much for her. He, however, experienced her help as constant criticism and control. He felt her attitude was highly intrusive and often humiliating for him. At times, an almost unbearable rage overcame him, and he wanted to get at her throat, but immediately felt guilty for it, and suppressed his anger since he depended on her assistance to pass his exams.

His deepest wish was to demonstrate one day his unique achievements in astrophysics to the public. Moreover, as the famous discoverer of a new world formula, he would then overshadow all famous physicists, and at the same time impress his ambitious mother with his genius.

When he visited his parents occasionally, he would not accept food from his mother because he did not want to be dependent on her any more. She was at a loss and couldn't understand his behavior.

CASE HISTORY: Moritz's father was a successful businessman. However, he was not satisfied with his marital life. He had numerous affairs and saw this as his right. This caused Moritz's mother great suffering over the years. She developed depression and eventually committed suicide.

In adulthood, Moritz developed schizophrenia with manic episodes. During one of his acute psychosis, he was convinced he was Jesus Christ who had to bring salvation to the world. He wrote political letters to the editor of a newspaper and insisted on having them published. He wrote about conflict resolution in the Middle East and made suggestions as to how one should go about to solving the matter.

COMMENTARY: Moritz, his father's pride, was the oldest of three sons. He had remained loyal to his mother, who had suffered of depression all her life, and felt obliged to soothe her distress. It came as a shock to him when she committed suicide. He had failed in his task as a helper child.

Professionally, he could not live up to his father's expectations. Moritz could barely keep himself above water. When he faced financial problems, he had to turn to his father for help, which meant he faced a hedgehog's dilemma. Although he held his father in contempt for his mother's suicide, he was forced to ask him for financial support. At the same time, he used his father's misconduct towards the mother as a means of exonerating himself. To escape the moral dilemma, Moritz tried to gain public recognition with his letters to the editor. His emotional state improved noticeably whenever he wrote his articles. Although he remained financially dependent on his father, he felt morally superior to him. Suggesting solutions to keep the world at peace with his grandiose delusion of being Jesus Christ strengthened his feeling of self-respect and superiority.

People who suffer from schizophrenia sense all too well the great vulnerability of their parents, and the precarious emotional balance in the family system. They protect their parents from internal accusation whenever possible and try to alleviate the parental fear of being confronted with the reality of their failed family life. Financial dependence, in addition to emotional dependence, as was the case with Moritz, is another reason why they cannot go against their parents. At heart, they are always plagued by the unbearable fear of destabilizing the family system. They continually invent new constructs of escaping the constraints of the family system but increasingly end up completely entangled within it.

Paranoia

Paranoia is the opposite of the delusion of grandeur. Wounded intrinsic value and failure to generate self-realization and self-respect on the part of patients gets projected onto an adversary as hidden aggressions, while the patients perceive themselves as passive victims. Persons with paranoia are basically anxious and feel easily overwhelmed by people they enter into a conflict with.

> **CASE HISTORY:** Erhard's mother was a teacher. His father ran the family farm and was known for his irascible temperament. The parental relationship was upset by continuous disputes. Erhard had suffered from their quarrelling since childhood. Their conflict was intractable and led to divorce.
> Erhard had the long-term plan to take over the farm from his father. However, after completing his agricultural schooling, he realized that the farm was heavily in debt. His dream of being his own boss was

suddenly destroyed. He became psychotic and had to be admitted to a psychiatric clinic on several occasions. He was convinced that he was exposed to radioactivity, and that the secret service was after him. He wanted to construct a radiation-proof lead cabin for protection. Another belief of his was that one of his enemies had planted electronic devices under his skin, and he repeatedly tried to remove them by scratching himself. He heard threatening voices and felt monitored via radio antennas.

COMMENTARY: Erhard could not confront his father, who had upset his plans and destroyed his desired career. Although he had followed in his father's footsteps, studied the same profession and remained loyal to him during the parental fights, he could not inherit the farm.

As a child, he was punished by his father with the leather belt if he dared to oppose him. Fearing punishment, he was unable to express his anger – even as a grown-up. In our therapy sessions, he couldn't say a bad word about his parents; he still suffered extreme fear of disapproval and punishment.

His father as well as his mother were spared from his aggression. Instead, he projected his rage onto all possible authority figures with whom he had the slightest conflict. At the same time, he felt constantly persecuted. Erhard's fear of parental punitive measures had been transformed into paranoia. He could thus protect his parents from his accusations and himself from being disloyal to them.

He even protected his mother though she blamed him for the divorce, saying that it was him, who had forced them apart. She said he was such a difficult child to raise. All their disagreements were about him. She even had him examined by a psychologist, but it was of no help. At the same time, she referred to him as the most sensitive of her four children. He most probably had undiagnosed ADHD.

> The adaptive function of paranoia can be interpreted as an appeal to the altruistic instinct of potential helpers in the sufferer's social environment.

CASE HISTORY: Erich's parents divorced when he was five years old, and both remarried. As an only child, he was spoiled by his mother, maternal grandmother and his aunt. At eighteen, Erich got into a fight with his mother and was admitted to a psychiatric clinic. He never got over this. In every therapeutic session, he was dwelling on the subject. He found it unjust that he was forced into hospital care without his consent. The consequences for his entire life where immense. He had no friends; he considered all his colleagues to be his enemies. In our therapy sessions, he reported that his superiors and co-workers bullied him all the time. Even passers-by would deliberately block his way. To prevent this, he deliberately ran in those who did not get out of his way. He thought that everything, including the chimney of the nearby factory or the late-night warbling of the neighbors, was directed at him. At night, he feared that he would die from a heart attack because of the stress he constantly suffered. It all became too much for him.

COMMENTARY: Several times a week, Erich called to complain about the evils of the world, and how he was persecuted by the noisy lovemaking of his neighbors. He felt ill-treated and remained completely isolated in his apartment. He would have liked to have friends but was unable to form relationships; he was far too scared.

As a single child, he had been the sunshine of his mother, grandmother and his aunt, who were eager to take care of him and protect him from any evil. But it turned out to be quite the opposite: he mentioned several times how difficult it was for him to exist and grow up between two sets of parents and one aunt; he even felt abused, any glimmer of self-determination was constantly exploited by his family members' attention and their own emotional needs. He felt overwhelmed and constantly intruded upon while trying to establish his inner world.

During the course of therapy, when Erich felt rising fear as a result of his clogged emotions, Erich spoke with me or sometimes contacted my secretary almost daily to inform us about his paranoid stories. He depended on my secretary's calming voice, and just wanted to relieve himself of his delusional fear. He was satisfied after each phone call, feeling safe without any further action. He did not ask for more.

Male delusional jealousy

Men who suffer from schizophrenia with delusional jealousy are often unaware of their dependency and unresolved attachment from their mothers. They consider their female partners as possessions and feel hurt when their claim of ownership is threatened. Men at risk of schizophrenia become overanxious as soon as they think they might lose their female partner. They feel threatened if another male approaches their possession and combat their unacknowledged insecurity by means of delusional jealousy. When considering themselves inferior, they project their sense of inferiority as hatred onto their supposed rivals. Delusional jealousy is quite common in middle-aged men.

> **CASE HISTORY:** Irma met Franco during a language course while staying in Italy. The two fell in love, and he moved with her to Switzerland. They married and had four children. Although Franco worked as a craftsman and then as a sales representative for many years, he never quite felt at home in Switzerland. Irma as a native Swiss, on the other hand, was socially as well as professionally well integrated in her home country. Franco was pathologically jealous. Any man who even came near his house, let alone entered it, became the object of his delusional jealousy. For years, he accused his wife of having relationships with the postman, the milkman, the chimney sweeper and various other handymen. Night after night, he harassed her until the early morning

hours. He had her swear on the Bible that she was not having sexual relations with any other male than him. She repeatedly obeyed his demand, but this did not provide him with the reassurance he had hoped for, and he continued to harass her. His family doctor eventually referred him to a psychosomatic clinic. Irma was so exhausted from the nightly interrogations that she was admitted to the same clinic a few weeks later. I had to evaluate them both as a psychiatric consultant of that clinic.

THERAPEUTIC INTERVENTION: I realized that Franco's delusional jealousy was emotionally fixated and not rectifiable, not even with medication. He had not cut the umbilical cord when leaving his homeland, and his familiar male patriarchal behavior that was practiced in his family of origin could not be changed either. Yet because his wife could no longer endure his behavior, I suggested that he return to Italy to re-establish his roots. Although Irma still loved her husband and did not want him to leave, even though he did not feel at home in Switzerland, she considered this a good idea. A few years later, she informed me by phone that her husband had eventually returned to his homeland and was doing much better.

COMMENTARY: Franco's delusional jealousy arose as an adaptation strategy, most likely out of fear that he would never be able to meet up to his Swiss wife's expectations and thus not be able to satisfy the hidden demands that he had put on himself. Through his nightly accusations, he established his male image and felt superior at least for a short while because he made himself believe that he was in the right, while his wife and her imagined lovers were in the wrong. With this system of delusions, he was thus temporarily able to nurture his injured self-esteem, thereby reducing his emotional tensions. His wife, however, could no longer handle his strategy of using guilt, accusations and humiliation to ward off his fears of insufficiency. The two ultimately had to divorce.

> All delusions primarily originate from a chronic painful emotional state, which is not acknowledged by the environment and cannot be expressed by the affected person. The conflicted feelings are therefore essentially outsourced as delusional constructs and projected onto the surroundings in which the person lives. They have to be viewed as and dealt with as such.

Seen from this perspective, delusions are an attempt at self-regulation and self-healing on a meta level. Projecting unpleasant feelings onto one's surroundings helps to relieve psychic stress.

At an imagined new level of reference, schizophrenia sufferers create their own view of the world and of themselves. In their fantasy, they create a substitute world according to their own emotionally-driven logic – a kind of ideological blinding – to make their unbearable reality more endurable for themselves. Through delusions, these individuals manage to escape the experience of utterly frustrating feelings caused by reality.

To avoid aggressive conflicts, and as protection against the naming and shaming of their families, they develop their own philosophy of a new world, seek shelter with a religious guardian angel, or envision themselves as important scientists. From a fantastically delusional superiority, persons with schizophrenia develop a mental position of inviolability, which is meant to protect them from social defeat in life. The fact that these carefully devised fantasy castles do not reflect reality is secondary. They are preoccupied with their emotional relief, preserving the dignity of their families, and are least concerned about the truth.

> Delusions have distinct mental functions and must be understood as a cognitive adaptive behavior.

Delusions of love

Delusions of love are another example of mental simulation to correct painful reality. They are a magical problem-solving method on a mental level, which can be used to compensate for a failed or lacking, but dearly wished-for a romantic relationship.

Sensitive individuals prone to develop schizophrenia become easily rattled and are often emotionally deeply grieved if their affection is rebuffed. Initially unsuccessful in establishing a romantic connection, they invent fairy tales. Even if the object of their affection clearly expresses that they are not interested in a relationship with them, schizophrenia sufferers still project their most intimate feelings and romantic love onto them and cling to their own story as reality. Their desire drives their delusional notion while suppressing reality altogether. Delusions of love help these sensitive individuals deal with their desire for affection.

> **CASE HISTORY:** When Hans was promoted to a prestigious professional position, he was still living with his mother. She was a dominant woman and he was very dependent on her.
> By happenstance, Hans met a foreign woman at work who had recently divorced from her husband and missed company as well as support. She was open to his affectionate attention since she needed help. However, she was not looking for a lover. Hans was not her type; a romantic relationship was out of the question for her. When she began to avoid him, he nevertheless continued to stalk her, though she had told him many times she didn't want a romantic relationship. One evening, armed with a knife, he climbed onto her balcony, entered her apartment and hid behind the bathroom door. When she returned from work and went to take a shower, he attacked her. She was injured in the ensuing fight but was eventually able to wrestle the knife out of his hands. On his knees, he begged her to kill him; he wanted to die as her lover in her arms.

COMMENTARY: Hans' fairy tale of a love had turned into an aggressive reality show with a dangerous outcome for his much longed-for woman. For him, her rejection was like a death sentence. The story finally ended in court. Hans was issued a restraining order following his dramatic assault. Though the court order was issued as a protection, it provided no security for his victim. She had been traumatized by his love delusion and would most probably remain so for the rest of her life.

The following is an example of a female who never had an intimate relationship with a male but had always longed for one.

CASE HISTORY: I got to know Gabrielle as a chronically ill schizophrenia patient. During puberty, she was traumatized by the violent death of her father. He had hanged himself in the attic of the family house, and she was the one who found him. She was convinced that she could have saved his life had she gone upstairs earlier, and therefore felt guilty for his death.
Gabrielle was a teacher but practiced her profession only for a short time. Disciplining her students was a key problem for her; she became completely overwhelmed with her first class. The stress of her job, and the stress of her father's suicide was too much for her. She became psychotic.
As a student, Gabrielle adored one of her teachers, but it never turned intimate. As a patient, she developed feelings for the doctor on her ward who had performed electroconvulsive therapy (ETC) on her during her stay in hospital. After being discharged from the clinic – her doctor was meanwhile professor – she was convinced that he was sending her secret love messages by radio and television. During each of my visits, she asked whether she had to be treated with ECT again. She was firmly convinced that such treatment was a deserved punishment for her sinful attraction.

COMMENTARY: The electroconvulsive therapy became an intimate part of her stay at the hospital and had a double meaning for Gabrielle. It symbolized the intimate affection for the revered professor as well as her medically camouflaged sexual arousal. Although thoughts of love elicited feelings of guilt because a relationship with a married man was a moral taboo for her, the nevertheless ECT triggered feelings of happiness; however, Gabrielle covered up her sexual desire by presuming that it was a punishment.

The violent and painful separation from her father caused her lifelong fear of being deprived of relationships to become interwoven with a traumatic longing for affection. The trauma was triggered by the experience of her father's suicide, which she still felt guilty about because she had not been able to prevent it. This turning point in Gabrielle's life caused her to become metaphorically glued to her father's self-imposed fate and prevented her detachment from him. Through repeated electroconvulsive therapy, she hoped to erase her terrible trauma while fulfilling her sexual desire for an orgasm at the same time. But Gabrielle could express her yearning for erotic experiences in a creative way; artistically talented, she was drawing portraits of nudes. However, she never entered into an intimate relationship with a male.

With her mother, she had a very distant relationship. She described her as a tough woman whom she could never get close to. Whenever she visited her, she felt patronized and criticized by her. Her mother could not provide her with feelings of security, and Gabrielle felt she was not taken seriously as an adult.

Married women in an unhappy relationship who have neither the strength to separate nor the courage to file for divorce may also develop delusions of love as a problem-solving strategy to escape from their unhappy relationship. They fixate on public figures such as movie stars, politicians and other famous personalities, or just a male acquaintance within their circle whose appeal is strong enough.

CASE HISTORY: Mango's mother had divorced in Turkey when Mango was very young and had left her in her grandfather's custody. She emigrated to Switzerland with her older daughter to look for work. Mango loved her grandfather and even adored him. Having been spoiled by him as a young girl, her relationship changed dramatically when she became a teenager. Suddenly, his largesse turned into strictness. The freedom she had enjoyed during childhood turned into rigid control. In his eyes, she had become a young woman, and another code of conduct was expected of her from now on. Mango, however, wouldn't accept her grandfather's restrictions. She abruptly left her homeland to join her mother and sister in Switzerland, thereby avoiding confrontation with him.

Once there, she met a young Swiss man who pursued and courted her. Since dating without getting married was not accepted in her native culture, her mother urged her to get married. Mango gave in, though he was not her heart's desire. For a few years, she led a very unhappy marriage and was hospitalized several times with the diagnosis of schizophrenia. During her psychosis, she always clung to the delusion that she was the mistress of Michael Douglas. Whenever she felt particularly unhappy, she heard his voice and conversed with him. This brought her consolation and relief in her unhappy marriage.

FOLLOW-UP AND COMMENTARY: Mango's marriage ultimately ended in divorce. The delusions of love had helped her to get out of the troubled relationship. Later, when talking about her childhood in Turkey, she thought of her grandfather, whom she still worshipped with nostalgia. She regretted having left him in a hurry, and maintained an ambivalent relationship with both countries, Turkey, her motherland, and Switzerland, her chosen homeland. She remained entangled in the detachment conflict from her divorced parents as well as her grandfather and was not free to pursue a relationship of her own choice. For years, she had sent part of her income to her relatives in Turkey.

But she finally settled in Switzerland and bought an apartment with her savings. As a recipient of social assistance, she was repeatedly prompted to sell it in order to be able to apply for social benefits. However, it was the only thing she owned. She successfully argued that her apartment reflected her roots and insisted that this was her safe haven. As her therapist, I strongly supported her position.

Sometimes, doctors end up as objects of affection or father figures as part of their patients' love delusions. Especially gynecologists are prone to being confronted with love delusions of unhappy schizophrenia patients, but psychiatrists are also possible targets: a young schizophrenia patient one day appeared naked at the front door of her male psychiatrist late at night.

Disguised sexual abuse

Sexual abuse in childhood is a traumatic event for a female that reaches far into her adult life. Moreover, it is often handled as a taboo in the family of the abused individual and thus hard to unearth in a therapeutic process. The secret of the sexual trauma sometimes can only be lifted on a meta-level in the form of a delusional psychotic state at an advanced age.

> **CASE HISTORY:** Olga had been sexually abused by an older boy as a child at an affiliated institution run by her parents. All these years, she had kept her secret; she had never told her parents nor her husband. Except for her negative body image – she felt that her labia were too large – she successfully repressed the sexual trauma.
> She trained as a nurse, got married and had three children. As they got older, she enlisted in a training program for biographical work. When she had to delve into her own past and started to write down her childhood years, she suddenly dug up her repressed sexual encounter of her

childhood. She felt compelled to write day and night. Initially, she suffered severe headaches that could not be alleviated by any pain medication, although she had gone to several renowned specialists. Then, she became psychotic. Olga developed the delusion of being related to the twelfth-century German Benedictine abbess Hildegard von Bingen. Noises in the radiators of her house and in the telephone handset were signs that she should continue writing down all her thoughts and associations.

COMMENTARY: Olga's father had a physical disability. As a little child, she had always felt sorry for him. The prestigious institution, mostly run by her mother, was another factor that prevented her from mentioning the sexual abuse. She felt protective towards her parents.

Up to the point at which she began her biographical work, she had kept the traumatic incident under wraps. She took full responsibility for the sexual encounter with this boy and made her large labia accountable for the abuse. Even now, she was unable to be reproachful towards her parents for not having protected her well enough. It was unimaginable for her to blame them. As a new moral reference, she called upon Hildegard von Bingen, or Saint Hildegard, in her delusional psychosis to come and help her with her childhood story, exonerating her parents to save them from being publicly shamed.

She had to spare her parents and felt compelled to support their fight for financial survival even though she was a sexually abused child. She shielded them from losing their livelihood on account of the sexual abuse, which had happened in their institution. Only in adulthood, as a mother of three grown-up children, while working on her biography, could her childhood trauma surface through psychosis – that was the price she had to pay.

Somatic delusions

The adaptation strategies of persons with schizophrenia are not entirely restricted to the psyche, they can also be projected onto the body. The involvement of the body in the delusional process is called *somatic hallucinations*. The object of projection, the body, thus conveys the emotional state of emergency through body language, as is the case with psychosomatic illnesses. A schizophrenia patient, for instance, who constantly felt criticized by her family, often complained that her body had shifted and no longer felt the same. Once her mental and emotional condition had improved, her body was suddenly put in order again.

Somatic hallucinations often occur in sexually inexperienced young men. Somatic medicine thus deals with the genital area of these men. The physical delusions are then treated by means of somatic medicine, meaning the patients seek help for inflammation of the prostate, urethritis or inguinal hernias. Antibiotics are prescribed, examinations are arranged, and surgery is performed on even the smallest of inguinal hernias presented by delusional patients.

> **CASE HISTORY:** After his first unsuccessful love at eighteen, Peter was admitted to a psychiatric clinic in a psychotic state and was diagnosed with schizophrenia. During his stay, he developed the delusion that a male nurse had caused him to develop a hernia because he had blocked his path. He was operated on twice for a small inguinal hernia. After the operation, he was in a panic because he thought that someone had severed his spermatic cord during the operation. He was constantly plagued by the fear that he was no longer capable of having children. He consulted numerous urologists and requested surgical reports to confirm that his spermatic cord was still intact. When masturbating, which he did occasionally, he felt that he was constantly being watched by his neighbors and was haunted by strong feelings

of guilt. He never entered a relationship with a female again. He had developed chronic schizophrenia.

COMMENTARY: Peter's delusions can be interpreted as a strategy to protect himself from the abyss of absolute inferiority and covert jealousy. He thought that everyone was watching him and saw potential rivals everywhere. He accused a male nurse of having caused him to develop a hernia; his doctor of having castrated him by severing his spermatic cord; and the neighbors of intentional annoyance by making love at night or watching him when he was masturbating on the toilet. On walks, he always carried a cane in case somebody was to get in his way.

All these elaborate delusional constructions are mental simulations on a new level of reference and reveal how much mental work is invested in schizophrenia in order to restore and maintain emotional balance.

> Delusional ideas are systematic mental constructions within an inclusive logic. They only function within closed cognitive systems and do not process any stimuli coming from the real world other than including it into the delusional system. Any kind of new psychosocial learning is thereby being obstructed.

The illness of schizophrenia, unsurprisingly, also occurs in intellectual families who do a lot of brainwork. The problem-solving strategies of these families are on a cognitive level rather than a practical one by trial and error. Problems are primarily dealt with through reasoning and not through actions.

Individuals who develop schizophrenia quite often possess above-average intelligence. Some experts even see a direct correlation between high intelligence and schizophrenia. They continue to be convinced that above-average intelligence is a prerequisite for developing paranoid schizophrenia. Nobel Prize winner John Forbes Nash, who was portrayed in the movie "A Beautiful Mind" (2001), is a well-known example of this hypothesis.

Replacing delusions with actions

The over-functioning of the prefrontal lobe, which leads to a spinning of thoughts in the cortex, may, in some cases, be halted by means of concrete action in the early pre-psychotic phase. If patients follow the clear instructions issued by a therapist specializing in problem-solving strategies, the development of full-blown schizophrenia can sometimes be prevented, as in the following case.

> **CASE HISTORY:** Ueli was an intelligent young man who had successfully completed his training at medical school. He worked as a doctor on the emergency ward for one year. However, he did not like the stressful atmosphere at the hospital and considered pursuing a second degree in dentistry. Ye, he still remained ambivalent, thinking day and night about what his professional future should look like. He created extensive checklists to determine where he would find most satisfaction. He gradually slipped into a pre-psychotic state. At this point, his mother asked me for help.
> **THERAPY AND COMMENTARY:** During therapy, it transpired that Ueli had never had an intimate relationship with a woman. During medical school, he was too busy with his studies to find time for it, though would have liked to have had a girlfriend. Therefore, I gave him the therapeutic task of learning how to approach women, which he dutifully fulfilled by writing the same romantic letter to all the women he had met. He eventually started a relationship with the woman who had reacted best to his advances. Ueli was overjoyed at his success. I also gave him advice for his career planning. Through concrete guidance, and putting the therapeutic task into action, his restless contempla-

tion regarding a suitable solution was interrupted, and his slide into psychosis had been halted. His newfound relationship lasted for several years. Unfortunately, his partner became terminally ill and died. But at that time, he was stable enough, and did not slip into psychosis. Some years later, when his career run into difficulties again, Ueli called me for help. Once again, he couldn't stop his brain from spinning endlessly, thus preventing him from sleeping. Meanwhile, he had completed his second program of medical training in dentistry and was considering an academic career. However, he felt bullied in his workplace and was unsure if he could withstand the tough competition at the university. I once more gave him very practical advice. Having his precision-seeking talent in mind, I told him not to pursue an academic career but rather seek employment in a dental practice to gain more practical experience in his profession, and thereby also become more rooted in life.

Several years later, he called me again – this time not in a crisis. He just wanted to tell me that he had followed my advice. Now he had settled, working as a dentist, and was very satisfied with his situation of being his own boss. Tackling his problems solely on a cognitive meta-level was no longer necessary for Ueli. At this point, he had acquired enough professional experience and was able to find his own way without therapeutic support or coaching. He had realized his ambition of achieving recognition and appreciation by choosing to settle down professionally in a highly prestigious resort. He had managed to find a work-life balance.

CASE HISTORY: Judith was a petite young woman with an impatient temperament and a sensitive emotional disposition. After passing her final exams in high school, she didn't succeed in her studies, which caused her parents great disappointment, and thus stress for Judith. They had expected her to pursue an academic career and be successful with it.

Her mother, who was a professional musician, inundated Judith with advice. Her father, an engineer, silently withdrew in helplessness. The bright future of their daughter, their last glimmer of hope for a better future which both had banked on, had faded. Moreover, it came to the fore that the relationship between the parents had been at an impasse for quite some time.

Judith on her part started to develop psychotic symptoms with a phobia of knives. She was scared to even go near a knife, plagued by the compulsive notion that she might grab it and lunge at someone. Her family doctor diagnosed psychosis and prescribed her medication. Because of her delusional obsession, she could neither study nor look for a job. Even daily tasks were a challenge for her at that point.

FOLLOW-UP AND THERAPY: Judith was referred to me for treatment by her parents. I supported her in moving to another city and looking for a job in order to become independent of her parents, which she successfully accomplished.

When we touched on the issue of the knives in one of the therapy sessions, I gave her the task of verbalizing in plain terms her aggressive feelings during situations of conflict. She followed my advice, be it when something bothered her with her boyfriend, or at work. She learned to assert herself and defend her own position. At work, she distanced herself from co-workers she had some problems with. From then on, the fear of knives disappeared, and she could discontinue her medication.

COMMENTARY: In Judith's case, the preoccupation with knives was an expression of severe impatience in a young woman whose aggressive feelings would immediately flare up for the slightest reason. Judith was raised in a middle-class family in which there were few outlets for her violent temper. Her family regarded such behaviour – especially in a girl – as inappropriate. Within her family, she had no choice but to suppress her angry temper. On top of this, she felt burdened by chronic parental conflict, which Judith was unable to do anything about. So, she had to move out of her parental home to gain breathing space, to express her temper and develop her personality.

With my support, Judith had moved to the French-speaking part of Switzerland, where she found work and became financially independent. She later began her studies, following in the footsteps of her mother, but later tended towards the natural sciences like her father. Finally, she pursued a course of study independent of her parents' talents. She ended up finding her own way and thus no longer required therapy.

TREATMENT

From Mistakes to Rules

Forty-five years ago, Christian Müller, an acclaimed expert in schizophrenia, told me in all honesty that a psychotherapist could actually only treat one single individual with schizophrenia during his entire professional career. With this in mind, providing psychotherapy for schizophrenia patients might seem an impossible task for professionals – and rightly so.

Treating schizophrenia can be puzzling indeed. Doctors of schizophrenia patients are often confronted with a fascinating variety of theatrical behavior that can easily make them lose sight of the bigger picture. Presented with a whole host of symptoms that accompany the illness, it is perhaps not surprising that mental health professionals are at a loss as to how best to treat schizophrenia patients – as well as their families – and retreat to drug treatment only.

Therapy as a learning process

Systemic family therapy, however, has adopted a different approach. New insights into the biographies of the individuals who suffer from schizophrenia, as demonstrated in the outline of their case histories earlier, expand our understanding of the illness and offer us new options for treating these patients, involving a continuous, attentive learning process not only for the patients and their families but for the therapists as well.

The art of therapy with schizophrenia patients can only be learned by constantly reinventing it anew – as Piaget once said: "Apprendre c'est réinventer". Maintaining a learning attitude and adapting the art of therapeutic intervention as part of an evolving process while the family system is going through the necessary changes, means that treatment of schizophrenia has the potential to be quite promising. Learning from therapeutic mistakes thus turns into a vital method of improving the art of therapy. With this in mind, here are some words of consolation to mental health professionals who make mistakes (as we all do):

> Every therapeutic mistake makes the system reveal itself a little bit more clearly.

Anxiety is not helpful

Acute schizophrenia is a functional disorder of the brain. However, the development and the course of the illness largely depend on environmental factors such as the family system, the larger social community like school and work, and last but not least, the medical profession responsible for handling the patient and the family. Therefore, the therapeutic approach to schizophrenia patients and their families plays an extremely important role for the outcome of this illness.

In contrast to physical illness, schizophrenia clearly demonstrates that the therapeutic environment can have an enormous impact on the course of the treatment. An anxious therapeutic attitude has a detrimental impact on the outcome, in that it is often a negative self-fulfilling prophecy and therefore not at all helpful.

An overcautious approach in therapy, failing to trust the developmental potential of individuals with schizophrenia, puts them in a helpless, passive position. Intrusive and overprotective behavior, on the other hand, often reminds patients of their patronizing fathers and anxious, overinvolved mothers, and may lead to regressive withdrawal, or to aggressive defensive outbursts. Consistently self-assured yet careful attentiveness on the part of the therapists, however, can enhance the patients' will to trust themselves, and motivates them to learn during the treatment process. Therapists should always bear in mind the consequences of their first encounter with families of schizophrenia and ADHD:

> "You never get a second chance to make a first impression" is a rule when encountering people with schizophrenia.

Therapists must ensure that the initial impression they make is one of self-confidence and calmness, since the threshold for a startled response is very low for the patients as well as their family members, both of whom are typically highly sensitive to their environment. If patients experience more agitation, they react with an immediate flight response, and the therapy ends before it has even started.

Symptom-hunting is futile

When it comes to treating individuals with schizophrenia, the medical profession is primarily geared towards hunting for symptoms. In schizophrenia, however, treating only the symptoms is nowhere near enough, or can even prove to be detrimental. It does not lead to sustainable improvement and never to full recovery. The bewildering symptoms of schizophrenia represent solely a distraction and concealment of the core issue of underlying problems in the family system. From a systemic point of view, treating only the social symptoms of the illness is entirely futile; it may be done as an acute intervention, yet as a long-term treatment procedure, it is not helpful. A useful piece of systemic advice is therefore:

- Always ask yourself what the symptoms of schizophrenia might reveal about the family system's dysfunction.
- Use a genogram of at least three generations as a vital tool for deciphering the family system's entanglements and their dysfunctional connection with the patient concerned.

Relationship versus medical model

Medical health professionals, including psychiatrists, have a hard time letting go of treating the symptoms, instead of exploring and searching for conflictual relationships in the family system. Meanwhile, psychologists and other non-medical health professionals tend to be more relationship-oriented. However, if they defend the patients as poor victims of their environment, they are immediately dragged into the dysfunctional family system themselves, triangulated by patients and parents, thereby further postponing – or even actively preventing – the natural process of detachment. Therapists should thus go by the following advice:

> Looking beyond symptoms towards a systemic approach is a prerequisite for successful treatment of families with schizophrenia.

When ordinary logic fails

Even the most experienced therapists are sometimes unable to prevent being impressed by their patients' unanticipated irrational behavior, distorted perception, and delusional hyped-up thinking, and thus apply reason as a means of bringing them back to reality. The parents, too, are tempted to use all rational arguments at their disposal to help their sick child. Be that as it may, individuals in a delusional state stubbornly defend their delusional constructs since they represent the only security they have at that point. They are sticking to their own interpretation of reality and bizarre ideas no matter how distorted they might be. They have their own *para-logic*.

Regardless of how plausible and reasonable the arguments by medical professionals and parents are presented, schizophrenic perception and stress-related paranoid ideation cannot be changed by rational means.

Indeed, all well-considered attempts to persuade schizophrenia patients out of their delusional, paranoid system into orderly, conventional logic will only worsen their condition. In case of schizophrenia, emotions dictate the patients' reasoning. Luc Ciompi described this phenomenon in his book on *affect-logic* – it's not reasoning that dominates the emotions, it's the other way around: emotions dominate reasoning. Therefore, I would regard the following advice as crucial:

> At first, calming down the emotional state of the family rather than just correcting the family member's irrational behavior and paralogical thinking is paramount.

Abstain from activism

A statement commonly heard from the parents of schizophrenia offspring is: "It cannot go on like this – something needs to be done right away!" This call for help repeatedly leads professionals to take rapid action, assuming the patient is in danger. As a result, they come up with concrete proposals for immediate changes to be made in the family system. The parents' demand for an urgent fix may give the impression that the family system is ready for a change. However, therapists should remind themselves that this is not (always) the case.

> Schizophrenia is a chronic disorder that keeps reinventing itself within a closed family system. There is no fast cure for it, nor is a quick approach effective when trying to cure this chronic disorder.

The impatient begging draws professionals into the family's vicious cycle of *functional helplessness*. Initial therapeutic approaches should therefore mainly consist of targeted questioning. However, if these questions are met with resistance, it must be read as a sign that parents are uneasy and feel threatened by questioning. Resistance of the family should not to be interpreted as a lack of cooperation. A deeper empathic understanding of the family's dilemma is needed at that moment. Suggestions for change cannot be made until the family system has calmed down and gained confidence in the therapist and the therapeutic approach.

> The therapeutic role is one of a trusted coach: professionals act as change agents for the family system.

Potential for change lies with the family system

A common medical approach to schizophrenia is the treatment of the affected family member. From a systemic point of view, however, it is the least advisable to direct all therapeutic interventions exclusively at the most vulnerable and weakest member of the family system. The focus of coaching should rather be on the strongest members of the family system, the parents. Such interventions are considerably more effective and more efficient.

Once parents have recognized how they affect their sick child and accept the need to change their own behavior, and even notice initial, positive results, considerable first steps in therapy are achieved. The illness of schizophrenia, which had the appearance of being a seemingly hopeless mental disorder, suddenly becomes a state of mind that can be influenced, offering hope of change for the better for both the identified patient and the entire family. To become a successful systemic therapist, you must be convinced of the following:

> The most significant therapeutic coaching in the treatment of schizophrenia is achieved through active cooperation with the parents. As a natural outcome, the sick family member will be able to develop, thus becoming the embodiment of a successful therapy.

Validating hardship

Parents want what is best for their children. In that respect, parents of schizophrenia sufferers are no exception. They often go to considerable extremes at great expense to help their sick child. Year after year, they have been trying to master their difficult family situation, always based on the strict principles of their families of origin, without asking for help.

When parents finally go for therapy, they first and foremost expect acceptance of, and understanding for, their previous efforts. If a therapist homes in on them too quickly, they do not feel valued for their long-standing emotional investment or their suffering. Therapists who fail to show empathic understanding and push for change too hastily without considering the parents' hardship and long-standing investment in their sick child are likely to encounter resistance. Thus, the parents reject any proposal that does not primarily focus on their sick child. All therapeutic suggestions should therefore follow the rule:

> Address the family system in its current situation, and not where you would like it to be, before making any intervention or suggestions for change.

Emotional turmoil

Families with schizophrenia quickly plunge into emotional turmoil when new problems and stresses emerge. The affected family member, as well as the entire family system, is marked by increased reactivity and a pronounced tendency towards escalation. Therefore, therapeutic presence and rapid crisis intervention is needed at such a moment. Leaving families to their own devices amidst such an impulsive storm of personality disorder can often result in another bout of acute psychosis with concomitant destructive interactions within the family system. I call this phenomenon the chaotic escalation of an *emotional turbo-effect*.

The emotional storm in the family, which prompts an *emotional monster wave of acute psychosis* in the patient, would not be dangerous as such if it is dealt with immediately. On-call availability in such emergencies and an offer to quickly restore order by telephone calm down the family's anxiety. For this reason, therapists of schizophrenia families should always stick to the following principle:

> Keep an eye on emerging unrest within the family system and respond to any potential crisis promptly but calmly. This is very reassuring for the family.

Effective therapeutic coaching

A neutral and non-partisan attitude in the conflictual family relationship puzzle is essential. It helps the systemic therapist to assert their independence whenever parents or patients attempt to force them to take their side so as to increase their power. Acting as an advocate for the affected child or siding with one parent in the partner conflict will make it impossible to provide effective therapeutic coaching for the family system.

> Family therapists have to adopt an *attitude of multidirectional partiality*, as Boszormenyi-Nagy calls it, which involves empathizing with each member, and acknowledging his or her viewpoint and position within the family conflict.

Don't cut the umbilical cord too soon

The symbiotic mother-child relationship has evolved in mammals to secure the survival of the young and preserve the species from extinction. In times of crisis and reduced resources, it takes priority over the partner relationship.

In families with schizophrenia, mothers usually have an extreme symbiotic relationship with their child patient, which lasts far beyond puberty and long into adulthood, sometimes remaining forever. Therapists are often tempted to cut this symbiotic mother-child relationship as quickly as possible since they consider it *pathogenic,* hence the term *pathogenic mother* as formulated by Frieda Fromm-Reichmann. However, mother and schizophrenia child resist such therapeutic interventions by all available means, and the treatment immediately turns into a power struggle between mother-child symbiosis and therapeutic interventions aimed at change. The dynamics of the mother-child symbiosis are biologically so significant and enduring, that the therapist almost always loses this power struggle. The intensity of the symbiosis and its dynamic is an extremely delicate matter and must always be handled with great care, never be cut off forcibly and, most notably, never at the beginning of therapy. Therefore, therapists are advised to do the following:

> Always gain the mother's consent before attempting a therapeutic change of the mother-child symbiosis.

Criticism of therapy – vital feedback

The family's questioning of the therapeutic instructions, and their criticism of the therapist's approach, should always be interpreted as a wish for participation in the shaping of the therapeutic process. Professionals might perceive it as resistance and become irritated, sometimes even angry. However, the family's questioning should be regarded as a request to review the process and rethink the timing, or even delay the interventions. Accordingly, the therapeutic procedure should be adapted to the family's needs. Therapists should not feel personally offended by criticism from the patient's family but rather look at it as a helpful feedback strategy:

> Professionals don't always know what is best. Listening carefully to the family system and cooperating with it is therefore helpful.

Unfulfilled parental expectations

Parental opposition during therapy frequently masks problems usually stemming from the families of origin. It is therefore worthwhile directing the therapeutic attention at the family history and the underlying unresolved attachments.

Fathers and mothers may silently harbor unfulfilled ambitions and wishes, which can have a debilitating effect on a child's maturation. It is therefore important to ask parents about their hidden career ambitions and unfulfilled dreams.

Even if these dreams might seem trivial in the light of acute schizophrenia, unfulfilled desires are often an issue and negatively affect the family's emotional development. Once these issues come to light, therapeutic interventions may enable transformation more easily, and help to develop towards healthier functioning:

Once parents become aware of their unfulfilled potential and own up to their hidden dreams, they accept therapeutic help more readily, and the family system can once again continue to make progress.

The Role of Systemic Therapy

How does systems therapy work?

Systems theory has its origins in the field of physics and was later used in psychiatry, particularly with respect to family systems. Schizophrenia research was one of the first areas in human medicine to use systems theory. Psychiatric researchers and scientists from other fields hoped to gain a better understanding of the illness of schizophrenia, and thus be able to develop more effective treatment methods. Enthusiastic systemic therapists in the USA even believed that they would be able to heal schizophrenia within a few therapeutic sessions.

In traditional medicine, psychiatry included, all the therapeutic methods address the symptoms first and foremost. The family system as a whole is by and large disregarded, or only comes into play at a much later stage. Furthermore, in psychiatric hospitals, the anxious parents are primarily viewed as a disturbing factor in the treatment program of the patient and are therefore often excluded from the therapeutic process.

In systemic therapy, however, the approach to symptoms and worried parents is completely different. Each clinical presentation, whether mental or physical in nature, is not treated exclusively on a symptom level. Instead, the illness is always interpreted within a broader context, and the treatment focuses on the entire family system. Thus, the family system is analyzed to determine how it may contribute to the illness and perpetuate the disorder, or how it could provide help. Thus, the systemic approach consists of providing a number of vital ways to tap the resources of the family and other helpers whenever possible during the therapeutic process.

> From a systemic point of view, parental changes in behavior are far more effective and efficient than any therapeutic attempt at controlling the schizophrenic symptoms of the family member.

Systems therapy – a resource-based method

Families with members who suffer from schizophrenia are often characterized by unresolved issues that are passed on from generation to generation in relatively closed family systems, a finding demonstrated in many of the case histories described previously. Although intergenerational problems bind family members together, they also result in their being sealed off from their surroundings. Many of the family members experience *functional helplessness*, especially the fathers – as described by Bowen – even when they are high achievers in their professional lives.

Parents, as a first reaction, often show strong resistance to the process of change that therapists try to induce using systemic therapy. Guilt feelings lead them to fear and struggle against suggestions for modification, which manifests itself in irritability, skepticism, and sometimes even outright aggression towards the therapist. Despite their deep distress, they find it difficult to even begin to imagine any change taking place within the family, cynical of systems therapy and the chances of its having positive effect on their child affected by schizophrenia. They point out time and again that it is not they who are sick and in need of treatment, but rather their child.

However, parents are not the only ones who harbor doubts about systems therapy. The indirect systemic approach, which does not primarily address the symptom of the illness but works with the entire family system, is diametrically opposed to standard medical procedures, as pointed out earlier. For many mental health professionals, it seems strange and downright implausible that schizophrenia can be cured by working with the family system.

To introduce the concept that schizophrenia is a systemic illness, and to overcome initial doubts, I therefore propose that therapists take the following approach:

- Provide an overview of the state of the art to the parents during the first meeting after having taken the genogram of three generations.
- Introduce the integrative process management of therapy.
- Explain how all stakeholders will be taken into consideration.
- Include family members and other important persons such as employers, teachers, social workers, as well as other therapists who are already in contact with the family system.
- Bear in mind that they all influence the course of the illness.
- Keep in mind that the family system, and all those persons connected with it, are part of the therapeutic process – they may have a positive or a negative influence on the outcome of treatment.

Parents as a resource – not an obstacle

There are quite a few parents who are extremely motivated and eager to learn something new and become engaged in the change process right from the beginning. Contrary to all those who resist, they voluntarily seek help and want to know from the therapist how they can improve themselves to facilitate the recovery of their mentally ill child. By disclosing their own background, they expedite the process of therapy to the benefit of the patient.

Parents who prepare questions before the next therapy session and search for insights of their own accord can thereby considerably speed up the therapeutic process of change. With this resource-oriented approach, schizophrenia patients can take their own first steps necessary for recovery.

Accordingly, the systems therapy approach to schizophrenia requires cooperation on part of the parents in order to be successful. A willingness to learn, and an unbiased, open attitude towards the therapeutic process is crucial. Parents are therefore encouraged to actively participate in solving intergenerational problems that still bind them together with their families of origin. If parents are willing and able to reflect on their behavior, they will initiate change for the entire family system. Although they might temporarily feel under pressure, they will undoubtedly benefit in the long term, as the change process is beneficial for all family members.

Successful systemic therapy requires, above all, that parents understand and fully realize that they are in total control of themselves in the procedure. Parents know their families better than anyone else. They are the ones who set the pace and timing of the therapeutic process of change. Parents are in charge and are therefore obliged to take responsibility for all their actions – not the therapist.

Another vital requirement is that parents are not allowed to pass the responsibility for any new behavior onto the therapist. If parents are not yet ready for a particular step proposed by the therapist, they are encouraged to say so, and to ask questions about it. Systemic therapy is a learning process that requires time and patience from both the parents and the therapist, as well as openness and a willingness to learn.

Systemic therapy is also a tool for cooperation that treats parents on equal terms. Consent is necessary before proceeding with new interventions, and it is crucial to remain patient even if parents do not always follow the therapeutic advice they are given. Non-compliance and rule violations are natural responses and have to be accepted by the therapist. They should use them to review the therapeutic interventions in order to be able to improve them. Furthermore, systemic therapy accepts the parents' momentary situation and position in their family system. Systemic therapy is not meant to rush the therapeutic process; any process of change moves at its own pace.

Loyalty conflict – fear of what?

Adults often view their personal development as having been successfully completed and therefore see no further need to update their emotional knowledge and to learn from failures. This type of attitude hinders parents of schizophrenia sufferers from reflecting on their own family system and scrutinizing deeply engrained behavioral patterns inherited from their family of origin. As a consequence, parents often have a tendency to resist therapeutic interventions for change since they dread breaking their loyalty towards their parents.

For therapists, it is therefore important to consider that parents do not resist proposed interventions by reason of disobedience but rather out of a deep-seated fear. But fear of what? Do they fear what is in store for them? They have mastered many difficult situations in their lives but the confrontation with their own parents is often an insurmountable challenge. Unresolved issues of attachment to the family of origin carry big risks. However, if not dug up, the deep loyalty conflict within the family system threatens to endanger further progress. Or could it be that parents resist simply out of habit? Habits endure because they are rooted in tradition. All these questions and more arise. Going against the unyielding iron clamp of loyalty towards their own parents is a task laden with anxiety. The fear that the family system might distance themselves completely if they break their loyalty to their parents is immense. They are tremendously afraid of following their own individual path, along which they may begin to question their parents' principles and belief systems, which, in turn, might result in losing their approval.

> The resistance to therapeutic interventions should always be regarded as an inherent right to self-defense.

Attachment problems in family cycles which get passed on to the next generation without ever being dealt with prevent the family system from evolving. The obligation to remain loyal to one's own parents has costly side effects. It hampers change and adaptation to new situations and gradually shuts off the family from outside influences. The rumblings of an entrenched, suppressed emotional disturbance ultimately create mental upheavals, running through the multi-generational family system, producing black sheep and drop-outs as well as mental disorder in the form of *emotional monster waves* in the most susceptible family member who finally receives the diagnosis of schizophrenia.

"Yes, but..." – resistance

Therapeutic suggestions for inducing change addressed at parents of schizophrenia patients inevitably prompt latent feelings of guilt. Initially, they often resist any recommendations for behavioral modifications on the assumption that if they accept change, it implies that they have done something wrong during their child's upbringing. "Yes, but..." is usually both their answer and their predominant attitude. They begin to explain that they had probably not fully clarified what it meant to have a sick child. Even though they suffer tremendously under the difficult circumstances of their child's schizophrenia, they nevertheless defend the status quo. Having to admit that despite their best intentions, they made grave mistakes is almost unbearable for them. They prefer to remain powerful in their familiar state of *functional helplessness,* and thereby cannot envision new ways of behaving because they resist having to confront their feelings of guilt. Smoldering conflicts within the parents' relationship, and those within their families-of-origin, remain buried and can therefore not be tackled with the help of systemic therapy.

> The therapeutic change process cannot start as long as the parents avoid dealing with their own feelings of guilt.

CASE HISTORY: Marcel was diagnosed with schizophrenia in adolescence. After being discharged from the psychiatric clinic, he was referred to social psychiatric services for aftercare. As the doctor in charge, I called his parents in for an interview. The father, a well-dressed gentleman in a pinstripe suit, immediately took a reproachful attitude towards me. He claimed that even though I was in charge, I apparently had not the slightest idea of how to approach the suffering of his son. He complained that I seemed to be utterly clueless about the seriousness of his illness, trying to cover up my own inability and ignorance by making them, the parents, feel guilty.

FOLLOW-UP AND COMMENTARY: I was unable to form a viable therapeutic alliance with Marcel's parents. The father cut off the relationship with his son, and the mother remained helpless. Marcel was living under appalling conditions, completely neglected. He developed chronic schizophrenia.

Long after – I heard no news about Marcel for many years – a well-groomed man appeared in my office with a book in his hand. It was Marcel. He proudly presented me his autobiography and dedicated it to my library in the waiting room with the remark that it might be helpful for other patients. His book narrated in powerful terms the calamity of his life, which might benefit others in similar emotional circumstances and prove that they were not alone.

Although Marcel had not kept in contact with me for many years, he nevertheless returned to where his life had gone astray. In his book, Marcel had shown that he had found his way and indirectly dealt with his deceased parents, who had rejected him at times of crisis in adolescence. He had documented his ordeal to hand a lifeline to others in similar circumstances; he had achieved self-integration by writing down his life in a book.

There are many schizophrenia patients with appalling life stories who are unable to find words to express their psychosis. However, I am of the firm belief that writing down their biography as a coherent narrative reconstruction is a powerful therapeutic tool for people with recurring recollection of trauma and can aid emotional self-integration.

Blind obedience

Blind obedience of a family in systemic therapy is just as unhelpful in the process of initiating change as total resistance. If parents show blind obedience without reflecting on whether the proposed interventions are appropriate or not, they don't take full responsibility for their actions as suggested by the therapist. They ignore the possible consequences of the intervention and place all responsibility with the therapist. As a consequence, the therapist must bear all the blame in case something goes wrong.

> **CASE HISTORY:** The therapist of Sven's mother gave her strict instructions to cut the umbilical cord to her son and stop responding to his calls for help. She even demanded that the mother affix the therapist's advice to the bathroom mirror as a daily reminder. One day, Sven once again phoned his mother in a desperate emotional state. He told her he was haunted by suicidal thoughts and begged her to come and pick him up. Sticking to her therapist's advice, she refused. Later that day, Sven was found hanging from a fruit tree.
>
> **COMMENTARY:** Sven's mother was heartbroken. She had put her trust in her therapist and followed all the instructions – unquestioned, and now she had to pay for it with the death of her son. She complained bitterly that if it had been up to her, she would have picked him up, yet she had ignored her inner voice and neglected her responsibility because of her blind obedience. From then on, Sven's mother no longer trusted therapists or medical staff, and she was full of resentment and

reproach. Deep in her mind, she was convinced it was the therapist's advice that had caused the tragedy.

> Blind obedience can be toxic.

CASE HISTORY: Prior to a large family gathering, Raphael's family consulted a group of renowned family systems therapists for advice in dealing with their son, who suffered schizophrenia, during an upcoming family reunion. These therapists worked exclusively with the psycho-educational model. They instructed the family not to specifically focus on the identified patient but rather ignore him in order to avoid singling him out as a special member of the group. All family members followed these instructions faithfully. Much to the family's – and the therapists' – consternation, Raphael committed suicide during the family gathering.

COMMENTARY: Here, we have a classic example of how blind obedience can lead to disaster if the special situation of the schizophrenia sufferer and their family is not considered by the therapist. The instruction not to focus on Raphael during the family gathering was far too abrupt a behavioral change for Raphael. He could not cope with this sudden neglect on the part of all the family members. In stark contrast to their overprotective attitude to his illness before the family reunion, it came as an unbearable shock to him that every family member had suddenly abandoned him.

> Parents always have to be reminded that they have to take full responsibility for all suggested therapeutic steps. They should never accept any proposed therapeutic prescription for change if they cannot fully stand behind it.

Fake consent

Parents who do not fully stand behind the recommended processes of change, but go ahead with them anyway, may be able to hide their reservations from the therapist – but they can never mislead their family member who has schizophrenia. Patients will sometimes mockingly point up their parents' misgivings regarding interventions by asking if they were instructed by their therapist to behave in this new way. Thus, they devalue their parents' position as well as the therapist's competence. By triangulating parents and therapist, they assume the position of the *obsessed diplomat,* expose the parents' lack of inner conviction, seize control of the family system and thereby block the therapeutic process of change altogether.

Parents' hidden reservations may even be dangerous for a family member with schizophrenia. In the case of *Sven,* pseudo-changes in parental behavior seemed like a betrayal of the family tradition. His mother's therapist had requested of her that she treat him like an adult family member. The reminder on the mirror should have encouraged her to let him go. However, deep down she believed otherwise. Most probably, she was not convinced that he would be able to live on his own, thereby undermining his search for autonomy. *Sven* must have sensed that his mother did not trust him to make his own way. By calling his mother for support, he was probably even trying to help her overcome her dilemma. Suicide was his only way out of the ambivalent symbiotic mother-child relationship.

> Pretended parental consent to a therapeutic step is ineffective at best and can be detrimental at worst.

Parents who don't agree with the therapeutic suggestions should be even encouraged to voice their disagreement in therapy sessions, and therapists should always listen to them.

Guided family groups

Guided family groups, in my experience, are an effective way of initiating a change process in parental behavior towards their offspring with schizophrenia.

For over thirty years, I have conducted regular family groups for parents and other relatives who have a family member with schizophrenia. Several parents receive coaching in a supportive group climate, and thereby participate in a learning process in the presence of others who are in similar situations. This has a motivating effect on all participants and induces an atmosphere of learning, even though not all of them may participate actively in every meeting. Some parents are given concrete advice and suggestions as well as answers to their specific questions, while others participate as listeners; they are not required to expose themselves if they are not yet ready to do so.

In one group session, the usual procedure involves three sets of parents telling their story of how they experience daily difficulties with their family member who has schizophrenia. Then I encourage them to ask one very specific question about the most pressing issue that troubles them. I answer their specific question as clearly and precisely as possible. Afterwards, the other members of the group are invited to put forward additional questions or suggestions on the same or similar topics, which I also address as explicitly as possible. From then on, I introduce general principles and rules of conduct for handling their identified patient and provide a theoretical summary of the problems discussed in the session, intended as food for thought for all the participants but not necessarily as an instruction to change their behavior.

Within these family groups, all participants are in a particularly comfortable learning position to observe newly acquired and successfully applied reaction patterns and behavior, as well as the more unfortunate and harmful responses, which lead to more of the same pathology. They can draw their own conclusions on situations and behavior they have witnessed without having to expose themselves. The motivation for change is indirectly generated by watching other families within the group who have already progressed in their process of change. By closely monitoring other parents' learning, they gain personal insights and witness the advice given to other parents, which they may adapt to their own situation.

This type of therapeutic setting makes it easier to circumvent parental resistance, since they can stay out of the spotlight, which contrasts enormously with single-family therapy sessions, during which they are the exclusive focus of the therapist. As soon as parents are willing to reveal their own problematic family histories, they are assured that they are not alone with their concerns since they may first listen to the other participants' problems and can always get support from them.

Parents often remark that: "Even though I didn't have the opportunity to present my own story, I still learned a lot by listening and observing". Examples of similar family stories in professionally guided parents' groups are an effective and efficient learning model for families with schizophrenia. Guided by a systemic therapist, the participating parents may learn without ever feeling pressured to change. These therapeutic family groups differ greatly from sessions in which mental health professionals explain to parents the ins and outs of the illness of schizophrenia.

Therapy of marital conflict

Parents of children with schizophrenia quite often have the attitude that relationship conflicts are a private matter and don't concern their identified patient. Therefore, they find it strange and become annoyed when systemic therapists focus on their relationship. They are generally highly skeptical of interference in their couple conflict and argue that they had come to the session on account of their sick child and not for couples counselling. They especially dislike the word *family therapy* because it implies that there is something wrong with the family. They stand firm by their belief that it's only about the problem of their child's illness, and the therapy is to treat their son's or daughter's problem, not theirs.

> For successful systemic therapy with an individual who has schizophrenia, the parents must reflect on their partner relationship conflict.

In my experience, it is essential that parents who doubt the benefits of discussing partnership issues should nevertheless be motivated by the therapist to discuss conflicts within their relationship. A prerequisite is, however, that the parents have trust in the idea that gaining further insights into their own relationship issues will help improve the chances of their child's developing in positive terms. A non-judgmental therapeutic attitude towards the parents' family of origin and their unresolved attachment allows them to get started on this type of change process without being embarrassed or feeling ashamed.

Therapeutic Tasks for Parents

Pseudo-mutuality

Parenting styles that differ in subtle ways are a typical feature of parents of children with schizophrenia. From a therapeutic perspective, it is therefore neither helpful nor realistic to strive for unity in their caring approach. It is far more sensible to offer parents a viable means of working out the clear contrasts in their educational models and point out the differences in their families of origin. Such an exploration of their respective biographies helps identify the main discrepancies in their parenting methods. Cross-cultural and cross-family differences should be discussed openly without any judgement as to which practices might be better. Allowing each other to practice their parenting styles authentically may offer them a viable way to avoid covert power struggles regarding their child rearing duties. However, as soon as parents are aware of their respective partner's distinct methods, they should respect them, and never undermine each other in front of their offspring, be kind about, and understanding of, the advantages and disadvantages of each parenting style.

Important questions about differing parenting principles relating to the prolonged puberty of their schizophrenic offspring may be discussed time and again. Systems therapists who mediate between the contrasting perspectives allow each parent to air their criticisms regarding their partner's approach towards their child's illness until both parents are prepared to decenter from their own point of view and also accept their partner's approach.

Division of tasks between parents

When parents have differing attitudes on certain important issues regarding child rearing, I suggest the following to avoid the destructive trap that drags teenagers into a pathological triangle expressed in the *malignant* symptoms of *schizophrenia* in puberty:

- Divide areas of responsibility when dealing with the young adult affected by schizophrenia.
- Parents should stand firmly behind their own range of duties. Each has full responsibility within his range of competence and should not expect any support from the partner.
- When one parent is interacting with the patient, the other is not allowed to interfere, thereby weakening the partner's parenting role.
- Even if interference is made with the best of intentions, unsolicited assistance or advice ultimately always undermines the actions of the partner.
- Each may offer his or her opinion solely when asked, otherwise, the partner's educational commitment is automatically being weakened.

Fathers' task

In the division of parental tasks, fathers usually take responsibility for financial matters such as budgeting and allowances. Arranging meetings with employers as well as visits to rehabilitation institutions are also within their domain. Initiating and enforcing hospitalization against the will of the patient is also a paternal responsibility. However, it is advantageous if the fathers' decision is backed by maternal support.

Fathers must keep in mind, however, that they are dealing with young adults. In therapeutic sessions, I am often confronted with the question: "Does the patient not want to obey or are they unable to?" In other words, fathers want to know whether their child is acting like a rebellious teenager, nasty and disobedient, or whether it is due to their illness. My usual reply is that adolescents must be defiant in order to leave their parents' orbit. Moreover, an authoritarian top-down instructional style is inappropriate for youngsters in the throes of maturation and developing their own personality. If anything, I ask fathers to understand that confrontations are a chance for serious exchange, and all questions should be considered; to engage with teenagers should not be regarded as a power struggle which must be won. It is an intense exchange between father and teenager, both taking up and defending their positions.

Fathers are obliged to step out of their role as paterfamilias and accept that paternal authority, deserves to be confronted by their young adults, and fathers ought to interact with them on an equal footing. They need to take the views and criticism of their adolescents seriously – even if they seem far-fetched, visionary or downright unrealistic to them.

Mothers' task

Mothers have to keep a different role in mind when it comes to the delicate handling of adolescents affected by schizophrenia. Concerned with maintaining a conducive emotional climate within the family as well as establishing rules for orderly housekeeping and taking care of relationships, they have to make sure that social rules are respected. If adolescents refuse to follow certain established rules, mothers are responsible for repeatedly reminding them, without losing their composure, without withdrawing their love, without inducing guilt or giving up altogether. Rules are to be practiced until they are internalized. Giving straight, top-down orders to adolescents runs counter to their learning process.

It is very important that mothers are aware of and reflect on any overindulgence of their children. Unfortunately, mothers too often steer in this direction: they increase their maternal service, unable to suppress their motherly protective instincts towards their sick child. When instructed by the therapist to abstain from such behavior, they continue to manipulate their teenagers, but do so clandestinely, because the instruction goes against their grain.

Time and again, I observe this type of maternal attachment behavior in personal sessions as well as in family group sessions. The ultimate urge to take responsibility for the emotional well-being of their offspring, no matter how old they are, can be discerned in hidden attempts at interference, and in the manipulative tone of voice, as well as the small, seemingly unimportant interjections. Though it is all cleverly disguised to ensure that no one, not even the therapist or the teenager, notices. Yet this maternal type of caring behavior stands in the way of their offspring's emotional autonomy and self-reliance.

Differentiation from the family of origin

Adolescents have the task of gradually assuming responsibility for their emotions, morals, actions and their autonomous role in life. Adolescents who retreat into the autistic emotional state of schizophrenia refuse to take up these basic duties and therefore miss out on the social exchanges necessary for acquiring social skills. With their mental development thus interrupted, they are unprepared for the challenges of adult life.

The parents of children with schizophrenia themselves are often caught in an unresolved detachment process with their own family of origin, meaning that the cross-generational handover of power and responsibilities has not yet been completed. This unresolved detachment process may relate to the paternal or maternal line of the respective family of origin.

The illness of schizophrenia brings to light the flawed decision-making and problem-solving patterns between family members of all ages. This lack of competence is generally cultivated and promoted with the cover-up of paternal and maternal conflicts.

Dealing with emotional issues resulting from one's family of origin as an adult means assuming responsibility for the handling of one's own emotions. The differentiation from the family of origin is the most important step in the therapeutic process. If parents do not detach from their families of origin, they will also hinder the detachment process of their adolescent affected by schizophrenia. Mothers, for instance, must refrain from overprotective interference, fathers from authoritarian arrogance carried over from their own upbringing. By not making this distinction and preserving patterns of behavior, they encumber both their own and their adolescent's development.

Mothers and fathers must repeatedly be reminded to treat and converse with their adolescents as adults who are equally entitled to voice their opinion, be heard during discussions and have their views taken seriously. A constructive and genuinely communicative parental approach concerning topics between parents and their teenagers on an equal footing, no matter how hurtful their teenagers come across, can clear the obstacle represented by schizophrenia.

> To practice controversial exchanges at eye level with their teenager without resorting to paternalism, without devaluing their adolescent in conflict, and without manipulative interference on the part of mothers, is the most important challenge for parents towards.

The toxic triangle

Parental strife puts an enormous emotional strain on the functionalized child who is actively woven into the triangular relationship between his parents. The broker-helper activity of their child – the patient – continues to exist even if the parents get divorced. For this reason, I also encourage divorced parents to ensure they have transparent agreements in place concerning their child's therapeutic help.

CASE HISTORY: Lucius was twelve years old when his parents divorced. After the mother moved into a new apartment with her boyfriend, he lived with his sister in the apartment next door.

Lucius was a sociable boy who was popular among his peers. During adolescence, he occasionally began to smoke cannabis and eventually became addicted. He was unable to complete his apprenticeship, developed anxiety attacks, and was completely dependent on his mother's support and protection. Constantly having to comfort and appease him became too strenuous for her. Once placed in a rehabilitation home, he still tried to get his mother's assistance, calling her at all hours, begging her day and night to take him home again. Although she was upset about his phone calls, she was unable to refuse them for fear that he would commit suicide. At the institution where he was staying, he boycotted all therapeutic efforts, resisting all the rules until he was discharged for being obnoxious to the staff.

Over the years, Lucius went through different therapeutic institutions until every single one of them lost patience and discharged him. Numerous efforts to arrange a joint discussion with Lucius' divorced parents failed. His mother rejected her ex-husband and had only contempt for him. And his father was not amenable to any therapy. Out of desperation, Lucius was placed in a home for chronically ill patients by the advising experts, even though he was only 26 years old.

FOLLOW-UP AND COMMENTARY: Years had gone by until his mother, utterly desperate, came for consultation. I coached her in how to stand up to Lucius while protecting herself from his complaints and guilt-inducing behavior, without distancing herself emotionally but still sticking to her own position.

One day, to my big surprise, his father approached me by phone. He was distraught over the referral of his son to an institution for chronically ill patients. He absolutely did not agree with the decision and wanted to arrange a therapy session, which I accepted. I began to involve him in the therapeutic process, giving him the task to help his son reintegrate into the working world. He was delighted and immediately willing to follow my advice. When Lucius was discharged from the institution, he offered to take him home, and to give him work in his own business. During the further course of treatment, the father unexpectedly suggested having a family session with the purpose of dealing with the past and planning the future. I welcomed his initiative. He gave me the task of organizing it. As chance would have it, the meeting took place just before Christmas. The family meeting was a positive experience for all of them, including me as their therapist. A few days later, the father invited the entire family for dinner; it was a real peacemaking Christmas meal.

After six months, the divorced couple returned on their own to my office for a further therapeutic session. In a quiet and cooperative manner, they had come to terms with the past without mutual recrimination, and we could set up clear rules and tasks between the two of them regarding their son. As they took hold, these changes were an enormous relief for Lucius' older sister. She had felt responsible for her younger brother ever since their parents' divorce. She told me "It took a huge load off my chest".

What previously seemed unthinkable, suddenly had become possible: with his father's help, Lucius was now ready to pursue an apprenticeship in a sheltered workshop. He moved into an apartment of his own and began to work regularly, supported by the disability insurance as a means of professional reintegration. Times had changed, as had his parents; Lucius' apprenticeship was well under way. A few years later, he began to prepare for the final exam, which he later passed successfully and continued to live independently on his own.

Defocusing on illness

After years of suffering, despite many self-sacrificing efforts, parents are disappointed and often desperate, having achieved nothing in terms of their child's recovery. They notice that their *always-meant-to-be-helpful-behavior* has gradually deteriorated into an endless, negative spiral with their patient. Criticism and condemnation, sometimes even anger and hate, replace patience and benevolence in the light of their unsuccessful endeavors. In family group sessions, I can sense frustration and despair when they describe family situations with their patient.

As soon as mothers become aware of their negative emotional helix, they immediately feel guilty and hide their anger behind increased and even more intrusive caring behavior. However, no matter how much they try to be helpful, the negative emotional undercurrent always resurfaces and is immediately picked up on by the schizophrenia patient.

Fathers who suppress the negative emotional undertone in their communication with the patient often tend to withdraw, erroneously believing that withholding criticism represents a positive change of heart and mind. In reality, being quiet and removed does not mean that they've ceased focusing on their offspring's illness, even though this is exactly what is required if the illness of schizophrenia is to be overcome.

> **CASE HISTORY:** The mother of Hildegard, a schizophrenia sufferer placed in a home for the chronically ill in a hopeless condition, came to my family group, and then to individual sessions. She wanted to know what she could do for her sick daughter; she didn't come for herself.
> I changed the focus and we began to work through a very complicated patchwork family history with an immigrant background. At her mother's request, I saw Hildegard a single time. When Hildegard's younger brother later came for a session on his own, he said that his sister had made great strides lately, ever since the mother had been in therapy

with me. He was unable to make sense of this since Hildegard had only attended one single session.

Indeed, Hildegard showed remarkable improvement once her mother started to work on her own biography. Hildegard was suddenly very cooperative in her supervised work program, though previously she had seemed to have all the symptoms of a chronic schizophrenia patient, resisting all rules and unable to work. She began to go jogging again, regularly pursued her job in a sheltered workshop and even contemplated starting a training program for a new job, a development no one had ever considered possible, nor realistic, before.

The willingness of parents to tackle their own unresolved detachment from their families of origin represents a sustainable change in the family system and thus reduces the likelihood of a recurrence of an *emotional monster wave* in the identified patient. Taking better care of their hidden aggression towards their husbands allows mothers to shift attention away from their sick child and focus more on their own ambitions. Fathers on their part have to be encouraged to re-engage carefully with their patient child whom they might have given up on a while ago.

Ambivalence hinders detachment

Emotional ambivalence within a symbiotic mother-child relationship is typical for families with schizophrenia. Ambivalence in the mother-child bonding process always leads to a vicious cycle and hinders the detachment process in the youngster. This type of mother-child behavior, which was originally intended as motherly care, becomes a dreadful obstacle during puberty.

CASE HISTORY: Shortly after her release from a psychiatric clinic, Anouk visited me together with her mother on a hot summer afternoon. She entered my office with large pink sunglasses, wearing white lace gloves and an impressive hat. The whole ensemble was like a protective outfit against her surroundings.

Anouk expressed her ambivalence towards her mother who was haunted by fear that Anouk would have an autistic relapse or become suicidal, and therefore used any pretense to visit her daily to check how she was doing. Her mother, however, a loving and good-hearted woman who only wanted the best, sometimes made Anouk so angry that she almost fainted. This was especially the case when her mother would burst into her apartment without knocking or calling first to ask whether she could come by.

Half a year later, the mother felt overwhelmed by having to take care of her all the time. She definitely had had enough, and openly voiced her frustration. Anouk immediately responded to her mother's intention to distance herself with self-destructive thoughts. She was obsessed with the idea of jumping out of the window or flinging herself in front of a car. At the same time, she would desperately try to assert her independence by taking long bus rides every day. She also scoffed at her mother, saying that if she were a mother herself, she would do everything possible to support her daughter at any time.

COMMENTARY: The ambivalent mother-child relationship could be related to the fact that Anouk's mother had frequently beaten her because she had been a very stubborn child. She had been using the same educational style she had suffered herself. Anouk's mother had been beaten by her mother as well. Her family of origin had followed very strict religious rules. Although she had denounced the educational style of her family of origin, she was unable to stop herself from applying it to Anouk. Deeply torn by guilt feelings, she tried to make amends by overprotecting and thereby infantilizing her daughter.

This ambivalent mother-child bonding meant that they made desperate attempts to distance themselves from each other yet yearned for closeness at the same time. The mother insisted that Anouk leave her in peace, as she was at the end of her wits, unable to give her any more support. However, Anouk forced her mother over and over to care more for her than her mother was actually able to. She threatened to throw herself out of the window or under a car. Both fought simultaneously for freedom and self-determination while also desperately asking for compassion from the other. Both were behaving in a destructive manner towards each other because they were fiercely intertwined.

Finally, the moment they yearned for arrived when Anouk's mother could take a clear position towards her own parents on an important personal matter. This also enabled her to stand up to Anouk, which changed the family situation all of a sudden. Anouk began to take on more responsibility for herself, started a relationship and moved in with her boyfriend without needing her mother's constant support.

Dealing with guilt feelings

> Mothers of schizophrenia patients are usually overanxious and therefore cling to their caring role far beyond their offspring's puberty.

When smother-love is rejected by teenagers *with schizophrenia*, mothers feel hurt, become rattled and react by withdrawing their love. But by denying children love, women violate their mothering instinct. As a consequence, they immediately feel guilty and compensate with overinvolved mothering behavior. Thus, they become caught in an ambivalent, vicious cycle of love and hate and guilt feelings towards their adolescents, which is disastrous for both of them.

Mothers of children with schizophrenia can't help worrying day and night. They try everything possible to protect their sick child from further emotional pain and are incessantly questioning what could be done to improve the situation, sparing no effort to alleviate the suffering of their offspring. They make the child's illness the main focus of their life. "My mother is solely focused on me", one of my schizophrenia patients complained. "She should better take care of herself!" Even a systems therapist couldn't express it better. Yet mothers' care behavior goes by the motto: "Only when my sick child is cured do I have the right to pursue my own life", and this attitude persists even if the offspring has long been of adult age. But the caring instinct is also a pretext for avoiding having to work on their own process of detachment from their family of origin. They do not realize that their symbiotic mother-child relationship only smothers their sons' and daughters' maturation process, while at the same time hampering their own personal development.

The therapeutic challenge with overprotective females is to help them to give up caring responsibilities without immediately becoming offended and withdrawn. If that happens, they are fundamentally resisting any therapeutic notion that proposes emotional autonomy for their child. In fact, it feels downright inhumane to them to distance themselves from their caring role. As an excuse for keeping their maternal encroachment, they eloquently argue that they never would let their teenagers know their worries, nor mention anything to them. However, their pretense at being emotionally detached is a form of self-delusion and their offspring is usually more than aware of their mother's real inner attitude.

> **CASE HISTORY:** Although the mother of Steve, a schizophrenia patient, understood that she should worry less about him and look after herself more, she nevertheless felt obliged to act on her gut feelings when she sensed that he was suffering. She did not realize that she was in fact mothering herself when she was doing something so-called nice for him, relieving him of all responsibility, treating him like a toddler while neglecting her own self-realization out of sheer benevolent altruism towards her son.

> Pampering and caring behavior towards the child with schizophrenia is very difficult for mothers to desist from; it feels entirely wrong. Even if mothers believe they have understood the concept of detachment themselves from their maternal role and handing over responsibility to the young adult, it is extremely hard for them to put it into action and then stick with it.

During my clinical work with mothers of adolescents with schizophrenia lasting more than four decades, I have observed countless times how these mothers accepted my instructions to refrain from overstepping boundaries, but still felt compelled to issue instructions and maintain emotional control over their sick children whenever difficulties arose. They clung to the conviction that they were the only one who could help.

> The maternal instinct is so central for most women that it overrules reason time and again, no matter how hard or carefully one works on this issue as a therapist.

Demanding from mothers that they withhold their basic caring behavior often causes them to throw their hands up in despair, as though they had to swim against the tide of their emotions – in fear of drowning. If I make them pay careful attention to their smothering behavior, they often attempt to get me to retreat a little by asking me with a reproachful undertone: "Could you, as a mother, really look the other way and refrain from helping your sick child?" Yet as soon as they get a handle on their overprotective attitude and see some improvement in their child, it strengthens their belief, and they are even convinced over time that this new behavior does indeed help restore the child's right to self-determination.

> **CASE HISTORY:** Jonathan, the youngest of three siblings, refused to go to school after a prolonged illness. During a consultation, his mother was up in arms and questioned why I assigned her the task of backing

off and looking after her own interests while handing her husband the job of personally accompanying their son to school every morning for two weeks.

Later on, she said that she had serious doubts about her husband's ability to get anything done in terms of Jonathan's school attendance. She was highly critical at first and did not cooperate with me. She didn't believe that my advice would make a difference. However, as soon as her son went back to school regularly, she felt very relieved. The father's comment was that he had always felt that his wife was overly concerned with their children, but he didn't want to interfere nor get entangled with her maternal care. Jonathan successfully started his apprenticeship two years later.

Disentanglement of Family Issues

During puberty, sensitive adolescents become increasingly aware of their mothers' vulnerable position as the less authoritative party in the chronic parental power struggle. They therefore don't want to hurt them because they sense that mothers can never win in their partner relationship. As a consequence, they curb and adapt their own rebellious behavior by suppressing their autonomy instinct to support the emotional needs of the family environment. However, the urge for autonomy, which is a key prerequisite for successful teenage years, still exists but remains subliminal, which puts them under permanent strain, which can sometimes have delayed fatal consequences in the form of a *monster wave of emotions*, leading to schizophrenia.

> **CASE HISTORY**: Alfredo wanted to be a gardener, but his mother did not agree that gardening should be his job for life. She urged him to pursue a career as a postman. As a government official, he would have a regular income and a good pension. Alfredo yielded to his mother's will. However, a few years later, in a uncontrollable fit of rage, he strangled her with a rope. He had become psychotic.
>
> **COMMENTARY:** With the best of intentions, Alfredo's mother had tried to steer his career choice to ensure that he would have a secure existence. She prevailed, yet Alfredo ended up feeling suffocated by her. His anger built up over the years, bursting into a monster wave of hatred, and he killed her. He then spent the rest of his life in an institution for mentally ill patients. However, within this closed setting, he was free to choose his profession. As fate would have it, Alfredo was finally able to pursue his desired profession – gardening. He eventually even received work to tend the parks in the community.

> **CASE HISTORY:** In another brutal confrontation between a schizophrenia patient and his mother, the patient had mounted a revolver to the door latch so that his mother had to shoot him while opening the living room door. With this end in mind, he had forced his mother into the role of the offender, thereby demonstrating to the world who was the victim.

Unresolved family issues

Mothers of schizophrenia sufferers who are questioned about their own adolescence during therapy sessions, often reveal emotional entanglements with their families of origin, especially in the form of unresolved detachment from their parents. This pending separation conflict unconsciously triggers mothers to involve their children in an undeclared yet conspicuous mission.

Schizophrenia during adolescence indicates that mothers are still stuck in a conflictual relationship with their families of origin. Their child's illness is a reminder of their own unresolved family issues. If one carefully follows the process of their conflicts, one can observe how familial disagreements, originating from their families of origin, are being passed on to their partners, and from there to their children, via the triangular relationship. Interestingly enough, the negative consequences of this dormant pathogenic conflict usually do not reveal themselves until their children reach puberty. Only then are mothers confronted with the adverse consequences of their own failed detachment process.

> The unresolved detachment process on the part of mothers is perceived by susceptible teenagers, leading to prolonged puberty features in psychotic adolescents.

Mothers, usually unaware of what is happening, unknowingly pass their conflicts on to their partner relationship. In endless arguments, they are quick to criticize their partners for their inadequate behavior and thereby alienate the father of their child. They also immediately take a protective attitude towards their child, opposing the father whenever he takes a hard line. This seems to be an inherent self-defense mechanism of mothers, which blocks any direct interaction between father and teenager suffering schizophrenia. The mothers' overprotective stance towards their offspring impinges on their teenager's right and need for a separation conflict with their father, while at the same time distracting from their hidden conflict with their own parents.

> Children with schizophrenia often function as a cover-up in a highly encrypted manner for unresolved partnership conflicts and hidden attachment problems in the family of origin.

Suffocated conflict creates monster waves

Fathers also play an important role, though in different ways, in the build-up of schizophrenia. Fathers who did not acquire practicable conflict-solving strategies in their family of origin yet implement authoritarian instructional strategies with regards to their children, lack confidence and firmness in dealing with their teenager's obstinate behavior. They restrain these youngsters as much as possible, falling back into the patterns of suppressed conflict management they have learned from their own fathers.

> **CASE HISTORY:** Astrid and her younger brother grew up in privileged conditions and were well cared for by their mother. As a child, Astrid had a close relationship with her father. Yet after finishing school, she could not decide what to study, which he considered a problem. He complained that she lacked the necessary perseverance and would never finish what she had started. He could not comprehend why she was wasting all her talents.

During one of her numerous jobs, Astrid fell in love with an asylum seeker, got pregnant and married him. After giving birth, she was completely overwhelmed as a young mother and wife. She became psychotic and had to be admitted to a psychiatric clinic. After discharge, she wanted to return to her parents' home with her child and husband. Her mother wanted to prevent her grandchild from being taken in custody at all costs. Back home again, Astrid behaved like a pubescent teenager and did as she pleased, left her room in a state of mess and constantly behaved insolently towards her father, which greatly angered him and prompted aggressive rants.

COMMENTARY: Astrid's father was deeply hurt by her behavior. He said his father had slapped him hard if he had rebelled or not performed his tasks in the family business. He knew only one set of rules from his family of origin: either you obey, or you will be punished. There had been no discussions between family members on equal terms. He had therefore had no opportunity to practice conflict resolution strategies. As a consequence, he lacked the resilience to motivate Astrid to take responsibility and change her behavior.

In our therapy sessions, I tried to entreat him to deal with his daughter as an equal. Yet he replied that all suggestions were to no avail: Astrid had stopped listening to him, he no longer regarded her as his daughter; his parents would never have let him behave like that. He didn't realize that his irascible outbursts had taught his daughter to do exactly the same. She avoided him, just as he avoided her. He cut off all contact with Astrid as a form of punishment. At the same time, he kept his parents' authoritarian educational model, although it didn't work with Astrid.

The irony of the story was not so subtle. She ignored his tantrums when he lost his temper and punished him by cutting all ties, but simultaneously tried to draw him into her problems by attracting his attention repeatedly through odd behavior, like talking to a power station at night.

The mother on her part criticized her husband's authoritarian behavior incessantly in a very condescending tone. This gave him every reason to turn his back on the entire family, convinced that he couldn't do anything right anyway. Astrid, meanwhile, made sarcastic remarks about her parents' dysfunctional marriage. One day, however, as the family ruminated on the sheer unsurmountable aversion against each other, the mother made the remark that they probably had been too strict with Astrid, and that's why she thought Astrid was now such a difficult teenager. She was talking as if she knew all the answers but didn't ask herself the question: "What is my part in it?"

> For fathers who want to participate effectively and productively in the therapeutic process, it is essential that they engage with the identified patient on equal terms while also reflecting on their own biography.

Fathers harm their pubescent teenagers affected by schizophrenia most by playing the adult role, believing they have shed their teenage skin and therefore have nothing new to learn. They refuse to reflect on their own teenage years, and how they were shaped by the educational style of their own family. Yet they have to go back in time and reflect on these years of confusion and learn from their own experience in order to become reliable counterparts for the next generation in ongoing disputes about day-to-day affairs with their offspring. Through such exchanges, youngsters mature and develop personal responsibility, and learn conflict management techniques to solve future problems encountering in life.

Paternal incompetence

In the following example, the father was in fact prepared to seek support through therapy for his parental role as father. Yet whenever he was alone with his son, he repeatedly fell back into the patriarchal command style rooted in the tradition of his family of origin – unaware that this experience had hurt his personal pride as a youngster and had left him fairly thin-skinned as an adult in confrontations with his son. Moreover, his rash behavior – belittling his son for not having any success in life – was an affront to his son's pride. It threatened to perpetuate the father-son situation across generations, whereby both would continuously feel the sting from blows to their personal pride. This attitude threatened to undo the father's intentions of receiving support through therapy with regards to his parental role.

> **CASE HISTORY:** Noah's father had made a genuine effort to engage in the relationship with his teenage son, who had ADHD with poor impulse control. However, he did not condone that his wife provided Noah – who was highly vulnerable because of his sensitivity – protection against his fatherly reprimands whenever Noah got himself into trouble. He thought Noah failed to take responsibility for his actions, while Noah's mother found herself unable to deny him the "nest" at home. The father consequently felt he could never assert himself in this matter, and the parents were constantly at odds about how to deal with their son's behavior.
> One day, Noah returned home unexpectedly and immediately rushed to the coffee machine. At that moment, his father made the remark that he had not been invited and should have at least asked first before helping himself to coffee. Noah felt offended, snapped back, smashed a sugar bowl, and berated his father for not even welcoming him home. When his father let him know that this kind of attitude was not acceptable, Noah stormed out of the house, took the garden gate off its hinges and hurled it against the front door.
> **FOLLOW-UP AND COMMENTARY:** When the father attended the next therapy session, his conclusion was that he did not wish to see his son for some time. We discussed his reaction to his misbehaving son. Con-

trary to his intention, I advised him to continue to meet Noah on a regular basis – but away from the mothers' nest, since home largely represented her domain, where Noah felt protected and entitled to behave rudely towards him. His mother had always come to his rescue when his father had raised his voice or punished him for bad behavior.

Noah's father was used to a far more authoritarian style back home. Therefore, I turned back the clock to his family of origin and focused on how he was raised. When discussing his puberty as a teenager, he recollected that he had been a very obedient adolescent, always adapting to the whims of his surroundings. He realized, however, that he could not automatically expect the same blind deference and respect from his own son as he had shown towards his father.

Noah's father had been able to unknot himself only partly from his family of origin and the educational style, which had shaped his character as a young man. He had tried to confront his father as an adult a few times but exclusively in writing. He never had a direct confrontation in person about issues that bothered him. Now being a father himself, he was experiencing the exact opposite. His son did not accept his authority. Noah, a child with ADHD, had poor impulse control. Resorting to a position of power, just as he had experienced it with his father in adolescence, was to no avail. Although Noah was often aggressive and abusive towards his father, he still needed his attention and support.

My instruction to Noah's father was to remain calm at the meetings, even if his son rejected him, and to endure difficult father-son confrontations without resorting to the same authoritarian style he was used to in his own family. I encouraged him to confront his son in a steady and consistent manner, always ready to cooperate for minimal agreements but without educational intent, moral reprimands or scathing criticism. I also reminded him that he should not punish his son by cutting him off, or threaten him sarcastically, even though Noah was likely to be rude.

From functional helplessness to competence

One of the reasons why fathers may easily reach an impasse when dealing with their teenager affected by malignant schizophrenia, is the fear of initializing a partner conflict. Even though they often hand over caregiving responsibilities to the mother, who on her part may criticize them for avoiding any kind of serious discussion with their pubescent child, they are nevertheless constantly trying to correct their own deficiencies in order to please their partner. The result is a nonstop struggle between a rigid paternal attitude and an overprotective maternal habit, and a never-ending attempt from the male side to please their wives. The outcome tends to be unsuccessful since mothers are more occupied with their child than with their partner. This ongoing clash between the parents unfortunately maintains the cycle of behaviors associated with schizophrenia, turning it into a chronic disorder.

> My advice to fathers: work on your unresolved issues from your family of origin in order to acquire the competence you're currently lacking in dealing with your pubescent child with schizophrenia. Be less dependent on your wife's or partner's approval.

In systems therapy, when the instrument of the genogram is applied, a careful reconstruction of the various entanglement patterns within the families of fathers and mothers brings unresolved issues of attachment into focus. They can finally be addressed and be partially resolved.

> **CASE HISTORY:** Mathias had been offered a senior position in his job, yet to everybody's surprise, he fell into a psychotic crisis instead of rejoicing. As the only son with two older and one younger sister, he had always assumed the role of the emphatic and mediating brother in all family conflicts. His two older sisters created plenty of difficulties for their parents, who also had serious unresolved issues between them-

selves. Mathias usually assumed a protective helper role towards his mother and younger sister. As for himself, he tried to behave as unobtrusively as possible in order not to burden his parents with additional worries. At the boy scouts, he had always taken the role of a leader. He therefore resented his sudden weakness, complained about his fate, and caught himself wallowing in his thoughts. Neither he nor his environment had expected him to react in such a way.

FOLLOW-UP: The mother of Mathias had already successfully worked through specific issues stemming from her family of origin on her own initiative to detach herself better from the emotional responsibility she assumed as the oldest child for her depressive mother, who had often threatened her with suicide throughout her childhood and adult life. Now, the father of Matthias wanted to work with me on his family of origin, too. Since his own parents had already died, I advised him to write a personal letter first to his father and then to his mother. He went on a short trip all by himself to write to his father. In the following therapy sessions, he informed me that he had progressed a great deal. Later, he also wrote to his mother.

COMMENTARY: Mathias was a functionalized child. His role as a "helper" was basically rooted in the family. He had always tried to protect his depressive mother from his impulsive father. If there were problems within the family, he immediately felt responsible for restoring peace. As such, he had later chosen a social profession consistent with his role in the family. His qualities were noticed and very much appreciated at work but when he was promoted to a leading position by his superior to take on more responsibility, he developed a psychotic episode. Therefore, I had him remove himself from the family system by temporarily placing him in a psychiatric hospital that offered psychotherapy. At the same time, I worked with the parents on their relationship issues, as well as their families of origin. Furthermore, I gave the father advice how he could strengthen his relationship with his son by meeting with him regularly, so they could get to know each other better.

Mathias had previously expressed that he had only scant knowledge of his father. He had always been afraid of his aggressive outbursts. After several one-on-one meetings, a warm relationship between father and son evolved. As time passed, the whole family achieved a new balance. Mathias recovered from his psychotic crisis and became a responsible father to his own family; his wife was expecting their second child. Much later, he felt sufficiently confident and self-empowered to accept a leading position in a social institution and was happy with job and family life.

Marginalization of fathers

The next case shows how difficult, if not impossible, it can be for males to exercise their paternal role when mothers cling to their symbiotic relationship with their offspring affected by schizophrenia.

> **CASE HISTORY:** After a long period of failed career choices, Adrian gradually developed a chronic schizophrenic condition with physical symptoms of weakness. He withdrew little by little and slipped into an autistic world of his own. He even felt too weak to walk to the railway station and insisted that his parents chauffeur him everywhere. Since he was an intelligent young man, he cleverly rationalized his pathological behavior using logical arguments, which made his mother always give in to his requests.
>
> One day, Adrian's father run out of patience and told Adrian that he was no longer willing to support him, and that it was finally time he started looking for a job. In response, Adrian went on a hunger strike with severe consequences; he had to be admitted to the emergency ward at the local hospital to be tube-fed.

FOLLOW-UP AND COMMENTARY: In a one-on-one therapy session, Adrian's mother mentioned that her husband was deeply committed to Adrian. He had enjoyed a particularly intimate relationship with him since birth yet had always been insecure in his role as a father. She could rarely count on his support while bringing up their children. She said it was even worse when Adrian was a child. Sometimes he was possessed by a delusional fear that he could poison Adrian.

In a later session with both parents present, I pointed out how they had, over time, adapted to Adrian's pathological behavior, and that his illness had thereby deteriorated. Referring to the intimate relationship with Adrian since birth, I encouraged the father to take a clear position towards his son but without exerting pressure. The father was skeptical and added that this would be the very last time that he would commit himself to a treatment program aimed at his son. Besides, he expressed the fear that his wife would criticize him behind his back no matter what, and reverse everything he decided.

My suggestion was discussed during the subsequent sessions with both parents. The mother gave her consent. Her husband was full of energy, made the next appointments with my secretary and coordinated everything with all the other professionals involved. He suddenly became the dedicated therapeutic process manager.

Six months later, however, the mother once again had taken direct control of handling the family, and the father was pushed to the side. She demanded from him that he once again chauffeur their son because of his physical weakness. In the meantime, Adrian had consulted another therapist, who diagnosed his symptoms as chronic fatigue syndrome. He also forbade his parents from attending further therapy sessions with me; the mother supported his instruction. She cancelled all therapy appointments which had been arranged by the father. The fears of the father had come true.

A few years later, out of curiosity, I called up. The mother told me that Adrian was doing much better and had just prepared to leave for

Canada. As parents, she said, they had regained their composure and learned to accept each other's duties and would approach everything with a little more serenity. The family system had evolved further in favor of Adrian, despite the initial resistance by the mother.

Tug-of-war in partnership

In parents' groups, I have met many mothers who complain about the aloofness and lack of compassion on the part of their husbands. At the same time, however, mothers frequently prevent their partners from having an independent-minded paternal approach to their children, which is usually quite different from the long-standing motherly caring behavior. Fathers of schizophrenia sufferers, as mentioned previously, often withdraw from their paternal role very early on. Their confidence eroded, they frequently feel unable to deal with the separation conflict of their pubescent child for fear of a tug-of-war with their wives.

However, if adolescents show aggression towards the overprotective maternal squeeze, mothers once again summon paternal authority, demanding fathers to come to their rescue. Under such circumstances, fathers who have long turned away from the family are in a precarious position.

> The crucial question is: can mothers abandon their overprotective caring behavior and make space for the fatherly role?

CASE HISTORY: Xaver was a child with ADHD. His parents as well as his teachers were unable to deal with this disorder. Upon professional advice, he was placed in an institution at the age of twelve but all efforts to help him there had failed. He was passed from institution to institution in quick succession. During this frustrating period, his mother attended my family group and sought my advice.

COMMENTARY: Xaver's parents were stuck in a tug-of-war in their relationship. The father had had an authoritarian upbringing. He had been an obedient child and had met all his father's expectations. Xaver, on the other hand, whom his mother described as having been a special child since birth, failed to live up to any of his father's ideals. Because he suffered from ADHD, the authoritarian, achievement-oriented educational model of his father's family was unsuccessful.

In the family sessions, I explained to Xaver's father new ways of handling his son. I gave him the advice to use his strictness with more flexibility. I also backed him when his wife complicated things further by continually interfering in his educational and disciplinary attempts. With time, he gained more confidence and experience.

However, the mother had difficulties controlling her attitude. Driven by anxiety, she responded to her son's frequent cries for help by pulling in more helpers and additional help systems. She herself had grown up as the youngest of four children with a domineering father and had left home early to escape his authority. Yet she was unable to free herself from the shackles of patriarchal authority by running away from her parents. On the contrary, she had internalized the authoritarian methods practiced by her father and was thus constantly involved in a tug-of-war, wanting to wield the scepter herself while also trying to break away from such an approach. The criticism of her husband was a projection of her own internalized patriarchal behavioral patterns. Both families of origin did not allow for significant changes in their interaction patterns.

Fathers' impact on therapy

Murray Bowen observed in the 1960s that rates of success of systemic therapy for families affected by schizophrenia correlated positively with the participation of fathers in the therapeutic process. At the National

Institute of Mental Health in Washington, D.C. he had hospitalized schizophrenia patients along with their parents for close observation. In his study of schizophrenia families, he found that a therapeutic alliance involving only mothers resulted in little if any progress in the treatment of schizophrenia patients. However, when the fathers were involved in the therapeutic process, a significant change in the course of treatment was observed.

I came to the same conclusion in my own separate, unpublished study of schizophrenia families. Treatment success depended on the therapeutic involvement of fathers. The scientific work of Reber (2009) on the protective factor of a good father-patient relationship correlated significantly with treatment success of schizophrenia in puberty and was perceived by the patients as a supportive resource.

With further research into the roles of fathers in families with schizophrenia, it became apparent that the forefathers were often already weakened by situational circumstances within the family or social conditions.

> Strengthening the fathers in their role through systemic therapeutic coaching with a three-generation approach may have a healing effect on the schizophrenia patient by resetting the family system.

CASE HISTORY: The father of Ben, a young schizophrenia sufferer with ADHD and dyslexia, desperately sought counselling because he consistently felt undermined by his ex-wife, Ben's mother, as well as by Ben's older sister. He was very unsettled and feared he would be unable to help his son to evolve into a successful adult. He had already sought help for himself and his son but had been disappointed and was extremely reproachful towards all therapeutic professionals, including me. His mother had also suffered from schizophrenia, which had left him with nothing but traumatic experiences with doctors as well as psychiatric hospitals in his childhood. In emails, he complained bitterly that no one would help him; his son would soon end up as a hopelessly lost, chronic sufferer of schizophrenia.

FOLLOW-UP AND COMMENTARY: The role of Ben's father in the family was weakened because of his childhood experiences. He always had to accompany his mother to the psychiatric clinic together with his father, which had been extremely stressful for him. His son's pubescent schizophrenia reminded him of his mother's condition and posed an existential emotional threat to him. However, he finally realized that his extreme criticism of all therapists and his constant arguments with his ex-wife did not soothe his pain; they were in fact a complete waste of energy. So far, he had not accomplished anything with his accusations, his complaints had even weakened his position as a reliable father and prevented him from being a rock in the stormy emotional sea his son was exposed to. Despite his extremely serious allegations, I supported him when his son became psychotic and he had to admit him once more to a psychiatric clinic.

During hospitalization, Ben's father suddenly found access to his son and could approach him in a calm and self-assured manner. With my support, he proceeded to deal with his son's pubescent attacks without devaluing him or taking offense. Moreover, he was now willing to accept my proposals for rehabilitation and even considered implementing them. He also began to be a lot more active and cooperative on important issues, accepting and understanding my advice in long-term planning. His son established a more stable relationship with his father, assuming responsibility, and even considered vocational training.

As a result of the improved relationship with his son, the father could reassess at the same time his own childhood trauma with his mother and her schizophrenia. A cross-generational healing process had taken place and the father took life into his own hands again. He no longer needed additional therapeutic support.

Divorce does not do away with split loyalty

Parents of children with schizophrenia, as well as mental health professionals, often assume that these children will be released from their experience of *split loyalty* following their parents' divorce. No longer caught in the helper role between them, they thus shed their roles as *obsessed diplomats*. However, they usually remain entangled in the unresolved conflict of their parents even after divorce, since fighting parents mostly continue with their tug-of-war, which weighs heavily upon the conscience of their children.

In cases where the schizophrenia patients remain with their mother, fathers are not exempt from their parental duties, since their continued involvement plays a decisive role in the detachment process. Only if fathers assume their responsibility and take an active role in the therapeutic process, can the patient be freed from the symbiotic bond with their mother.

> **CASE HISTORY:** As a small child, Gudrun often had to do without her mother because she spent weeks or even months in a clinic on account of a chronic illness. Additionally, she was exposed to the silent conflict between her parents from infancy to puberty. At the age of sixteen, Gudrun developed an eating disorder. Eight years later, one year after her parents' divorce, she developed paranoid schizophrenia.
>
> When Gudrun became psychotic for the third time, her divorced parents contacted me for help. Neither wanted their daughter to be admitted again to a psychiatric clinic because she had suffered badly each time. On top of that, Gudrun's mother was at a loss as to how to care for her daughter on her own. She was therefore willing to accept her ex-husband's help.
>
> Follow-up and commentary: I gave Gudrun's father the task of taking her under his wings for a while. Although he was at a breaking point himself, he nevertheless accepted my advice, and administered her medication during her entire psychotic episode. They went for long

walks in the countryside, and gradually, Gudrun started to gain confidence in her father. For the very first time, she no longer saw him through her mother's eyes as she had done before and developed a trusting relationship.

Gudrun's mother had to work on her unresolved attachment from her family of origin. It turned out that as a child, her father had spoiled her. But now, even as a sixty-year-old woman, she could still could not assert herself against him and therefore lacked the skills to communicate her disagreement to her husband. Instead, she constantly vented her frustration about her unhappy relationship to her daughter, who had become a captive of the silent conflict between her parents over the years. Gudrun mentioned that she had never actually seen her parents quarrel.

After a few years, she became psychotic again because of conflicts at work, and the family sought my help once more. This time, Gudrun mentioned to me that she sometimes felt obliged to take on a parental role towards her divorced parents; they would often behave in a childish way, wayward and irresponsible, trying to pull her in. She protested that this was not her job and found it utterly unfair that her parents exposed her to their unsolved conflicts even after their divorce.

Gudrun had realized for the first time that her designated role in the family was to mediate between her parents. Now, she even could express it openly during therapy. This insight provoked a huge step forward towards independence. Nevertheless, Gudrun's mother was still focused on her daughter's illness and insisted that she go for therapy. Gudrun, however, didn't want to become dependent on a therapist. I accepted her decision and offered Gudrun and her parents to contact me any time they needed support.

The Deeper Function of Madness

The obsessed diplomat

Let us return to the functionalized role of children, which fosters the development of schizophrenia. These individuals always have a mission to fulfill within their family system. They are *helper children* for sustained family conflicts, as well as for unresolved cross-generational undercurrents passed on over many years. At the same time, they are also duty-bound to keep conflicts and taboos under control. In fact, they behave like decoys acting on their family's behalf, drawing attention to themselves with their problematic, enigmatic behavior to deflect from embarrassing family matters. As a diversionary maneuver, they supply sufficient red herrings to attract professionals with their symptoms, thereby deflecting from the deeper problems in the family system, protecting it from public shame.

> Schizophrenic family members serve as objects of projection in the family's deception maneuver. They ultimately become scapegoats for all dysfunctions within the system.

From a systemic perspective, individuals with schizophrenia might be referred to as *obsessed diplomats*. They play their role using an encrypted, psychotic means of communication, often illustrating very clearly their diplomatic function within the system. The madness of schizophrenia patients indicates that there is a hidden message, a taboo, a chronic injustice within the family system, but the riddle of what it is and how it has to be addressed first needs to be deciphered.

> The function of madness is to bring to the surface the fact that the system is in urgent need of an update or change.

The Deeper Function of Madness

CASE HISTORY: An individual with schizophrenia said that his mental condition was like a reflection of his family. When things went bad, he would no longer feel like himself. When things went well for his family, he also felt better. At that moment, he could turn towards living his own life again.

One could also say that schizophrenia patients as functionalized children are assigned a congenital "therapist's role". They sense the parental needs at an early age, sometimes from the womb to the tomb. Schizophrenia patients also help camouflage their parents' marital problems, as well as conflicts originating from their families of origin – which is why they must remain absolutely loyal to both parents. The family system cannot allow them a phase of adolescence in order to mature because the system-preserving function has to be maintained at any price.

> As *obsessed diplomats*, family members with schizophrenia remain involved with the chronic conflicts of their parents as well as the extended family network, not knowing that they embody the connecting element in the intricate family system.

Obsessed diplomat as guardian

Individuals with schizophrenia, because of their heightened sensitivity, regularly also play a very specific part in the lives of mothers who don't take a clear position vis à vis their abusive partners or own fathers. They thereby assume the role of bodyguard, acting as heroes, a part that elevates them above everybody, in particular their own father. As such, they avoid the conflictual detachment phase in adolescence. Trapped in this vicious cycle of unresolved family issues, they become targets of suppressed parental rage. I have heard quite often frustrated fathers say in such situations: "Either me or the child; one of us has to move out!" Facing this dilemma, mothers will always side with the sick child, and the fathers are the ones who back off or even leave the family. In this pathogenic triangle, offspring risk losing the vital relationship with fathers for good, which prevents them from developing into adulthood.

Liberating the obsessed diplomat

Carl A. Whitaker, a noted psychiatrist and family therapist from the United States, a therapeutic expert of experiential therapy in the 1970s, working with families of schizophrenia sufferers, played the role of "crazy patient" in each of his family meetings. By way of example in the therapy sessions, he behaved even crazier than the schizophrenia patients with the surprising result that they suddenly became quite reasonable and began to assert themselves. With his experiential therapy, Whitaker forced patients with schizophrenia out of their roles as obsessed diplomats towards self-responsibility.

Another imaginative approach beside Carl A. Whitaker's is to encourage mothers and fathers to take up new positions in the family system, thereby restructuring and transforming their parental roles. This reset will help to stop the endless loop of the pathogenic triangle of parents with schizophrenic teenagers, thus rendering the role of *obsessed diplomat* redundant.

Whenever parents cooperate in the abovementioned process, the patient is freed from their functionalized role by the systems therapist, who comes to occupy the patient's pathological role instead, acting as "the professional diplomat" who intervenes in the parents' conflict as a *patron saint* of sorts with their expertise and skills to deflect latent noxious effects. Quite often, patients resist giving up their role as heroes or obsessed diplomats and oppose the therapist. However, therapists need to bear in mind that "all things come to those who wait", and the healthy process continues.

Once this reset has been consolidated, and the changes perceived by everybody as positive, the family system once again becomes *autopoietic*, but this time in a healthy way. The therapeutic person is consulted by individual members selectively, only in critical situations, as a coach. Further progress of each family member toward greater autonomy within the system runs its natural course and needs no further assistance. Thereafter, the family system comes to function at a higher level.

> **CASE HISTORY:** Luc, the second of three children, was born at a time when his parents were experiencing considerable marital problems. As a sensitive child, his mother had an especially close relationship with him. He soon became her confidant; she entrusted him with all her worries because he was a good listener.
>
> In adolescence, Luc began to smoke cannabis on a regular basis and became psychotic shortly before his final exams in high school. In the throes of his paranoid delusions, he was convinced that he was the older brother of his father as well as the father of his mother. He insisted that he had to take care of his entire family. At the same time, he felt that he was possessed by the devil and had to be punished because he could not save his family from all evil.
>
> **COMMENTARY:** Luc's delusions clearly revealed the position he had in his family. Accordingly, he had to conceal the marital conflicts and assume the role of the understanding father towards his mother. At the same time, he also had to take on the role of father's older brother to encourage his father to be more self-assertive and masculine.
>
> Luc's mother was a very emotional woman. As an only child, she had a close relationship with her father, who idolized and spoiled her to the extreme. Therefore, as an adult, she expected the same special treatment from her husband. She was disappointed, even deeply hurt, when he could not meet her expectations. So she took an acquaintance of her parents as her lover who satisfied all her wishes and needs. How-

ever, her lover introduced a new conflict into the family system; he was also quite needy, which showed in his possessive behavior.

Luc's father, who wanted to avoid any conflict with his wife, had become a silent sufferer. Taking an authoritarian role towards his wife, as his own father had done with his mother, was out of the question. He could therefore not challenge his wife nor confront his rival, her lover. In this sense, he remained loyal to his own mother, for whom he always had felt compassion and pity.

Both parents were still entangled with their families of origin and had brought into their partnership behavior patterns that were detrimental. Luc, as the obsessed diplomat, felt responsible for both of his parents and their problems. He had to free them from their familial entanglements, thus taking on the burden of the family history, which turned into an unbearable strain and inhibited his further development.

The parents of Luc were willing to work on their problems inherited from their families of origin. With therapeutic support, Luc was freed from his role as obsessed diplomat and could address his own life and professional career. Not surprisingly, he chose psychology. Thus, he professionalized the therapeutic role that was bestowed on him as a functionalized child by the family system.

Differentiation – Tool for Change

Il faut reculer pour mieux sauter – stepping back to jump further – is a French saying which might prove useful for parents, reminding them that working through hidden family issues and assessing differing parenting patterns always requires an additional emotional effort, but is worthwhile when reflecting on the partner conflict. Going back to and contemplating the stories and values of the families of origin has a lasting, far-reaching effect on the development and rehabilitation of the child with schizophrenia as well as on one's own well-being.

Differentiation from the family of origin

Differentiation and detachment from the family of origin involves autobiographical digging. This method was developed and practiced by Murray Bowen as one of the corner stones of his therapy. The procedure is roughly as follows:

- Systematic regular involvement with one's family of origin, collecting a maximum amount of objective data on all the various family members to get a more nuanced picture of the different biographies and their impact within the family system. Data on taboo subjects should be included, although one might have to make a vigorous push to get them.
- Becoming aware of one's own position and role in the family of origin.
- During family visits, the task is to be an observer, to hold back any reactive response to imminent emotional family issues.
- In case there are broken relationships between members in the family of origin, it is beneficial to establish contact again with all those mem-

bers that have been cut-off from the family system, including the black sheep.
- In case of a strong dependency on the family of origin, the contact should be reduced. More distance is recommended to further the detachment process and sharpen one's independent judgement and position in the family system.
- Conflictual issues with parents should be addressed as explicitly and unambiguously as possible, be it with father or mother, but always without trying to convince them of one's own viewpoint.
- Parents should be approached from an adult's position and not from the position of an angry teenager, or with childlike emotional demands and silent expectations.
- To approach one's parents in a submissive and obedient manner to avoid conflict is not beneficial either. Instead, it is advisable to express one's own opinion unambiguously and straightforwardly, but in a calm way.
- Trying to convince parents of one's own position represents dependency and a need for their acceptance, and thus signifies incomplete detachment. One should neither expect agreement nor acceptance from them.
- The relationship patterns in the family of origin have to be studied in order to recognize and become aware of one's own behavior patterns.
- The different relationship patterns in the family of origin should be analyzed in terms of how they affect the partnership in certain ways, as well as the handling of the schizophrenia patient.
- Need for affection within the partnership should be communicated clearly and in a calm fashion without a reproachful attitude, and not as an order or demand, always observing carefully one's own emotional reactions.

Differentiation from deceased parents

Differentiation and detachment from deceased parents poses a more daunting, though not impossible, task. Under these circumstances, I encourage individuals to address their deceased parent by writing a letter, as demonstrated in a previous case history. Poets and philosophers have used this method, writing down their feelings and thoughts as clearly and exactly as possible for their own as well as their readers' understanding. This is a classic, well established means of enduring the drama and suffering of life. Even neuropsychology supports this method nowadays: "If you can name it, you can tame it."

The deceased father and mother should, however, always be addressed separately. "How" and "why" questions should be reflected upon first and not spewed forth in a flush of anger. Still overwhelmed with pain, and frustrated about disappointments in childhood years, heaping accusation upon accusation of unresolved issues onto the deceased is not helpful. To assert oneself to the deceased as an adult, defining the causes of this lasting harm to one's psyche and putting them into words, helps us to regain our inner peace and dignity.

These letters to the deceased father and mother should never end with a damning indictment, which is likely to have an effect, especially a negative one, on the writer. Recriminations continue to hold us in a state of dependency and ensure that unresolved emotional undercurrents remain fixed in the psyche, as well as in the biographical content of family stories, contaminating the next generation.

The objective is to free oneself from needy expectations. This method benefits the writer as well as his or her family system. Extending this process of differentiation and detachment towards the family of origin with the method of *narrative reconstructivism* can enable the family system to move through developmental stages, thereby gaining freedom from harmful dogmas which limit all the family members.

> It is of great benefit to the maturation process of schizophrenia patients when parents address conflicts in their families of origin, even if their parents have long since departed.

CASE HISTORY: Robert's divorced parents came to my office to seek advice regarding their son who suffered from schizophrenia. His mother had a very close relationship with him. The father had long given up his role as a guiding hand and withdrawn completely from family life to avoid constant confrontations with his ex-wife. The wealthy maternal grandmother spoiled her grandson out of pity, as she put it.

FOLLOW-UP AND COMMENTARY: First, I gave Robert's father the advice to keep up contact with his son on a regular basis. The mother was given the advice to hold back somewhat the care and attention bestowed on her son.

Then, I instructed the father to discuss certain issues with his own father, Robert's grandfather. On his own initiative, he thanked his father for having insisted that he finish high school and not allow him to drop out.

Until then, Robert's father had taken a derogatory attitude towards his own father. He thought of him as narrow-minded and therefore had distanced himself from him. His own mother he described as unapproachable; he had never had a warm, cordial relationship with her.

Robert's father felt more secure in his parental role after his open discussions with his own father. This positive experience had strengthened his position towards his son, ill with schizophrenia. He could resume his fatherly duties, which he had previously neglected entirely.

Therapy with the help of a lie

> Reconnecting with the family of origin may resolve certain entanglements and lead to a reset of the dammed-up emotional undercurrents in the family system.

CASE HISTORY: Haiko, the elder of two boys, successfully completed his apprenticeship and worked for several years in his profession. However, he lost his job twice in a row because both companies filed for bankruptcy. After the second time, he was unable to bounce back. His family doctor diagnosed him as pre-psychotic.

A few years later, following the advice of their family doctor, his parents contacted me because they were seriously concerned about Haiko's future. When he told them that he was in therapy with me, they felt relieved and regarded their therapy session as an additional support to his treatment. They were all the more shocked, to discover that Haiko had never come to see me, but they did not discontinue their therapy session.

His mother had spent five years in psychotherapy because of a traumatic experience as a child. When exploring the genogram, it came to light that the mother had been sexually abused when she was five years old by a man from the neighborhood who had also sexually abused twenty-seven other girls. When she was officially questioned at that time whether she had been abused too, her mother answered for her instead: "No, my daughter would never do anything like that". No further inquiries were made. Therefore, Haiko's mother never received psychological support as a child. She kept her secret, which was a family taboo until she was fifty years old. However, over the years she had nightmares and often sleepwalked. In her dreams, she screamed so loudly that her two sons woke up and rushed to her bed in awful fright. Time and again, she would feel something was stuck in her throat; she had to regurgitate.

When she finally went to see a therapist, Haiko constantly asked her what she discussed with him, but she only made vague allusions, and never gave him a clear answer. Although she felt better after dealing with her childhood trauma, and only rarely had nightmares, she still felt ashamed and refused to reveal her secret to her son.

COMMENTARY: She must have been extremely afraid of being judged by Haiko and his brother. She was also scared of me as a therapist. She had projected the punitive attitude of her mother outwards. She viewed the therapy sessions, which had been arranged by her family doctor, almost as a court hearing.

I gave her the advice to break the taboo and inform her two sons as accurately as possible. She was visibly relieved after the session and was willing to implement my proposal immediately. I did not invite her anymore for therapy sessions, nor did the parents together need further therapy with me.

Haiko had made his parents attend therapy with a strategic lie, which is the typical therapeutic task of schizophrenia patients. He exposed his mother's sexual abuse, thus breaking the taboo of the maternal grandmother, and helped her to reveal her sexual taboo from childhood to her two sons. All of these lies therefore served the purpose of enabling Haiko's mother to finally denounce her loyalty to her own mother.

In this rare case, the patient cooperated with me as a therapist in an almost ideal way, even though I had never met him. However, it is usually not possible to approach a family's core issues that fast. It is even rarer that a patient manipulates his parents into attending family therapy through a lie. In Haiko's case, the lie was extremely helpful because it uncovered the family taboo imposed by the grandmother that had inhibited Haiko's mother for decades. The taboo could be lifted as early as the first family therapy session and dealt with in the family.

Psychotropic Medication

Medication as an agent of change

Nowadays, the regular treatment of schizophrenia with psychotropic drugs is considered state-of-the-art by professionals as well as family members. However, being under the control of psychotropic medication is always a delicate matter for the patients. They often refuse to take medication at the very beginning of their illness because they interpret any form of insistence as a violation of their psyche, and an intrusion into their personality, which is in fact correct.

> All psychotropic medications change the affective condition and mental state of a person; they are meant to control emotions and behavior.

Patients with schizophrenia who realize that the person handing out the medication is anxious and tense perceive medication as even more of a threat. Under some rare circumstances, however, medication may be administered by a trustworthy member of the family. Since schizophrenia patients usually cannot sleep in the initial phase, the medication can be given just once a day as a "sleeping pill" in case they refuse medication. Under no circumstances, however, should emotional pressure be applied, since many patients will immediately react with intensified symptoms and aggressive rejection, and become less cooperative.

Medical professionals administering medication should always be aware that a trusting relationship with patients is more important and has a better calming effect than the intake of medication. Quiet confidence is still the best "medication" and has in itself a strong stress-reducing effect. Should an interpersonal struggle arise, however, the intake of the medication has to be postponed until the relationship between caregiver and patient has calmed down. After the emotional atmosphere has settled, a new attempt can be made to hand out medication.

In the following case, the patient's father was considered the person most trusted to administer the psychotropic medication to his son, who had strictly refused to consult a doctor.

CASE HISTORY: Kaspar smoked cannabis on a regular basis from the age of thirteen. First, a joint every day before school, and the next one during the breaks. He completed an apprenticeship but left the job because he didn't like the profession, and also had difficulties with his superiors. He quarreled with his parents and was aggressive towards his siblings. He left home without further notice, worked odd jobs for a short period, and slept under bridges. Eventually, he withdrew entirely from his social network, and in a visibly neglected state, his parents almost had him admitted to a psychiatric hospital against his will.

FOLLOW-UP AND COMMENTARY: Kaspar's categorical refusal to accept any medical help was enough to drive his parents to despair and seek counselling at the very last moment. The parents' description of Kaspar indicated that he was experiencing the onset of psychosis. Yet because he strictly refused to see a doctor, I instructed the parents on how to handle their son. To reduce Kaspar's flight reaction, I advised the mother to restrain herself emotionally and stop giving him anxious maternal advice. The father, meanwhile, was given the task of guiding his son with a steady hand, and to assign him simple manual work on his farm, yet without criticizing him. I also put him in charge of medication. He was convinced that he was able to persuade his son to take the medication from him, one pill every night; it worked. With the successful administration of medication by his father, a psychiatric hospitalization could be avoided. Kaspar gradually calmed down over a period of two weeks. His parents could talk to him again and even persuade him to come to my office for a consultation. Although this young man had not yet found his professional orientation, he was able to cope with his everyday life on his own again.

Covert drug administration – a no-go

Parents of schizophrenia patients regularly get instructed by psychiatric professionals that regular intake of neuroleptics is essential to prevent a relapse of psychosis. They take this information very seriously and are at a loss if the patient refuses the medication. If the patient continuous to resist, some parents cannot withstand the temptation to mix medication secretly into food or drink. For systems therapists, however, this is an absolute no-go since it is a demonstration of the manipulative parental control of the young adult's emotions, and inevitably fosters paranoia.

> **CASE HISTORY:** Felix was the youngest of three siblings, and the most well-adapted child. However, his behavior changed abruptly during puberty. He showed a lack of contact with reality, rejected parental orders, and dropped out of his apprenticeship. His parents ultimately had him admitted to a psychiatric clinic, where he was treated for psychosis. After he was discharged, he vehemently refused to take his medication. Contrary to my clear instruction, Felix's mother, who was a nurse, secretly mixed medication into his food and drink, and continued to do so for many years. She said that she wanted to prevent him from being admitted to a clinic again and make his rebellious behavior towards her more bearable.
>
> **COMMENTARY:** Over the years, Felix never left home; he always stayed at his mother's side. He neither led an independent life nor did he ever have a job. However, when his mother became old and bedridden, the roles suddenly reversed. Ultimately, she became entirely dependent on him. Felix repeatedly used this new situation to neglect her; he left her unattended in bed for hours and withheld her food. He clearly demon-

strated that he was in charge now and had the final say, and she had to submit to him. Felix continued in this manner until his mother died.

> I always advise parents against covert medicine administration. As tempting and instantly effective this approach may seem, it encroaches on the patients' privacy and undermines the maturation process of their personality.

Under particularly favorable conditions, such as a low-stress environment with reliable caregivers, the acute psychosis of teenagers can be treated on an outpatient or halfway house basis, sometimes even without medication.

The Soteria model of Loren R. Mosher is such an example. The idea behind the model was to create a low-stimulus environment. Soteria is a residential community, or so-called halfway house, providing young schizophrenia patients with a non-threatening atmosphere, shielded from overstimulation, and in which a primarily non-medical staff work together with the patients. The patients retain all their personal rights, can maintain their social contacts with the outside world, and take responsibility for daily chores. Medication, if any, is administered only as a second therapeutic tool and at the lowest possible dosage.

Grandparents may also take on such a role as caretakers. They do not feel the same level of responsible for their grandchild with schizophrenia as parents do and can therefore remain calmer and less reactive.

Medication intake lies with the patient

The best long-term results with drug treatment of schizophrenia patients is achieved when they learn to take responsibility for the medication themselves. Yet one should bear in mind that this goal can only be achieved one step at a time. Several relapses may occur before they learn when and how to take their medication.

Being told by the doctor, the therapist or parents that they have to take medication is experienced by many as an invasion of their private sphere. They mostly view medical professionals as an extended arm of their parents or, in the broadest sense, of society, which they automatically resist. If they are being ordered or even forced to take medication, they feel patronized. Therefore, it is important that medical professionals do not present themselves as authority figures but act as coaches who give advice rather than orders. It is only by trial and error that schizophrenia patients may finally take responsibility and learn to administer medication on their own.

> **CASE HISTORY:** Arthur was an intelligent but headstrong boy. From early childhood until beyond puberty, he often engaged in power struggles with his mother. In most cases, he prevailed; his mother gave up and suffered in silence. His father, for the most part, abstained from the conflict between mother and son, practicing his instrument – he was a musician by profession.
> After having completed a second master's degree abroad, Arthur started his first job back home. Not for long, however. He had problems with his superiors because he constantly came up with suggestions for improvement, which were neither asked for nor appreciated. He took offense at being told do his job and felt as though he was not being taken seriously, so he tried even harder but ended up being fired. Soon afterward, he accepted a new job in another company but was plagued by the fear that the same thing could happen to him again. He therefore sought therapeutic advice from me. Unfortunately, he couldn't control his impulses and gave his new boss suggestions for improvement. Even though his behavior was tolerated, he was scared of losing his job once again. Panic-stricken, he suffered from delusions and travelled throughout Switzerland to escape his supposed persecutors. He had become psychotic.

One day, the company social worker got involved. She worked out a specific contract with strict rules for Arthur, which he had to sign. Shortly thereafter, the social worker informed me that Arthur couldn't adhere to the rules and asked me to prescribe medication because she thought Arthur was seriously ill, yet he refused to take any.

FOLLOW-UP AND COMMENTARY: The company doctor sent Arthur for a special evaluation to have him diagnosed properly. After many tests, the diagnosis of an initial period of psychosis I had made long before was confirmed.

At this point, his father contacted me. I instructed him to bring his son for a consultation as soon as possible but without putting pressure on him. I prescribed medication for him. At a subsequent meeting, I explained to Arthur that his brain was running like a turbo engine, preventing him from sleeping. This made sense to him, and he allowed me to oversee the therapeutic process. From then on, he was willing to take a small dose of neuroleptics. He also took my advice to quit his job since it was too stressful for him. After taking some time off, he looked for new employment. The new workplace was better for him, and he could soon discontinue his medication. I only saw him once every two or three months. In one of those rare sessions, he informed me that he had taken his medication again before an important meeting with his boss because he sensed that he was starting to have paranoid thoughts again. Arthur had learned to independently administer his medication whenever the situation required it.

Parents, stay out of it!

Schizophrenia sufferers often refuse medication in the acute phase, as noted previously, because psychotropic drugs are representative of external control. For that very reason, parents have to leave the drug treatment in the patient's own responsibility. They would do well to seek support for themselves in how to manage their adolescent but refrain from focusing just on medication.

Making anxious inquiries into the subject of the patient's medication is not helpful. Parental interference, likewise, is at best a hindrance. At worst, the temptation to mix medication into their offspring's food or drink, as in Felix's case, is inevitably feeding the patient's paranoia and fosters his dependency on parental control. Even with the best of intentions, parental condescension does not prevent relapses. The patient has to be self-motivated when it comes to learning how to prevent relapses. In any case, parents should accept that their affected offspring may have relapses but can nevertheless still make progress in their development towards adulthood.

> It is the patient's responsibility to prevent a relapse – not the parents'. Relapses are inevitable but will not impede learning.

Schizophrenia patients have to learn over the course of therapy when to take their psychotropic drugs. This is particularly important as these drugs can in fact interfere with one's personality. All psychotropic drugs have a different status than drugs for physical illnesses. The willingness of schizophrenia patients to take responsibility for their behavior, managing their medication intake on their own, is an important part of their autonomy and self-determined life. It gradually develops during the therapeutic process.

Vocational Rehabilitation

Rehabilitation programs are not sufficient

The choice of profession in Western societies plays an important role in everybody's life in terms of self-support and public recognition. It is also vital for developing a healthy self-respect and self-esteem. This also applies to individuals with schizophrenia. Systemic therapy and counselling should therefore always promote and support vocational training and rehabilitation in addition to family therapy and therapeutic treatment of the patient.

There are, however, very limited opportunities in the medical system of today for successful vocational rehabilitation of young schizophrenia patients. The existing services on offer are not sufficiently geared to the particular needs of this group of patients.

Standard procedures are not effective

The official vocational rehabilitation process begins when the patient and the psychiatrist have completed the government's disability claim forms. These medical documents should help the disability insurance to obtain the necessary information about the nature of the disorder, thereby enabling a more successful vocational rehabilitation.

These insurance forms are primarily designed for patients with physical or mental disabilities, even though nearly 50% of applicants for disability benefits nowadays suffer from psychiatric disorders. There is limited opportunity for therapists to submit detailed supplementary information on patients' interaction patterns with their environment. The decision-making body of the disability fund seems only marginally interested in this type of information. Furthermore, the decisions for disability benefits are primarily judged from a legal perspective as well as a focus on the diagnosis of the illness, rather than on the potential resources and resilience of that person.

However, if the application for vocational rehabilitation is approved, the next step is a routine placement in a sheltered workshop to assess the patient's working ability. Unfortunately, sheltered workshops, which are multi-purpose institutions, are primarily set up for physically and mentally disabled patients and therefore not very effective, and even less suited for vocational rehabilitation of young schizophrenia sufferers who mostly have high intellectual potential.

Individuals with schizophrenia are extremely touchy about having to tolerate evaluations by institutions, which often have a critical attitude towards them. Owing to their sensitivity and insecurity, they easily feel underappreciated in terms of their cognitive potential, and also as a person.

For that reason, several research programs have concluded that standardized rehabilitation programs are not very effective in vocational rehabilitation of young persons with schizophrenia.

Job coaching – the alternative approach

As an alternative to placing psychiatric patients in sheltered workshops, there are currently new programs such as job coaching and supported employment. Such procedures are designed to support individuals with schizophrenia as they seek jobs on the open market. This approach to vocational rehabilitation was evaluated by several research programs and proved to be more effective and thus more promising than the traditional programs in sheltered workshops. The guiding principle for this new form of vocational rehabilitation of psychiatric patients can be summarized as follows:

> First place, then train.

Placing young schizophrenia patients in jobs on the open market in regular apprenticeship programs, vocational education or even in academic training, differs greatly from the traditional programs, which are geared towards observing patients and evaluating their behavior in artificial settings where the performance level is rather low and the task often meaningless for the patients.

Direct placement of patients in the free job market, however, always requires an experienced job coach who guides patients as well as employers. An important detail is that patients have to make their own decision based on their skills and personalities. Job coaching and supported employment are personalized, rehabilitative measures for young psychiatric patients. The routine procedure of job coaches is as follows:

- First consult with the patient and their therapeutic professional to find out what kind of job suits their inclination, skills and personality.
- Search for suitable workplaces, look carefully at skills and personality, and to what extent they match with the job requirements.
- Pay special attention to the personalities of superiors and co-workers and assess how well they may fit with the patient's personality.
- After deciding that a job is likely to be suitable, visit the potential employment site with the patient.
- If a job looks fitting, introduce the patient to the superiors at the arranged workplace.
- Whenever superiors and co-workers are willing to engage in the experiment and match with the patient, a temporary placement is arranged.
- The job coach continuously provides advice and support to the supervisors and co-workers, while keeping in contact with the patient and their therapist at the same time.
- In case the temporary appointment proves to be successful, it is transformed into regular employment.

- The job coach, however, must continue to provide support to the workplaces and the patient, and stay in contact with the therapist, although less frequently.

Providing job coaching to schizophrenia patients is an important part of systemic therapeutic rehabilitation. It can be carried out by specialized job coaches or by systems therapists themselves.

The vocational rehabilitation of persons with schizophrenia by means of therapeutic support and job coaching is, as I stated previously, often much more advantageous than long periods of observation and training in sheltered workshops. Those institutions usually don't match the individual skills of the patients to the right job, meaning they are often performing below their intellectual ability, which is a blow to their ego.

Contrary to common belief and long-held practice, young people who have undergone an acute psychotic episode do not necessarily require a longer stay in a rehabilitation facility. Such type of long-lasting rehabilitation might even hinder the development of responsible conduct and prevent patients from achieving autonomy. Instead, it rather increases patients' fear of a future regular job and thus has a negative impact on their self-esteem. For that reason, I advise against staying in institutional rehabilitation programs for too long. Instead, I encourage young people with schizophrenia to look for a job as soon as they are ready, even enroll at a university for a regular course in a suitable educational program or get into a regular training program such as an apprenticeship that matches their inclinations and aptitude.

When difficulties arise in the chosen pathway and the patient has a flight reaction – tempted to run away as is often the case – job coaches, therapists, superiors and social workers have to get together again to guide the patient through the crisis and encourage them to persevere. However, flight reactions may also imply that the choice of job or study program was wrong, and a closer evaluation should be made.

Parents as obstacles to job coaching

On the one hand, parents are always influenced by their own high ambitions, which come into play when their children choose their profession. However, another instinct is to shield them. Parents of young schizophrenia sufferers are even more inclined to protect their children from disappointment since they assume that they are easily discouraged by failure, which might apply to many patients on account of their high sensitivity as well as reactivity. For this reason, I always try to include the parents in the process of vocational rehabilitation.

The job coach or therapist asks the parents for their opinion to ascertain where they stand on this issue, and how they judge their patient's skills and preferences. Quite often, parents do not believe that their child is able to meet the conditions of regular employment or higher education. They all too frequently cast doubt on their endurance and prefer to wait and see. Parental caution of this kind, however, tends to put the brakes on the patient's intellectual ability and hinders all efforts of the job coach. Especially mothers are typically not aware of being overprotective, presenting an obstacle to professional integration. Moreover, patients with schizophrenia get easily affected by their parents' anxiety and indecisiveness and thereby become discouraged about making their own decisions.

Mental health professionals who are risk-averse frequently have a similar protective attitude concerning their therapeutic interventions and tend to assign young schizophrenia patients to sheltered workshops to evaluate their endurance and ability to perform. However, this type of mindset is a wasted opportunity for young persons with schizophrenia to be successfully rehabilitated in the regular job market.

> **CASE HISTORY:** After graduating from high school, Hans started university. Overwhelmed and disoriented, he pursued all sorts of other activities. His mind was turbo-charged, he became ever more restless and could not sleep any more. He was diagnosed as manic-depressive and

admitted to a psychiatric hospital. His parents were dismayed by their son's psychotic episode – his career was blocked by his illness – and asked for professional advice and support.

COMMENTARY: Hans was under the assumption that he had to go to university to satisfy his parents' expectations, but it was not where his interests lay. As a first step, I had to build up his parents' shaken confidence. They were completely rattled and questioned his ability to ever make it in the real world. Dropping their fundamental concerns did not come easy to them. As a second step, to take the pressure off, I had to free his parents from their fears, doubts and disappointments; both were teachers. However, they managed to give Hans some time to reorient himself and establish a new network of relationships, so that he could decide on his career choice without their interference. Hans' first job as a pizza deliverer was clearly below their expectations but they nevertheless accepted it. After a while, he was promoted in his workplace but he didn't stay on. As a next step, he took a job at a printing company in a different city and started an apprenticeship, which he successfully completed three years later. Hans eventually settled with his own small printing business, satisfied with life and job.

After the great shock and uncertainty caused by acute psychosis, patients are often not yet ready to re-engage in a competitive activity. They feel ashamed, having lost face or been ridiculed – fears that are not entirely unjustified. Therefore, it is advisable to allow them time to reorient themselves. Caution should be applied: pushing them too fast, too hard, will only cause harm.

Successful cooperation with employers

Successful integration of young schizophrenia patients in the open labor market not only depends on the willingness of companies, the use of job coaches, the attitude of parents, and the general economic situation but – as in all rehabilitation efforts – also on the patient's motivation and readiness to get involved in ordinary life, as demonstrated in the case history of *Hans*.

Young schizophrenia patients, prepared to resume work, should be given support in finding an appropriate temporary placement or in signing up for a suitable apprenticeship. Integration efforts should be based on a resource-oriented approach that prioritizes talents, skills and special interests while always maintaining or promoting social contact and using existing networks for guidance and as resources. Consulting a career counsellor may also be helpful as a supportive measure.

Placing young people with schizophrenia in the open labor market could even be advantageous for the respective companies. Employers sometimes welcome the advice of qualified job coaches or systems therapists and are interested in receiving psychological consulting. They even consider job coaching a form of internal training in management skills, which are valuable for learning how to handle difficult personnel in various situations.

I have frequently experienced that superiors are more committed to rehabilitation efforts than is commonly assumed. Moreover, cooperation with employers, coaches or teachers is quite often associated with fewer conflicts of competence than is frequently the case with the personnel of vocational rehabilitation institutions.

Final Words to Parents

Learning from mistakes

The end of this book is intended to encourage desperate parents with a few words of advice. You might have noticed the therapeutic suggestions I made at many different stages, pointing out harmful developments that build up over generations, which you – as members of your families of origin – have a stake in. I neither wish to assign blame nor condemn your actions. Guilt and condemnation have no place in systemic family therapy – however, mistakes do. We all learn from our mistakes. If we do not recognize our mistakes, we are unable to seek advice. We should aim to overcome this emotional trap and ask ourselves how we can approach and deal with unsolved emotional undercurrents in our system.

Courage to accept imperfection

Signs of discouragement are widespread. Who likes the feeling of having done something wrong, this nagging sense of guilt? We need the courage to be imperfect to shift our attention to new objectives and a forward-looking vision. To achieve this, we should neither rely on perfection nor despair. Both paralyze and cause a standstill. Admitting our mistakes – especially as parents – may lead us to believe that we have lost some of our dignity and self-worth. However, denying mistakes equates to weakness. Having the courage to accept past, present and tomorrow's mistakes – that is strength. Mistakes keep us flexible, allowing us to adjust our mindset.

Ready for change

I cannot emphasize enough the importance of diversity between men and women, as well as the significant and, at the same time, calming influence of the different child rearing methods used as part of maternal and paternal roles. The striking difference of instructional strategies does not trigger schizophrenia. But by fighting each other over who has the better method, you harm yourself as well as your children. Differences between parents that are openly stated and acknowledged encourages a differentiated perception in the children. The social adaptability is also strengthened when you communicate clearly with each other and, at the same time, show respect towards the different attitude of your partner. Children thereby receive a flexible basic mental structure of thought and are thereby strengthened for future conflicts in daily life.

The best of all things possible

By seeking help for yourself, you are helping your sick child. If you don't learn to seek help, then no one can help you.

But always remember that it takes time to change. More time than you might like. However, the courage it takes to achieve small steps will inspire you to take the next one.

Emotional maturity does not mean perfection. It means a sense of achieving what is possible. Make it possible for yourself; your child may mature accordingly.

Readiness for change in the family setting is for you to determine – as a parent. But don't forget your own biography. Knowing the history of your family of origin and learning how to interpret and deal with it – including the taboos – frees the next generation from unsolved turbulent undercurrents of accumulated emotions, so-called *emotional monster waves*. Heed my advice to listen to the echo of your family system, which reproduces the affective disorder in your family of origin.

Glossary

ADD: Attention deficit disorder without hyperactivity, a congenital special neurotype, not accompanied by diminished intelligence.

ADHD: Attention deficit and hyperactivity disorder. Congenital special neurotype, not accompanied by diminished intelligence.

Allergy: Overreaction of the immune system to bacterial, chemical, or any other noxious stimuli, including stress.

Amotivational syndrome: Loss of motivation, apathy, and lethargy caused by the regular use of cannabis.

Anorexia: Eating disorder, a refusal to eat, popular with teenage girls, usually triggered by emotional problems.

Anticipation: Feeling of something that is going to occur in the near future.

Antisocial personality disorder: Psychiatric diagnosis characterized by disregard for social norms being replaced by self-declared norms and rules.

Anxious mother with a loud mouth: Mothers who at first glance seem to be strong but in fact are stressed, which is reflected in overactive loud verbal behavior, a term coined by Murray Bowen.

Apathy: Lack of interest, enthusiasm and concern.

Associative communication style: Non-linear thought process, jumping from one topic to another, typical for people with ADHD, ADD and schizophrenia.

Attractor: A concept from the theory of dynamic systems. In family systems, it describes an individual's situation which attracts the attention of the social surrounding up to the point that the individual gets easily drawn into the role of a scapegoat for all emotional issues in their social environment, in particular the family.

Autism: An extremely withdrawn state in schizophrenia. Behavior that is unusually centered on the self. Term from adult psychiatry but also used for children who are severely withdrawn, limiting their development of social and communication skills.

Basic neurological disorders in schizophrenia: Concept created by Lilo Süllwold. Minimal brain dysfunctions which are genetically determined and can be measured in family members and patients before the outbreak of acute schizophrenia.

Big Bang moment for autonomy: The ultimate drama of breaking away from parental control.

Biographical work: Life history calendar method. Interpretation of individual biographies within their family system. Historical data of the different family members are interpreted in a contextual way.

Bipolar disorder: Mental illness characterized by extreme mood changes with phases of severe depression and manic episodes.

Blackout: A temporary failure of cognition and memory during a period of extreme stress.

Brainstorming: Using the brain's hyperactivity for problem-solving. A method to find new unconventional ideas and solutions.

Bulimia: Bulimia nervosa. Massive binge-eating followed by self-induced vomiting, a diagnosis more common in women.

Case history: Medical recording of life events and medical history.

Catatonia, catatonic stupor: Blockage of speech and motor capacity caused by extreme hyperarousal, a dangerous state of acute schizophrenia.

Cerebral edema: Swelling of the entire brain, occurring with infections and trauma, or highly elevated state of arousal during the acute phase of schizophrenia, in the worst case resulting in death.

Chronically stable: Permanent disability with no active disease process.

Cluster risk: Combination of various risk factors for a specific disease.

Cognition: Conscious processing capacity of the brain, thought formation and planning of thoughts as well as actions.

Color conflict method: Method to test the inability of handling conflict in a family (A.

Holte). A card set with different colors is handed out to the family members with the misinformation that all family members have received the same set. In families with a low ability to handle conflict, the family members oppress their own perception of existing color differences in order to maintain peace by consensus, and thereby stability of the family system. This type of behavior is present in families with schizophrenia.

Communication deviance: Communication styles differ greatly from the norm observed in families with schizophrenia patients (Lyman Wynne and Margaret Singer).

Comorbidity or concomitant illness: Two or more diagnostically separate conditions which occur together in the same patient.

Compliance: Compliance in therapy means that the patient follows all the treatment orders in the therapeutic process.

Non-compliance: Patients who don't not follow the medical treatment orders given by the doctors are called non-compliant. Discontinuation of therapy is the most extreme form of non-compliance.

Concordant: The same illness, e.g. schizophrenia, in two genetically identical twins.

Conditional love: A person's love for another individual is subject to conditions such as following rules or obeying orders.

Cortex: The outer part of the brain, called cerebral cortex, which accounts for most of the mass of a human brain. It mostly developed in the primate lineage leading to modern humans.

Cortisone: A hormone that is released under stress, also used as medication.

Decentralization: A term coined by Jean Piaget, an essential developmental step during adolescence, overcoming the childlike ego-centric view of the world, being able to look at something from another perspective.

Delegation: A projection process, delegating unsolved problems or unfulfilled goals in the family onto one or several children of the next generation.

Delusions: Subjective ideas and interpretations of reality not congruent with common sense.

Delusional jealousy: Exaggerated jealousy for which there is no objective reason. It can be interpreted as a projection of one's own inferiority complex towards potential competitors.

Delusion of reference: Perceiving events and conversations in the environment as personal signals and messages to self.

Detachment from the family of origin: Becoming independent from the family of origin.

Differentiation: A systemically defined individuation, leading to emotional independence from the family of origin, and to emotional autonomy without losing contact or breaking off.

Unresolved detachment: An incomplete detachment from the family of origin in adolescence. It leaves the individual concerned with a sense of entitlement, which is projected in adulthood onto a partner, children, a superior or other important authority figures.

Divided loyalty: Loyalty of a child or an adult to two primary relationship persons who are in a chronic conflict with each other but are not living together under the same roof, so the child can relate to each of them separately.

Double-bind: Communication style which passes on contradictory messages at different levels at the same time, and punishment follows either way. Therefore, the individual is always caught in a trap.

Emotional psychosis: Acute psychotic reaction of short duration triggered by extreme stress of short duration.

Emotional monster wave: Escalation of emotions which spin over from the emotional brain, the limbic system to the forebrain, the prefrontal cortex, leading to the onset of psychosis. This mechanism is comparable to the natural phenomenon of a monster wave in the ocean, causing destruction when hitting the shore.

Empathy: The ability to sympathize with another person's feelings.

Empowerment: Assigning competence and power to a person who feels unable to act.

Endogenous psychosis: Psychosis that has arisen from within the patient and is not caused by any external factors.

Entitlement: A concept by the family therapist Ivan Boszormenyi-Nagy, relating to the right of a person to have their needs met as an adult for what they have missed out on owing to emotional deprivation in childhood.

Ephemeris: The phenomenon when hidden values or issues in a system suddenly come to the fore.

Equally valuable: A term coined by Jesper Juul, describing a parental attitude towards children and adolescents by which their perceptions of reality are taken just as serious and valuable as those of adults – should not be confused with equal rights.

Exogenous psychosis: Psychosis or schizophrenia which is triggered by outside influence such as poisoning or massive stress coming from the environment.

Experiential therapy: The experiential therapeutic approach relates to Carl A. Whitaker who as family therapist behaved unexpectedly crazier than his schizophrenia patient, hereby surprising them and their family, almost forcing them into normal behavior.

Family group therapy: Group of parents of schizophrenia patients or other psychiatric patients led by a systems therapist with the goal of promoting a learning and developmental process in the participants.

Fight reaction: One of the three primitive automated stress reactions triggered in schizophrenia sufferers in situations perceived by them as threatening or potentially hurtful.

Flight of ideas: Accelerated thought process, racing of thoughts in an increased state of arousal. Lots of thoughts push into consciousness simultaneously, a formal thought disorder during the state of acute schizophrenia.

Flight reaction: One of the three primitive automated stress reactions triggered in schizophrenia sufferers in situations perceived by them as threatening or dangerous.

Focusing factors: Specific family constellations under which a child is born or traits, abilities, disabilities, which all lead to increased emotional attention of the family towards that child. Other family problems may additionally get projected onto that child too.

Forced admission: Admission of patients into a closed institution against their will because there is danger of self-harm or harming others. This procedure always requires a medical examination, allowing the doctor to admit the patient.

Formal thought disorder: Speech patterns run at a higher speed in a state of high arousal, logical coherence of formal thought processes are no longer guaranteed in an acute episode of schizophrenia.

Freeze reaction: One of the three stress reactions whereby motor and cognitive responsiveness are completely blocked, but consciousness is not altered.

Functional helplessness: A term coined by Murray Bowen during his schizophrenia research at NIMH, relating to fathers who were successful as individuals in their job but were utterly helpless and insecure as father figures within the family.

Genogram: Recording of a family tree, capturing essential individual data of the various family members over three or more generations as well as relationship data between the different family members.

Hallucinations: Imagined sensory perceptions, such as hearing voices, that do not come from external stimuli but are self-generated within the brain, a phenomenon typical of schizophrenia.

Hebephrenia: Schizophrenia of young patients who behave in a regressive fashion but usually do not have a sophisticated delusion system.

High Expressed Emotions or high EEs: A communication style which is hostile, critical and emotionally overinvolved.

Hospitalization: Admission to a clinic or a hospital.

Hyperarousal: Overexcited state of the primitive reptilian brain leading to sleeplessness.

Hypervigilance: Increased alertness with extremely high brain activity, leading to overinterpretation of stimuli or hallucination.

Hyperfrontality: Hyperactivity of the pre-frontal lobe in acute schizophrenia.

Hypofrontality: Under-functioning of the pre-frontal lobe of the brain in chronic schizophrenia patients caused by lack of stimulation due to their withdrawn life, as well as long term neuroleptic drug treatment.

Hypoglycaemic coma: State of unconsciousness, achieved by a lower blood glucose level with high insulin injection as a treatment method for schizophrenia patients who have been unsuccessfully treated with conventional therapeutic measures such as neuroleptic medication.

Hypophysis: See pituitary gland, is directly attached to the lower part of the middle brain, the limbic system, responsible for emotions and motivation.

Il faut reculer pour mieux sauter: Withdrawing in order to improve one's chances of subsequent progress and success.

Intimidation: To bully somebody.

Job coaching or supported employment: Individual vocational rehabilitation measure in which a consultative expert supports patients in finding a job in the free market and helps them to keep the job by also coaching the supervisor, thus the expert is a supportive partner of both the employee and the employer.

Kin selection: Survival strategy of a group of individuals who are genetically related.

Largactil: First psychiatric medication discovered from an antihistaminic medication in France, 1951.

Life events: Stressful events in one's life history.

Life history calendar method: Retrospective, going through important biographical events in the life of a person and constructing a coherent narrative as an attempt to explain the development of an illness (see Belli, Shay, Stafford, 2001; Cassi et al., 1996).

Love illusions: A love affair which exists only in fantasy, projected onto a non-existent or real person who has no interest in a relationship.

Malignant puberty: Adolescent phase which reaches far into adulthood and has psychotic features, including self-destructive behavior, caused by the suppression of aggressive emotions in the separation conflict. This pubertal aberration is typical for schizophrenia patients. It hinders the development towards adulthood.

Mania: Phase of mental illness marked by high levels of arousal, strong inner drive, feelings of euphoria, lack of distance in social contact behavior combined with high irritability and a significantly reduced need for sleep.

Manic-depressive disorder: Extreme emotional fluctuations between depressive phases, followed by phases of mania called mood swings.

Megalomania: Exaggerated form of mania with crazed perception of self and an absence of rational judgement.

Meta-level: Abstract level of perception where imagined social interaction, social structures or communication are treated as facts, and everything has only symbolic meaning.

Missing link: Missing information in an incoherent and inconsistent family narrative or family history as a result of taboos.

Monoamines: Substances naturally occurring in the brain which have a stimulating and activating effect.

Monoaminooxidase: An enzyme that breaks down monoamines.

MRI: Magnetic Resonance Imaging. Noninvasive three-dimensional imaging technology through magnetic uploading of cellular structure, producing three-dimensional detailed images.

Multifactorial genesis of schizophrenia: Theory that assumes genetic as well as environmental stress factors involved in the development of schizophrenia.

Mystification: Blurring, unclear communication style observed in families with schizophrenia, a term coined by Ronald D. Laing.

Narcissistic: Exaggerated self-centered and self-referential information processing, highly sensitive to any criticism.

Narrative reconstructivism: A therapeutic method in which patients tell their life stories, and the therapeutic expert only asks questions for clarification without providing any interpretations. A method which promotes a new feeling of coherence of self.

Neuroleptics: Drugs used for treatment of schizophrenia which act on the dopamine system of the brain.

Neurotransmitter: Messenger substance which transmits impulses from one nerve cell to another.

Olfactory bulb: The Olfactory Bulb is a brain structure responsible for our sense of smell. Located at the tip of the olfactory lobe from which our forebrain and cortex developed.

Paradigm: A concept accepted by the majority

of people because of its effectiveness within a culturally or ethnically defined group in explaining a complex issue.

Paradoxical intervention: Therapeutic intervention in family systems which at first appear to go against every logic or common sense, intended to provoke change in family systems through its shocking effect.

Paranoia: A negatively biased perception, attributing ill meaning to all action coming from the social environment or a certain person.

Parentification: A child that is drawn into a parental role whenever the parents can't fulfill their role as caretakers.

Pathogenic: Factors which lead to an illness.

Patrilineal: The male line of inheritance of goods and tradition in a family system.

Persecution complex: Thought disorder, projection of one's own fear onto another person with whom one has a conflict, attributing ill intention to that person. Such a delusion may be caused by hidden aggressions and, at the same time, fear of punishment owing to guilt feelings.

Personalized therapy: Therapy which does not follow standardized rules but is adapted to the person's individual biography as well as family history.

PET: Positron Emission Tomography, an imaging technique of the brain.

Phobia: Anxiety disorder. The central feature is an unfounded, persistent fear of situations, objects, activities, persons, or fear of being observed in public, therefore avoiding such situations.

Pituitary gland or hypophysis: Central endocrine gland situated at the interface of the emotional brain and the hormonal system, receives direct impulses from the brain and has control over the entire hormone system in the human body.

Play Dead reflex or Freeze reaction: One of the three stress reactions, also called scared stiff. The spontaneous flow of thoughts as well as movements are completely blocked but no change of consciousness occurs.

Pre-frontal cortex: Part of the cerebral cortex located in the frontal area, which is between the limbic system and the outer cortex, important for focusing.

Pre-psychotic: Mental condition just before the outbreak of acute psychosis. The cognitive functions are not yet fully impaired but hyperarousal, increased irritability and concrete thinking are noticeable.

Personality development: Psychological development during adolescence as interaction of genetically inherited traits and social environment.

Pseudo-individuality: Personality based on the needs of the family system and not on talent and character traits.

Pseudo-mutuality: Outwardly agreeing with each other while having deep-seated conflicts, a term coined by Theodore Lidz.

Psychiatric hospitalism: Adapting to life in a psychiatric institution, not being able to live independently outside of the institution any more.

Psycho-educational method: Educational therapy held in groups in which the participants, such as parents of schizophrenia patients, are instructed how to behave towards their sick family member. The method may also be used with schizophrenia patients themselves as a type of behavioral therapy in groups.

Psychosis: Serious mental illness with thought disorder, thus losing touch with reality. Patients experience their surroundings as having changed rather than realizing the changes within their own perception and behavior.

Psychosomatic illness: Physical illnesses which have a psychological background, often not recognized or accepted by patients or doctors.

Psychotropic drugs: Drugs which change the functioning of the psyche, thus act upon the brain, thereby inducing a change of mood, emotions, thinking as well as behavior.

Puberty: Developmental phase during which young people fight for self-governance, responsibility and independence from their caregiver in order to develop their own personality and way of life.

Puppy license: Concept from animal psychology. Puppies are tolerated by their mothers even when they attack them and are therefore protected from adult aggression. The same principle can be applied to teenagers when they fight their parents.

Pyrrhic victory: The term goes back to the bloody victory of King Pyrrhus over the Romans, which had been achieved through high losses and finally amounted to failure. The winner was weakened by the conflict to such a degree that he could not build on his success.

Regression: Falling back as an adult into an earlier stage of development with childlike behavior.

Relational disability: Typical for schizophrenia patients who are incapacitated by their increased sensitivity and therefore have difficulties in forming and maintaining relationships. They easily feel offended and, as a consequence, withdraw at the slightest criticism.

Relationship history: Description of emotional interaction over a longer period of time, e.g. in a symbiotic relationship between mother and child.

Replacement child: Child born shortly after the death of an older sibling, has the task of helping the family to cope with their grief.

Rule of thumb for the prognosis of schizophrenia: 1/3 healing spontaneously, 1/3 stabilizing at a lower level, 1/3 becoming chronically ill.

Schizophrenia: The literal meaning of the Greek term is "split mind", or split psyche. The term schizophrenia was coined by Eugen Bleuler, referring mostly to the ambivalence of schizophrenia patients.

Schizophrenia with manic features: Strong manic episodes with euphoric emotions and delusional ideas of greatness but without paranoid thoughts of persecution.

Schizophrenogenic mother: This term was introduced by Frieda Fromm-Reichmann in 1948. Her hypothesis was that mothers of schizophrenia patients contribute to the development of schizophrenia in their children. The term later came into disrepute because of its guilt-inducing effect: it implicated mothers while ignoring the role of the fathers.

Second opinion: Asking for the medical opinion of another doctor.

Sheltered job: Special jobs organized for patients in the open labor market, supported by coaching and wage subsidies.

Sheltered shop: Specialized institutions helping patients to adapt to regular occupations in order to be reintegrated later in a regular job.

Social inheritance: Passing on behavior and thinking patterns from generation to generation by model learning, and also formal moral and ethical instruction in contrast to genetic inheritance.

Soteria: Communal living model, conceived by Loren Mosher, for young schizophrenia patients. In a low-stimuli environment, patients live together with non-medical personnel. The patients' rights are respected, their social network is retained and responsibilities for everyday chores shared within the community. Medication, if at all, is used as little as possible.

SPECT: Single-Photon Emission Computed Tomography.

Split loyalty: Bonding behavior of a child with two significant caretakers such as parents who are in constant conflict with each other while in the presence of that child.

Structural responsibility: The oldest sibling usually feels responsible for the functioning of the entire family, keeping up the family system's structure, such as hierarchy as well as family rules.

Supported employment or job coaching: Vocational rehabilitation by helping the patients find a job in the free market with continuous support for the patients as well as their superiors.

Symbiosis: Refers to a close and prolonged interdependent relationship of two individuals or organisms.

Symbiotic mother-child relationship: Close and prolonged mutual dependency between mother and child which leads to a better chance of survival for the offspring in its infancy but obstructs the development towards autonomy in adolescence.

Synapses: Nerve endings where "messages" are transmitted from one nerve cell to another.

System overflow: The brain is unable to process and adapt to an excess of simultaneous stimuli.

Systems therapy: The relationship system is the focus of therapeutic interventions, promoting change in the patient.

Thought disorder: Delusions and hallucinations, complex intellectual constructs not based on external reality but rather stimulated by emotional pain, a symptom of schizophrenia.

Thrift theory: Poverty is not considered a cause for the development of schizophrenia, but rather a consequence of the illness in a chronic phase.

Glossary

Timing: Optimal choice of time for therapeutic interventions.

Top-down behavior in therapy: Hierarchical therapeutic interventions giving medical orders which must be followed by patients and their families without being questioned.

Trial and error: Method of learning by doing and correcting along the way whenever failures occur.

Triangle: Three-person-relationship, e.g. between mother, father and child. The child is usually dragged into the parents' partnership conflict, but one parent can also be dragged into the conflict the other parent has with the child, term coined by Bowen.

Triangulating behavior: Dragging somebody into a conflict one has with another person as helper or "protector".

Tsunami: Seismic sea waves caused mostly by underwater volcanic eruptions or earthquakes with devastating destructive effects on coastal areas upon arrival of the wave.

Unconditional love: Support, nurturing love and affection without any conditions attached, typical for maternal behavior.

Vulnerability: Special susceptibility to stress or certain conflictual conditions due to genetically determined sensitivity.

Word salad: Scraps of unintelligible words which may be grammatically correct but are semantically confused to the point that the listener cannot extract any meaning from them.

Bibliography

Benton A. J.: Developmental dyslexia: Neurological aspects. In: Friedlander W. J.: Advances in Neurology, vol. VII. Raven Press, New York 1975.

Bernau S.: Hilfen für den Zappelphilipp, das Selbsthilfe-Elternbuch, Herder, Freiburg 1995.

Biederman J.: Attention-Deficit/Hyperactivity Disorder. A Life-span Perspective. In: J Clin Psychiatry 1998, 59: 4–16.

Biederman J.: ADHD and juvenile mania: an overlooked comorbidity? In: Academy of Child and Adolescent Psychiatry 1971, 3: 997–1008.

Biederman J., et al.: Pharmacotherapy of ADHD reduces risk for substance use Disorder. Paediatric Vol. 104, 1999.

Biederman J., et al: Further evidence for family-genetic risk factors in ADHD: patterns of comorbidity in probands and relatives in psychiatrically and pediatrically referred samples. Arch Gen Psychiatry. 1992, 49: 728–738.

Biederman J., Faraone S., Milberger S., Guite J.: A prospective 4-year follow-up study of attention-deficit hyperactivity and related disorders. Archives of General Psychiatry, 1996, 53 (5), 437–446.

Bird H.R., et al: Estimates of prevalence of childhood maladjustment in a community survey in Puerto Rico, Archives of General Psychiatry, 1987, 44.

Bleuler E.: Lehrbuch der Psychiatrie. Revised fifteenth edition by M. Bleuler, Springer, Berlin 1983.

Bleuler M.: Die schizophrenen Geistesstörungen im Lichte langjähriger Kranken- und Familiengeschichten. Thieme, Stuttgart 1972.

Bock T., et al: Schweizer Archiv für Neurologie und Psychiatrie, Vol. 163 Nr. 4, 6/2012.

Bodenmann, G.: Die Folgen von Scheidung für Kinder aus psychologischer Sicht. In: Rumo-Jungo A., Pichonnaz A.: Kinder und Scheidung. Schulthess Verlag, Zurich 2006.

Bowen M.: Family Therapy in Clinical Practice, Jason Aronson, New York 1978.

Bowen M.: Die Familie als Bezugsrahmen für die Schizophrenieforschung. In: Schizophrenie und Familie. Suhrkamp, Frankfurt a. M. 1992,181–219.

Brenner H. D., Böker W.: Verlaufsprozesse schizophrener Erkrankungen. Hans Huber, Bern 1992.

Brent D., et al: Personality disorder, tendency to impulsive violence and suicidal behavior in adolescents. In: Academy of Child and Adolescent Psychiatry. 1993: 32: 69–75.

Brent D., et al: Psychiatric risk factors for adolescent suicide: a case-control study. In: Academy of Child and Adolescent Psychiatry. 1993, 32: 521–529.

Brewin C. R., et al: Attribution and expressed emotion in the relatives of patients with schizophrenia. Journal of Abnormal Psychology. 1991, 546–554.

Brown G. W., Carstairs G. M., Topping G.: Post-hospital adjustment of chronic mental patients. The Lancet 2, 1958, 685–689.

Brown G.W., et. al: Influence of family life on the course of schizophrenic disorders: a replication. British Journal of Psychiatry. 1972, 121, 241–258.

Buhrmester D., Camparo L., Christensen A., et al.: Mothers and fathers interacting in dyads and triads with normal and hyperactive sons. The University of Texas at Dallas, School of Human Development, Richardson, US Developmental Psychology. 1992, 28 (3), 500–509.

Burns T., Catty J., Becker T., Drake R. E., et al: The effectiveness of supported employment for people with severe mental illness: a randomized controlled trial for the EqolIise Group.

Butler F. S., et al: Affective comorbidity in children and adolescents with attention deficit hyperactivity disorder. In: Clin. Psychiatry 1995: 7: 51–55.

Cantwell D.: Genetics of hyperactivity. J. Child Psychol. Psychiatry. 1975, 16, 261–264.

Cantwell D.: Psychiatric illness in the families of hyperactive children. Arch Gen Psychiatry. 1975: 27: 414–417.

Caspi A., Moffitt T.E., Thornton A.: Life History Calendar Method. Journal of Methods. In: 1996 – psycnet. apa.org.

Catafan A. M., et al: Prefrontal and temporal blood flow in schizophrenia: resting and activation technetium – 99 m-HMPAO SPECT patterns in young neuroleptic – naive patients with acute disease. J. Nuc Med.,1994, 35: 935–941.

Chua S. E., McKenna P. J.: Schizophrenia – a brain disease? British Journal of Psychiatry. 1995, 166, 563–582.

Ciompi L.: Affektlogik. Über die Struktur der Psyche und ihre Entwicklung. Ein Beitrag zur Schizophrenieforschung. Klett-Cotta, Stuttgart 1982.

Ciompi L.: Die emotionalen Grundlagen des Denkens. Vandenhoeck & Ruprecht, Göttingen 1997.

Ciompi L., Hoffmann, H.: Soteria Berne. An innovative milieu therapeutic approach to acute schizophrenia based on the concept of affectlogic. World Psychiatry 3:140–146, 2004.

Ciompi L., Panksepp, J.: Energetic effects of emotions on cognitions-complementary psychobiological and psychosocial findings. In: Ellis, R., Newton, N. (eds), Consciousness and Emotion, John Benjamins Publishing Company, Amsterdam/Philadelphia, 23–55, 2005.

Ciompi L., Endert E.: Gefühle machen Geschichte. Vandenhoeck & Ruprecht, Göttingen, 2011.

Ciompi L.: Vier fundamentale Mediatoren in der Langzeitentwicklung der Schizophrenie. In Böker W.: Schizophrenie als systemische Störung. Springer Verlag, 1989.

Cleghorn J. M., et al: Increased frontal and reduced parietal glucose metabolism in acute untreated schizophrenia. Psychiatry Res., 1989, 28, 119–133.

Cohen P., et al: An epidemiological study of disorders in late childhood and adolescence. J. Child Psychol. Psychiatry. 1993, 34: 851–867.

Cunningham C. E., Benness B. B., Siegel L. S.: Family functioning, time allocation and parental depression in the families of normal and ADDH children. Journal of Clinical Child Psychology. 1988, 17(2), 169–177.

Cross-Disorder Group of the Psychiatric Genomics Consortium, Identification of risk loci with shared effects on five major psychiatric disorders: a genome-wide analysis. The Lancet 2013; 381(9875):1371–9.

Cupa Z.: Konflikte, Beziehungsabbrüche und Fokussierungsfaktoren in Familien mit einem Schizophreniekranken. Doctoral thesis with D. Hell, supervised by U. Davatz, Zurich, 1997.

Damasio, A. R.: A second chance for emotion. In: Lane, R. D., Nadel, L.: Cognitive neuroscience of emotion. Oxford University Press, Oxford 2000.

Davatz U.: Fusion and Differentiation, 1980. Washington D.C.

Davatz U.: Zusammenhang zwischen Erziehungsstil und Stressbewältigungsstrategie und der Entwicklung einer Schizophrenie. Forthcoming publication.

Day R.: Social stress and schizophrenia. From the concept of recent life events to the notion of toxic environments. Handbook of Studies on Schizophrenia, 1986-wpic.pitt.edu.

Der Spiegel: Die Seuche Cannabis. Drogen an Deutschlands Schulen. Nr.27/2004.

Deutsche Gesellschaft für Kinder- und Jugendpsychiatrie und Psychotherapie: Leitlinien zur Diagnostik und Therapie von psychischen Störungen im Säuglings-, Kindes- und Jugendalter. Deutscher Ärzte Verlag, Cologne 2000.

Deutsche Gesellschaft für Kinder- und Jugendpsychiatrie und Psychotherapie Köln: Arbeitsgemeinschaft der wissenschaftlichen medizinischen Fachgesellschaft AWMF. Leitlinien-Register Nr. 028/019, 2001.

Doane J. A., West K. L., Goldstein M. J., et al: Parental communication deviance and affective style. Archives of General Psychiatry. 1981, 38, 679–685.

Doane J. A., Goldstein M. J., Rodnick E. H.: Parental patterns of affective style and the development of schizophrenia spectrum disorders. Family Process. 1981, 20 (3), 337–349.

Ehrat F., Mattmüller-Frick F.: POS-Kinder in Schule und Familie. Haupt Bern, 5. Auflage, 1994.

Eiser H.: Hyperkinetische Störung. In: Steinhausen H.: Handbuch Verhaltenstherapie und Verhaltensmedizin bei Kindern und Jugendlichen. Weinheim, Beltz 1993.

Ernst C., Angst J.: Birth order. Its influence on personality. Springer, Berlin 1983.

Falloon I. R., Libermann R. P., Lillie F. J., Vaughn C. E.: Family therapy of schizophrenics with high risk of relapse. Family process. 1981, 20, 211–221.

Bibliography

Faraone S., et al: Evidence for the independent familial transmission of ADHD and learning disabilities: results from a family genetic study. American J. Psychiatry 1993, 150: 891–895.

Faraone S.V., Biederman J.: Neurobiology of attention-deficit hyperactivity disorder. 157th Annual Meeting, American Psychiatric Association, New York 2004a.

Fisek G. O.: A cross-cultural examination of proximity and hierarchy as dimension of family structure. In: Family Process. 1991, 30, 121–133.

Fisher B., Beckley A.: Attention Deficit Disorder. CRC Press, Florida 1998.

Freed J., Parsons L.: Zappelphilipp und Störenfriede lernen anders. Weinheim, Beltz 1997.

Fromm-Reichmann F.: Notes on the development of treatment of Schizophrenics by psychoanalytic psychotherapy. Psychiatry Washington. 1948, 11, 263–73.

Galtung J.: Theory and methods of social research. Allen & Unwin, London 1967.

Gillis J. J., et al: ADD in reading-disabled twins: evidence for a genetic etiology. J. Abnorm. Child Psychol., 1992, 20: 303–315.

Gittelman R., et al: Hyperactive boys almost grown up. Arch Gen Psychiatry, 1985, 42: 937–947.

Goldstein M. J.: The UCLA high-risk project. Schizophrenia Bulletin, 1987, 13: 505–514.

Goldstein M. J.: Family Factors that antedate the onset of schizophrenia and related disorders: The results of a 15-year prospective longitudinal study. Acta Psychiatrica Scandinavica. 1985, 319, 7–18.

Goodman R., Stevenson J.: A twin study of hyperactivity – II J. Child Psychol. Psychiatry 1989, 691–709.

Gottman J. M., Fainsilber Katz L.: Effects of marital discord on young children's peer interaction and health. Developmental Psychology. 1989, 25, 373–381.

Gottman J., Markman H., Notarius C.: The topography and marital conflict: A sequential analysis of verbal and nonverbal behavior. Journal of marriage and the family. 1977, 39, 461–477.

Grabas E. G.: Zusammenhang zwischen minimalen cerebralen Dysfunktionsstörungen mit Verhaltensauffälligkeiten in der Kindheit und späterer Schizophrenieerkrankung. Doctoral thesis with D. Hell, supervised by U. Davatz, Zurich 2005.

Gutzwiller F., Zellweger U., Wydler H., Mohler-Kuo M.: Trend in health status and behaviour among young Swiss adolescents between 1993 and 2003. Swiss Medical Weekly 2005.

Haefner H., Thurm I.: Perceived vulnerability, relapse risk and coping in schizophrenia. European Archives of Psychiatry and Neurological Sciences. 1987, 237, 46–53.

Hahlweg, K.: Einfluss interpersoneller Faktoren auf Verlauf und Therapie psychischer und somatischer Erkrankungen. Verhaltenstherapie. 1995, 5, 1–8.

Hallowell E. M.: Zwanghaft zerstreut (ADD – die Unfähigkeit aufmerksam zu sein). Rowohlt, Reinbek bei Hamburg 1998.

Hans S., Marcus J.: A process model for the development of schizophrenia. Psychiatry. 1987, 50, 361–70.

Harbauer H., Lempp R., Nissen G., Strunk K. P.: Lehrbuch der speziellen Kinder-Jugendpsychiatrie. Springer, Berlin 1976.

Harms V.: Biomathematik, Statistik und Dokumentationen, Harms, Kiel, revised 5th edition, 1988.

Harten H. U., et al: Statistik für Mediziner. VCH Verlagsgesellschaft, Weinheim 1993.

Hechtman L.: Long-term outcome in attention deficit hyperactivity disorder. Psychiatric Clin North Am, 1992, 1: 553–565.

Hell D., Fischer-Gerstenfeld M.: Schizophrenien. Verständnisgrundlagen und Orientierungshilfen. Second edition, Springer, Berlin 1993.

Hoffmann H.: Schizophrenietheorie und Gemeindepsychiatrie. Folgerungen aus aktuellen Modellvorstellungen für die Versorgung. Psychiatrische Praxis. 1995, 22, 3–8.

Hogarty G.E. & Anderson C.: A controlled study of family therapy, social skills training and maintenance chemotherapy in the aftercare treatment of schizophrenic patients. In: Psychosocial Treatment of Schizophrenia. Toronto, Hans Huber 1987.

Hollis C.: Child and adolescent (juvenile onset) schizophrenia case control study of premorbid developmental impairments. British Journal of Psychiatry. 1995, 166, 489–495.

Hollis C.: Childhood antecedents of schizophrenia. Pediatrics. 1996, 9 (2), 31–36.

Holte A., et al: Confirmatory feedback in families of schizophrenics: Theory, methods and preliminary results. In: Hahlweg K., Goldstein M. J.: Understanding mental disorder: the contribution of family interaction research. Family Process Press, New York 1987.

Holte A., Wichstrom L.: Disconfirmatory feedback in families of schizophrenics. Scandinavian Journal of Psychology. 1990, 31, 198–211.

Holte A., Wichstrom L.: Confirmatory and disconfirmatory feedback in families of schizophrenics, pathological controls and normals. Acta Psychiatrica Scandinavica. 1990, 81, 477–82.

Hooley J. M.: The nature and origins of expressed emotion. Family Process Press, New York 1987, 176–194.

Hubschmid T.: Von der Familientheorie zur Angehörigenarbeit oder vom therapeutischen zum präventiv-rehabilitativen Paradigma in der Schizophreniebehandlung. Fortschr. Neurol. Psychiat., 1985, 53, 117–122.

Ingvar D. H., Franzén, G.: Abnormal distribution of cerebral activity in chronic schizophrenics. The Lancet 1974-Elsevier.

Jacob I.: Family interaction in disturbed and normal families. A methological and substantive review. Psychological Bulletin. 1975, 82, 33–65.

Jansen F., Streit U.: Eltern als Therapeuten. Springer, Berlin 1992.

Johnston C.: Parent characteristics and parent-child interactions in families of non-problem children and ADHD children with higher and lower levels of oppositional-defiant behavior. Journal of Abnormal Child Psychology. 1996, 24 (1), 85–104.

Jones P., Roger B., Murray G., et al: Child development risk factors for adult schizophrenia in the British 1946 birth cohort. The Lancet, 1994, 344, 1398–1402.

Juul J.: Dein kompetentes Kind. Rowohlt, Reinbek bei Hamburg 2009.

Juul J.: Grenzen, Nähe, Respekt. Rowohlt, Reinbek bei Hamburg 2009.

Juul J.: Die kompetente Familie. Kösel, Munich, 2007.

Kavanagh, D. J.: Recent developments in expressed emotion and schizophrenia. Brit. J. Psychiat. 160: 601–620, 1992.

Keppler W.: Ergeben sich aus Schwangerschaft und Geburtsanamnese Hinweise auf einen Zusammenhang zwischen Schizophrenie und frühkindlicher Hirnschädigung? Dissertation an der Universität Tübingen 1978.

Keppler W., Lempp R., Pascheday D., et al: Die frühkindliche Anamnese der Schizophrenen. Nervenarzt, 50, 719–724, 1979.

Klosterkötter J.: Kognition und Psychopathologie der Schizophrenie. In: Fortschr. Neurol. Psychiat. 1999, 67, 44–52.

Koehler K., Saur H.: Huber's basic symptoms: another approach to negative psychopathology in schizophrenia. Compr. Psychiatry. 1984, 25: 174–182.

Kooj S.: ADHD macht Erwachsene zu Chaoten, im Artikel vom Zentrum für Agogik, Zurich 1999.

Krause K. H., et al: Increased striatal dopamine transporter in adult patients with ADHD. Neuroscience Letters 285, 2000, 107–110.

Kuipers L.: Expressed emotions: A review. British Journal of Clinical Psychology. 1979, 18, 237–243.

Laing R. D.: Mystifizierung, Konfusion und Konflikte. In: Schizophrenie und Familie. Fourth edition, Suhrkamp, Frankfurt a. M. 1992, 274–304.

Lambert M., Conus P., Lubman D. I., et al: The impact of substance use disorders on clinical outcome in 643 patients with first-episode psychosis. Acta Psychiatrica Scandinavica, Volume 112, Issue 2, 141–148, August 2005.

LeDoux J.: Das Netz der Gefühle. Wie Emotionen entstehen. Hanser, Munich/Vienna 1998. (The emotional brain. The mysterious underspinnings of emotional life. Simon and Schuster, New York 1996).

Leff J., Vaughn C. E.: Expressed emotion in families: Its significance for mental illness. Guilford, New York 1985.

Lempp R.: Psychosen im Kindes- und Jugendalter, Hans Huber, Bern 1973.

Lempp R.: Vom Verlust der Fähigkeit, sich selbst zu betrachten. First edition, Hans Huber, Bern 1992.

Lennard H.L., et al.: Interaction in families with a schizophrenic child. General Psychiatry. 1965, 12; 166–183.

Lidz T., Cornelison A., Fleck S., Terry D.: Spaltung und Strukturverschiebung in der Ehe. In: Schizophrenie und Familie. Fourth edition, Suhrkamp, Frankfurt a. M. 1992, 108–126.

Lukoff D., Snyder K., Ventura J., Nuechterlein K. H.: Life events, familial stress and coping in the developmental course of schizophrenia. Schizophrenie Bulletin. 1984, 10, 258–92.

Lurija A. R.: Das Gehirn in Aktion – Einführung in Neuropsychologie. Rowohlt, Reinbek bei Hamburg 1993.

Machleidt, W., Haltenhof, H., Garlipp, P. (eds): Schizophrenie – eine affektive Erkrankung? Grundlagen, Phänomenologie, Psychodynamik und Therapie. Schattauer, Stuttgart/New York 1999.

Mannuzza K., et al.: Adult outcome of hyperactive boys. Educational achievement, occupational rank and psychiatric status. Arch Gen Psychiatry. 1993 50: 565–576.

Mannuzza S., et al.: Hyperactive boys almost grown up. Replication of psychiatric status. Arch Gen Psychiatry. 1991, 48: 77–83.

Markmann H. J., Notarius C. I.: Coding marital in family interaction: Current status. Plenum Press, New York 1987.

Mattejat F., Remschmidt H.: Die Bedeutung der familialen Beziehungsdynamik für den Erfolg stationärer Behandlungen in der Kinder- und Jugendpsychiatrie. Zeitschrift für Kinder- und Jugendpsychiatrie. 1991, 19, 139–150.

Meynert T.: Klinische Vorlesung über Psychiatrie. Wien 1990.

Michaud P. A., Tschumper A., Inderwildi L.: SMASH 2002. Swiss Multicenter Adolescent Survey on Health. www.umsa.ch.

Miklowitz D. J.: Family Risk Indicators in Schizophrenia. Schizophrenia Bulletin, 1994, 20 (1), 137–149.

Miklowitz D. J., Goldstein M. J., Nuechterlein K. H.: Verbal Interactions in the Families of Schizophrenic and Bipolar Affective Patients. Journal of Abnormal Psychology. 1995, 2, 268–27.

Minuchin S., et al.: A conceptual model of psychosomatic illness in children: Family organization and family therapy. Archives of General Psychiatry. 1975, 32, 1031–1038.

Mishler E. G., Wexler I. N.: The sequential pattering of interaction in normal and schizophrenic families. Family Process 1975, 14, 17–50.

Moffitt T.E., Caspi A., Rutter M.: Measured Gene-Environment Interactions in Psychopathology. Article in Perspectives on Psychological Science I:1745–6924, January 2006.

Moore TH., Lewis G.: Meta-analysis. Cannabis use linked to psychotic illnesses, University of Bristol, The Lancet 2007.

Morrison J. R., Stewart M. A.: A family study of the hyperactive child syndrome. Biol. Psychiatry. 1971, 3: 189–195.

MTA Cooperative Group: A 14-Month Randomized Clinical Trial of Treatment Strategies for ADHD. Arch Gen Psychiatry 1999, 56: 1073–1086.

Murray R. M.: Neurodevelopmental schizophrenia: The rediscovery of dementia praecox. British Journal of Psychiatry. 1994, 165, 6–12.

Mirski A.: The Israeli high-risk study. Raven Press, New York 1988

Neuhaus C.: Das hyperaktive Kind und seine Probleme. Ravensburger Buchverlag, Ravensburg 1996.

Neuhaus C.: Hyperaktive Jugendliche und ihre Probleme. Ravensburger Buchverlag, Ravensburg 1998.

Norman R. M., Malla A. K.: Stressful life events and schizophrenia. British Journal of Psychiatry 162: 161–166 (1993).

Nuechterlein K. H., Dawson M. E.: Information processing and attentional functioning in the developmental course of schizophrenic disorders. Schizophrenia Bulletin. 1984, 10, 160–203.

Nuechterlein K. H., Dawson M. E.: A heuristic vulnerability/stress model of schizophrenic episodes. Schizophrenia Bulletin 1984, 10: 300–312.

Nuechterlein K. H., Ventura J., Snyder K., Lukoff D.: Life events, familial stress and coping in the developmental course of schizophrenia. Schizophrenia Bulletin. 1984, 10, 258–92.

Olbrich R.: Expressed Emotion (EE) und die Auslösung schizophrener Episoden: Literaturübersicht. Nervenarzt, 1983, 54, 113–121.

Onstand S., Skre I., Togersen S. E.: Family interaction: parental representation in schizophrenic patients. Acta Psychiatrica Scandinavica, 1994, 90, 67–70.

Os J., et al.: Continued cannabis use and risk of incidence and persistence of psychotic symptoms: 10-year follow-up cohort study. BMJ Research 2011, 342: d738, doi: 10.1136/bmj. d/38.

Panksepp, J.: Affective neuroscience: A conceptual framework for the neurobiological study of emotions. In: Strongman, K. T. (ed.): International review of studies on emotion, Vol. I. John Wiley & Sons, New Jersey 1992, 59–99.

Pharoah F., Mari J., Rathbone J., Wong W.: Family intervention for schizophrenia. Cochrane Database of Systematic Reviews 2006, Oct 18 (4) DD000088.

Pliszka S.: Comorbidity of Attention-Deficit/Hyperactivity Disorder with psychiatric disorder. J. Clin Psychiatry. 1998, 59: 50–58.

Psychiatric Genomics Consortium Cross-Disorder Group Correspondence to: Smoller, J. W.: Identification of risk loci with shared effects on five major psychiatric disorders: a genome-wide analysis. Published online February 28, 2013: www.thelancet.com, http://dx.doi.org/10.1016/S0140-6736(12)62129-1.

Pugh M., Bigler E. D.: Schizophrenia and prior history of "MBD". Neuropsychological findings. International Journal of Clinical Neuropsychology. 1986, 8 (1), 22–26.

Ratey J. J., Johnson C.: Das Schattensyndrom. Klett-Cotta, Stuttgart 1999.

Reber N.: Die protektive Rolle des Vaters im Verlauf von schizophrenen Erkrankungen bei jungen Patienten. Doctoral thesis with D. Hell, supervised by U. Davatz, Zurich 2009.

Rebmann M. E.: Lassen sich aus der Kindheitsanamnese Hinweise auf einen Zusammenhang zwischen Schizophrenie und frühkindlicher Hirnschädigung gewinnen? Doctoral thesis, University of Tübingen 1977.

Retzer A.: Familie und Psychose. Fischer 1994.

Riedinger M.: ADHS und Sucht. Kohlhammer, Stuttgart 2016.

Rifkin L., et al.: Low birth weight and schizophrenia. British Journal of Psychiatry. 1994, 165, 357–362.

Rosso, I. M., et al.: Obstetric risk factors for early onset schizophrenia in a Finnish birth cohort. Am. J. Psych. 2000, 157, 801–807.

Rousseau J. J.: Die Bekenntnisse und Träumereien des einsamen Spaziergängers, writtne in 1782, published posthumously in Munich 1978.

Ruf-Bächtiger L.: Das frühkindliche psychoorganische Syndrom. Third revised edition, Thieme, Stuttgart 1995.

Rumo-Jungo A., Pichonnaz A.: Kinder und Scheidung. Schulthess Verlag, Zurich 2006.

Rund B. R., Blakar R. M.: Schizophrenic patients and their parents. Acta Psychiatrica Scandinavica. 1986, 74, 396–408.

Rund B. R.: Cognitive disturbances in schizophrenics: What are they, and what is their origin? Acta Psychiatrica Scandinavica. 1988, 77, 113–123.

Scharfetter C.: Allgemeine Psychopathologie. Second revised edition, Thieme, Stuttgart 1985.

Scharfetter C.: Schizophrene Menschen. Third revised and extended edition, Urban & Schwarzenberg, Munich 1990.

Schneider K.: Klinische Psychopathologie. Thieme, Stuttgart 1958.

Schöpf J.: Psychiatrie für die Praxis. Springer, Berlin 1996.

Schreiber J. L., et al.: Expressed emotions. Trait or State? British journal of Psychiatry. 1995, 166, 647–649.

Schubert C., et al.: Schizophrenie und soziale Anpassung. Springer, Berlin 1986, 120–141.

Seikkula J., Alakare B., Aaltonen J., et al: Open Dialogue approach: Treatment principles and preliminary results of a two-year follow-up on first episode schizophrenia. Ethical Human Sciences and Services. 2003, 5 (3), 163–182.

Seikkula J., Arnkil T. E.: Dialoge im Netzwerk. Neue Beratungskonzepte für die psychosoziale Praxis. Paranus: Neumünster 2007.

Sharon M.: Survival of the Sickest: The surprising connections between disease and longevity. Harper Perennial, New York 2008.

Siegel S.: Nonparametric statistics for behavioral sciences. McGraw-Hill, New York 1956.

Solden S.: Die Chaos-Prinzessin: Frauen zwischen Talent und Misserfolg (Women with Attention Deficit Disorder). Bundesverband Aufmerksamkeitsstörung BV-AH Verlag, Forchheim 2001.

Steinhausen H. C.: Leichte und schwere hirnorganische Störungen im Kindesalter. Schweizerische medizinische Wochenschrift, 1992, 4 102–111.

Stevenson J., et al.: Hyperactivity and spelling disability: testing for shared genetic aetiology. Child Psychol. Psychiatry, 1993: 34: 1137–1152.

Stierlin H.: Delegation und Familie. First Edition, Suhrkamp, Frankfurt a. M. 1982.

Stierlin H.: Von der Psychoanalyse zur Familientherapie. Klett-Cotta, Stuttgart 1992.

Süllwold L., Huber G.: Schizophrene Basisstörungen. Springer, Berlin 1986.

Summers F., Walsh P.: Symbiosis and Confirmation between the Parents of the Schizophrenic. Family Process. 1981, 20, 319–330.

Sydney H., Joseph M.: A Process Model for the Development of Schizophrenia. Psychiatry. 1987, 50, 361-370.

Tallmadge J., Barkley R. A., Marquette U.: The interactions of hyperactive and normal boys with their fathers and mothers. Journal of Abnormal child Psychology. 1983, 11 (4), 565–579.

Tarrier N., Vaughn C. E., Lader M. H., Leff J.: Bodily reactions to people and events in schizophrenics. Archives of General Psychiatry. 1979, 36, 311–315.

Thölke D.: Bedeutung der Interaktion zwischen Erziehungsverhalten und POS-Kind in der multifaktoriellen Schizophreniegenese. Doctoral dissertation with D. Hell, supervised by U. Davatz, Zurich 1998.

Tienari, P., Sorri, A., Lathi, I., et al: Interaction of genetic and psychosocial factors in schizophrenia. Acta Psychiatrica Scandinavia. 1985, 71, 19–30.

Tienari P., et al.: Interaction of genetic and psychosocial factors in schizophrenia. Acta Psychiatrica Scandinavica. 1985, 319, 19–30.

Tienari P., et al.: Die finnische Adoptionsfamilienstudie über Schizophrenie: Mögliche Wechselwirkungen von genetischer Vulnerabilität und Familien-Milieu. In: Böker W., Brenner H. D., Schizophrenie als systemische Störung. Hans Huber, Bern 1989.

Tienari P., et al.: Interaction between genetic vulnerability and rearing environment. In: Psychotherapy of Schizophrenia: Facilitating and Obstructive Factors. Scandinavian University Press, Oslo 1992 (b), 154–172,

Tienari P., et al.: The Finnish adoptive family study of schizophrenia. Implications for family research. British Journal of Psychiatry. 1994, 164, 20-26.

Tölle R.: Psychiatrie. Ninth edition, Springer, Berlin 1991.

Toman W.: Family constellation: Its effects on personality and social behavior. Springer, New York 1976.

Vaughan K., et al.: The relationship between relative's expressed emotion and schizophrenic relapse: an Australian replication. Social Psychiatry and Psychiatric Epidemiology. 1992, 27, 10–15.

Vaughn C. E., Leff, J.: The influence of family and social factors on the course of psychiatric illness. A comparison of schizophrenic and depressed neurotic patients. British journal of Psychiatry 129: 125–137, 1976.

Vaughn C. E.: Annotation. Expressed emotions in family relationship. Journal of child psychology and psychiatry. 1989, 30, 13–22.

Virtanen T. A., Moilanen I. K.: Stress und Stressbewältigung bei Müttern von Kindern mit leichten zerebralen Dysfunktionen. Praxis der Kinderpsychologie und Kinderpsychiatrie. 1991, 40 (7), 260–65.

Virtanen T. A., Moilanen I. K., Ihalainen M. M.: What causes stress for mothers of children with MBD? Scandinavian Journal Social Medicine. 1991, 19, 47–52.

Vogel E. F., Bell N. W.: Das gefühlsgestörte Kind als Sündenbock der Familie. In: Schizophrenie und Familie. Fourth edition, Suhrkamp, Frankfurt a. M. 1992, 245–274.

Vollenweider F.: Neue Aspekte der PET- und SPECT-Forschung In: Fleischhacker W. W.:

Schizophrene Störungen, Integrative Psychiatrie Innsbruck 1998.

Vollenweider F., et al.: Positron emission tomography and fluorodeoxyglucose studies of metabolic hyperfrontality and psychopathology in the psilocybin model of psychosis. Neuropsychopharmacology. 1997, 16, 357–370.

Walker E., Emory E.: Infants at risk for psychopathology: offspring of schizophrenic parents. Child Development. 1983, 54, 1269–1285.

Walker E., Lewine R. J.: Prediction of adult onset schizophrenia from childhood home movies. American Journal of Psychiatry. 1990, 147, 1052–1056.

Walsh F.: Breaching of family generation boundaries by schizophrenics, disturbed and normal. Comprehensive schizophrenic research program, Dept. of Psychiatry of Michigan, Rees Hospital and the University of Chicago. Family Therapy, 1 (3) 1979.

Walsh F.: Concurrent grandparent death and birth of schizophrenic offspring. An intriguing finding. Family Process, 1979, 17, 451–463.

Walter U.: Mein wildes liebes Teufelchen. Hinweise für den Umgang mit hyperaktiven Kindern. Second revised edition, Verlag Gesundheit, Berlin 1993.

Weakland J. H.: Double Bind-Hypothese und Dreier-Beziehung. In: Schizophrenie und Familie. Fourth edition, Suhrkamp, Frankfurt a. M. 1992, 221–248.

Weiss G., et al.: Psychiatric status of hyperactives as adults: a controlled prospective 15-year follow-up of 63 hyperactive children. Am. Acad. child Psychiatry 1985, 24: 211–220.

Wender P. H.: Das hyperaktive Kind. Ninth revised edition, Otto Maier, Ravensburg 1991.

Willermann L.: Activity level and hyperactivity in twins. Child Develop. 1943–44.

Wilson, E. O.: Die soziale Eroberung der Erde. C. H. Beck, Munich 2013.

Winokur G., et al.: Further distinctions between manic-depressive illness and primary depressive disorder. In: J. Psychiatry 1993, 150: 1176–1181.

Wolfensberger C.: Merkblatt: Das infantile psychoorganische Syndrom. In: Ehrat F. und Mattmüller-Frick F.: POS-Kinder und Familie, Paul Haupt, Bern, 1994, 29–35.

Wood B. L.: Proximity and hierarchy. Orthogonal dimensions of family interconnectedness. Family process. 1985, 24, 487–507.

Wood B. L.: Jenseits der "psychosomatischen Familie". Biobehaviorales Familienmodell bei kranken Kindern. Family Process. 1994, 123–147.

Wood B. L., Watkins J. B., Nogueira J., et al: The "Psychosomatic Family": An empirical and theoretical analysis. Family Process. 1989, 28, 399–417.

Wynne L. C., Singer M. T., Bartko J., Toohey M.: Schizophrenics and their families: Recent research on parental communication. In: Tanner J. M., Psychiatric Research: The Widening Perspective. International University Press, New York 1976, 254–286.

Wynne L. C., Ryckoff I. M., Day J., Hirsch S. J.: Pseudogemeinschaft in den Familienbeziehungen von Schizophrenen. In: Schizophrenie und Familie. Fourth edition, Suhrkamp, Frankfurt a. M. 1992, 44–72.

Yazdi K.: Die Cannabis-Lüge. Schwarzkopf und Schwarzkopf, Berlin 2017.

Zammit S., et al.: Cannabis use and risk of psychotic or affective mental health outcomes: a systematic review. The Lancet, Vol. 370, issue 9584, 319–328, 2007.

Zubin J., Springer B.: Vulnerability. A new view of schizophrenia. Journal of Abnormal Psychology, 1977, 86, 103–126.

Züblin W.: Zur Anamnese adoleszenter Schizophrener. Schweizer Archiv für Neurologie und Psychiatrie, Band 136, Heft 2, 29–41. Bern 1985.

Copyright © Ursula Davatz, 2019

All rights reserved.
No part of this publication may be reproduced, stored or transmitted in any form by any means, electronic, mechanical, photocopying or otherwise, without the prior written permission of the author and publisher.

The right of Ursula Davatz to be identified as Author and Publisher of this work has been asserted by her in accordance with the Copyright, Designs and Patents Act, 1988

ISBN 978-3033070776

www.ingramcontent.com/pod-product-compliance
Lightning Source LLC
Chambersburg PA
CBHW061343300426
44116CB00011B/1965